FROM **BLACK SOX** TO **THREE-PEATS**

from Black Sox

to Three-Peats

A Century of Chicago's Best Sportswriting

from the *Tribune*, *Sun-Times*, and Other Newspapers

EDITED BY RON RAPOPORT

THE UNIVERSITY OF CHICAGO PRESS Chicago and London

RON RAPOPORT was a sports columnist for the *Chicago Sun-Times* for more than twenty years and also wrote for the *Los Angeles Times, Los Angeles Daily News*, and the Associated Press. He served as the sports commentator for NPR's *Weekend Edition* for two decades and has written a number of books about sports and entertainment. He lives in Los Angeles.

The University of Chicago Press, Chicago 60637
The University of Chicago Press, Ltd., London
© 2013 by The University of Chicago
All rights reserved. Published 2013.
Printed in the United States of America
22 21 20 19 18 17 16 15 14 13   1 2 3 4 5
ISBN-13: 978-0-226-03660-1   (paper)
ISBN-13: 978-0-226-03674-8   (e-book)
DOI: 10.7208/chicago/9780226036748.001.0001

Library of Congress Cataloging-in-Publication Data

From Black Sox to three-peats : a century of Chicago's best sportswriting from the Tribune, Sun-Times, and other newspapers / edited by Ron Rapoport.
    pages cm.
    Includes index.
    ISBN 978-0-226-03660-1 (pbk. : alk. paper) — ISBN 978-0-226-03674-8 (e-book)
    1. Sports journalism—Illinois—Chicago.   I. Rapoport, Ron.
    PN4784.S6F765 2013
    796.09773'11—dc23

                                                    2013009171

⊗ This paper meets the requirements of ANSI/NISO Z39.48-1992
(Permanence of Paper).

CONTENTS

INTRODUCTION

When Hugh Fullerton was a young baseball writer in Chicago in the mid-1890s he received $400 in expenses and set off to cover the Cubs in spring training. He had no sooner arrived than four players learned of his bankroll, invaded his hotel room, sat on top of him, and searched through his clothes until they found the cash.

"Ignoring my wails of protest," Fullerton wrote, "they divided it into five equal parts, handed me my eighty dollars, remarking that was enough for any reporter, and invited me to go to a party with them."

The era when sportswriters were that close to their subjects has long since ended, but the amusement Fullerton derived from the incident illustrates an opinion he was the first to suggest and with which future students of writing about baseball would later concur.

Which is that baseball writing as we know it today—and, by extension, sportswriting as a whole—began in Chicago.

While writers in New York and other cities that had baseball teams in the late nineteenth century viewed the games they covered as solemn occasions and their articles as opportunities to show off their knowledge in an often ponderous fashion, newspapermen in Chicago, and not just those writing about sports, took a different approach.

"The papers in Chicago in those days were unlike any printed anywhere else," Fullerton wrote in "The Fellows Who Made the Game," in a 1928 edition of the *Saturday Evening Post*. "They were written largely in the language that the wild growing young city understood. . . . There was nothing sedate or dignified about them except the editorial pages and the stockyard reports. They were boisterous, at times rough; they lacked dignity, perhaps, but they were readable, entertaining and amusing."

These qualities were not lost on Fullerton's protégé, Ring Lardner, who did not develop his radical new prose style in a vacuum. After Fullerton recommended the twenty-two-year-old Lardner for his first job in Chicago, Lardner became fascinated by the wit and irreverence of several of the writers with whom he worked. Lardner trailed after Charles Dryden, then the highest-paid sportswriter in the country, with such determination that the ballplayers nicknamed him "Charlie's Hat." Nor did it take long for New York and the rest of the country to catch up to the Chicago writers who were making sports and the men who played them seem like so much fun.

"The result of the change in style of writing was evident immediately in the attendance upon games and in increased circulation of the newspapers, revealing the fact that there was commercial value in good reporting," Fullerton wrote. "Readers, laughing at the accounts of games and the doings of players, commenced to go see for themselves. The style of reporting baseball changed all over the country."

More than a hundred years have elapsed since Fullerton was forced to share and share alike with the players he was writing about, but I believe that the sportswriters who have worked in Chicago since then continue to occupy a special place in American journalism.

There is something about the city's visceral relationship to its sports teams, its heart-on-the-sleeve reaction to their ups and downs, that has seemed to draw strong writers, those with distinctive voices, to Chicago's newspapers. The best of them quickly learned that if they could find a way to tap into their readers' passions they would be rewarded with a loyalty that would last a lifetime. And more than a few of them did indeed spend thirty, forty, or even fifty years writing about sports in Chicago.

Even those who were just passing through quickly came to understand that there was something different about Chicago. "It's the best sports town in the country," says Skip Bayless, who worked in Miami, Los Angeles, and Dallas and then spent three years writing a column for the *Chicago Tribune* before becoming a commentator at ESPN. "I miss it."

I served two tours as a sports columnist for the *Chicago Sun-Times*, from 1977 until 1988 and, after some time in the sun at the *Daily News* in Los Angeles, from 1998 until 2006. Then, after forty years of daily journalism, I moved back west to engage in more leisurely pursuits.

Recently, I began thinking back on how enjoyable my time in Chicago was and trying to remember if I had ever bothered to appreciate it fully. Occasionally, I would discuss this with friends I had worked with and none of us had a definitive answer. Perhaps we had been too busy working to sit back and reflect, we agreed, and I wondered what I would find if I went back and tried to reconstruct that period.

So many of the writers I had worked with were so skilled, so intelligent, so funny—so *good*—that I wanted to read some of them again. And there was the excitement of the teams and events we covered—Michael Jordan's Bulls, Mike Ditka's Bears, and various Cubs disasters were just the tip of the iceberg—and the fascination with the people we talked to and wrote about. How would our work stand up all these years later? I wondered. Would it bear collecting in an anthology?

I started making some calls to the writers I had worked with who had spent all or most of their careers writing for newspapers in Chicago—Ray Sons, Bob Verdi, Don Pierson, Robert Markus, Mike Imrem, Sam Smith, Jeannie Morris, Melissa Isaacson, Joe Goddard, Carol Slezak, Taylor Bell, and more—and those who had come to Chicago after establishing themselves elsewhere or had worked in the city for a while and then moved on—Rick Telander, Rick Morrissey, John Schulian, David Israel, Mike Downey, Bernie Lincicome, Jay Mariotti, Gene Wojciechowski, Greg Couch, and others. All of them, I was pleased to discover, expressed enthusiasm for the project and many began searching their files and their memories for some of their favorite articles and columns.

Any doubts I might have had were quickly put to rest. So many of the pieces they sent me were terrific, perfectly capturing the moment in which they were written and eminently readable today. A search through the on-line archives of the *Tribune*, the *Sun-Times*, and the *Defender* was equally rewarding, and it soon became clear I would be dealing with an abundance of riches. Especially when I realized I would have to cast a wider net.

I had worked with some of the best-known Chicago sportswriters from an earlier era—Jerome Holtzman, Bill Gleason, David Condon, Tom Fitzpatrick—and though they are gone now I wanted to include them in this book. And then I began wondering about the generations that had come before them.

I knew Lardner had been one of many to write the *Tribune*'s "In the Wake of the News" sports column, which continues to this day, but had anybody read any of them recently? I certainly hadn't. I knew Arch Ward invented the baseball and football All-Star Games, but I had never read his "Wake" columns. I was aware of how popular Jack Griffin, John P. Carmichael, Wendell Smith, Warren Brown, and some others had been but was not familiar with their work. The same was true of Brent Musburger, who

3

wrote sports columns for the now-defunct *Chicago American*, a scrappy Tribune-owned afternoon paper that was converted to the tabloid *Chicago Today* in 1969, before he set off on a long career that has put him behind a microphone at just about every televised sports event imaginable. I wanted to know more.

And so I went on a treasure hunt through the archives that turned up one golden nugget after another. There were James Cruisinberry's reports in the *Tribune* on the 1919 Black Sox, written not after the fix had come to light a year later, but while the games were being played. There was Fullerton's article in advance of the 1906 World Series, celebrating what remains the only meeting of the Cubs and Sox in that event. There was I. E. Sanborn's eyewitness testimony to the fact that once upon a time the Cubs did—they really did—not only play in a World Series but win it. Two in a row, in fact. There was Westbrook Pegler, of all people, writing about Babe Ruth's called shot in Wrigley Field, Dryden on Ruth pitching a 1–0 shutout over the Cubs in the 1918 Series, Brown writing about the Bears' unparalleled triumph in the 1940 NFL championship game, and the Cubs' humiliation in the 1945 World Series. There was Wendell Smith holding baseball's feet to the fire as he single-handedly brought about an end to segregated player housing in spring training. And there was some excellent work in the *Chicago Defender*, which few people in white Chicago had ever read.

Though there is some straight reporting in this collection, and a number of feature articles, most of it consists of sports columns, which originally appeared under their writers' names in large type and often under their pictures. And as they began coming in, I found myself puzzling over a question that seemed almost metaphysical: What is a sports column, anyway? Certainly, the approach and the styles of the writers in this collection could hardly be more different and distinctive. From Goddard's just-the-quotes-ma'am approach in his long-running "What's Up With" series in the *Sun-Times* (which I have long thought should be collected in a book) to the graceful prose of Verdi, the take-no-prisoners pugnacity of Mariotti, the whimsy of Lincicome, the stand-up comedy of Downey, the tell-me-this-isn't-literature virtuosity of Schulian, columns come in all shapes and guises.

This very variety, it seems to me, illustrates some of the ways in which sportswriting has changed over the generations. Anyone reading Brown's pieces about the Bears and the Cubs that are reprinted here will see they rely heavily on play-by-play—touchdown-by-touchdown in the case of the Bears—in a way that would be unthinkable today. The reason, of course, is television, which, as it moved like a glacier over the sports landscape, ruthlessly ground the article based on what a writer *saw* into so much rubble. (The coming of the Internet a generation later merely served to pulverize the dust even finer.) "I already know what happened," any self-respecting sports editor tells his writers today. "I need you to tell me *why* it happened—and what you think about it."

Soon, the game story, once the very essence of sportswriting, became a dying art form as not just columnists but beat writers too responded to the new reality by working more player profiles, opinions, attention-getting phrase making, and whatever rhetorical devices they could muster into their articles. After a time, it became difficult to tell where the beat writer's territory ended and the columnist's began, and in fact some of the contributors to this book moved back and forth between writing columns, features, and game stories, sometimes all the same time.

But it was not just new technology that brought about changes in how sportswriters viewed their jobs. In the last decades of the twentieth century, a darker and more skeptical outlook began to take hold as the world in general, and the world of sports in particular, started coming to terms with the fact that its heroes are not always what they seem to be and that even those athletes who are altogether admirable have demons to confront.

Compare David Condon's 1975 column in the *Tribune* on White Sox second baseman Nellie Fox with Barry Rozner's in the Arlington *Daily Herald* on Cubs second baseman Ryne Sandberg thirty years later. Though Condon's column appeared three weeks before Fox died of cancer at the age of forty-seven, it is a breezy romp through his career and treats Fox's disease as just another opponent he will surely defeat. Rozner's column ran the day after Sandberg was elected to baseball's Hall of Fame, yet it focuses as much on the hard-fought battle that led to the greatest individual honor a player can achieve as on his enjoyment of it.

As I began arranging the book, I could see that certain themes were beginning to emerge. Many of the articles were touching on some of the high moments in Chicago sports lore—and a lot of the low ones, too—and on its greatest personalities. So while this book is by no means a comprehensive history, perhaps it can serve as an anecdotal review of the past hundred-plus years.

Beyond that, though, I saw this collection occasionally veering sharply off the beaten track, away from the big names and the big events, and with gratifying results. I was in a Chicago bar listening to Eric Nesterenko talking to Bob Greene about life. In a modest Los Angeles apartment hearing Lou Novikoff tell Fitzpatrick he might as well be dead. On a country road in Tennessee with Telander in search of a bitter and elusive Doug Atkins. In Slezak's mysteriously occupied garage in Wrigleyville. And in venues only tangentially related to sports: San Francisco, during the earthquake that rocked the 1989 World Series, with Sons; Oklahoma City, some years after the bombing of the Federal Building, with Bayless; Tampa, before a Super Bowl as US armed forces were going to war, with Imrem; Dachau, after the massacre in Munich during the 1972 Olympics, with Markus.

I also began moving beyond the sports page. Since Chicago's teams and athletes are so important to the city—sometimes I think they are the only common bond it really has—they do not remain the exclusive province of sports columnists. Mike Royko, for instance, the most celebrated general news columnist the city ever produced, occasionally wrote about sports, though certainly he was not the only one. Two of my favorite Royko columns are reprinted here, along with those by city-side columnists Mark Brown, Bob Greene, Dave Hoekstra, John Kass, and Richard Roeper.

And though this volume is heavily tilted toward general sports columnists, it also includes the work of a few specialists: Holtzman, whose baseball coverage in both the *Sun-Times* and *Tribune* can best be described as indefatigable and whose invention of the save rule revolutionized the game; Pierson, whose consistently strong columns and game coverage of the Bears and the NFL in the *Tribune* earned him an award from the Pro Football Hall of Fame; Sam Smith, whose coverage of the Bulls and the NBA in the *Tribune* during the three-peat era were supremely knowledgeable and authoritative; Wojciechowski, who wrote knowingly and cleverly about college sports for the *Tribune*; Bell, whose passion for Chicago's lively high school sports scene for the *Sun-Times* made his work required reading for those who followed it.

Enjoyable as putting this all together was, I found a troubling aspect to it, too. In a number of conversations with my former colleagues—some of them retired, others doing some freelancing, a few still turning out as many as four columns a week—we found ourselves marveling over the fun we'd had and wondering if, in light of the changes that have overtaken and overwhelmed daily journalism, ours might have been the last generation of sportswriters and columnists to enjoy that kind of freedom. There was that question again, the one that had been nagging at me all along. Had we lived in a golden age of sportswriting and not been paying attention?

These days, I occasionally attend lunches held at a restaurant near my home by the Badge of Honor Society, a group of former sportswriters for the *Los Angeles Times*. Though I worked at the *Times* early in my career so my membership in the group is legitimate, I feel like something of an interloper. When I left the paper in the 1970s, it was because I had a job waiting for me in Chicago. When many of the others sitting around the table left in the decades that followed, it was because they had been laid off. That was their badge of honor. And now they had no place to go.

The disintegration of the American newspaper is painful to observe on many levels, but none is more compelling to me than seeing the opportunities that my colleagues and I took for granted disappear. Each round of budget cuts, each announcement of another newspaper shrinking, and in some cases eliminating, its print edition in favor of the Internet is invariably accompanied by more pink slips, by more good men and women thrown out of work.

As for the sportswriters who do have jobs, they find themselves judged not by the quality of their work as much as by "hits," those meticulously measured number of readers drawn to every word they write on the web. It's all there in black and white, no dissent or discussion allowed. Writing has been turned into math. This affects what columnists write about, of course, and how they write it. Better to deal with a topic that everybody is talking about—and to do so at the top of your voice—than with something offbeat in a measured way, no matter how expertly crafted. Better to throw your fastball on every pitch and save the changeup for your memoirs.

I also look at the workload of sportswriters today and am reminded of something my father said when he saw me writing on my first computer. Dad, who grew up in Chicago during the Depression, learned electronics in the Navy, and never had an electrician in the house. Or a plumber, carpenter, television repairman, or workman of any other kind, for that matter. When something needed fixing, he figured out a way to do it himself. Trial and error was his method and he was confident that no inanimate object could defeat him if he stayed at it long enough.

But the minute he saw the glowing screen and the tappety-tap plastic keyboard that were my new tools, he said, "I'm glad I missed this," and turned and walked out of the room.

That's how I feel when I see sportswriters today blogging before games, tweeting during them and podcasting after them. When do they have time to *think*? I wonder, let alone write something they can be proud of the next day. It's a mystery to me and I'm glad I missed it.

But this is not meant to be a lament for what has been lost. Let the one hundred columns by the fifty-nine writers in this book, some of which appear in a somewhat different format and under different headlines than when they were written—and a few for which I can't determine the exact date they appeared—serve as a celebration of the sportswriters who worked for Chicago newspapers for more than a century and as an invitation, however wary, to those who will join them.

And let one more story from Fullerton, this one about his first opening day covering the Cubs, stand as an example of why many of us who became sportswriters love it so.

"The team was opening the season in Louisville," Fullerton wrote, "and in those days a street parade was always the feature. The Chicago reporters had an open hack and a place in the procession. A small round table was carried out from the bar of the Louisville Hotel, a dozen mint juleps placed upon it, and we joined the parade, being cheered along the entire line of march. The Courier-Journal the next day said, 'Carriage Number 6—Chicago reporters and mint juleps.'"

PIONEERS

I t is hard to know where Ring Lardner's newspaper columns left off and his fiction began, and for good reason. While Lardner's popularity and influence extended far beyond the sports page—Ernest Hemingway wrote articles for his high school newspaper under the byline Ring Lardner Junior and Virginia Woolf, who didn't know second base from Westminster Abbey, was an admirer—the truth is he never really left sportswriting.

Almost until the end of his life, even while writing the classic stories that made his reputation and his fortune, Lardner continually returned to sports in syndicated newspaper columns and magazine articles. His grandson James wrote in the *New York Times* in 1985 that as Lardner was turning out seven columns a week for the *Chicago Tribune* between 1913 and 1919, he also found the time to write *You Know Me Al*, *Alibi Ike*, *Gullible's Travels*, *Champion*, and many other short stories.

Let me repeat that. The man wrote a column every single day and *still* found the time to write some of America's most enduring fiction. The mind reels. The fact that the overall quality of his columns was so high, says Lardner's biographer, Jonathan Yardley, "must be counted among the extraordinary accomplishments of American journalism."

So perhaps it is no surprise that Lardner's "In the Wake of the News" columns in the *Tribune* bear all the hallmarks of his stories: loopy dialogue, misspellings, haphazard punctuation, and odd abbreviations. He must have driven his copy editors crazy. The column reprinted here is one he wrote before the 1919 World Series, which turned out to be not so funny after all.

The other pioneers in this section were also Chicago originals, in the press box and the arena. Frank A. (Fay) Young was a dining-car waiter for the Chicago and Northwestern Railroad when he started working at the *Chicago Defender* as it was being founded in 1906. He collected whatever newspapers he could find on his runs out of town and clipped articles about black athletes. When he finally quit his day job, Young went on to train and set the stage for writers at black newspapers around the country for the next half century. The article reprinted here is on a topic the black press returned to again and again but which few white readers ever came across. More's the pity.

Arch Ward, who ran the *Chicago Tribune* sports staff from 1930 until 1955, has been called the most powerful sports editor who ever lived. He is best remembered for inventing baseball's All-Star Game—he describes its perilous origins in the column reprinted here—and the NFL's College All-Star Game, which survives today in a different format as the Pro Bowl. Ward was also, in that more ethically relaxed journalistic era, a one-man conflict of interest. He once quit his job to become a promoter and, while still at the *Tribune,* started a new pro football league. Ward was so busy with outside activities, in fact, that *Tribune* writer Ed Prell told Jerome Holtzman in *No Cheering in the Press Box* that he and four other writers took turns ghosting his "In the Wake of the News" column. I'll bet Lardner wishes he'd thought of that.

Along with Dave Hoekstra's twenty-one-gun salute to Double Duty Radcliffe, baseball's oldest player, this section contains tributes to Chicago sports pioneers by some well-known columnists who just happened to be among their closest friends. Jack Griffin and George Halas, David Condon and Ray Meyer, Jerome Holtzman and Bill Veeck.

Sports columnists all over the country mourned Veeck's passing—I wrote a tear-stained tribute myself—but I think Bill would have liked Holtzman's, in which old friends tell their favorite stories about him. Some of them might even be true.

A Hot Tip from the Umpire

RING LARDNER

Chicago Tribune October 1, 1919

CINCINNATI, O—Gents: The world serious starts tomorrow with a big surprise. A great many people figured that the White Sox would be scared out and would never appear. But sure enough when we woke up this morning and come down to breakfast, here was the White Sox as big as life and willing to play. The first bird I seen amist them was Ray Schalk, the second catcher.

"Well, Cracker," I said, "I never expected to see you down here as I had been told that you would quit and would never appear." "Well, Biscuit," was his reply, "here we are and that's the best answer."

So after all that is said and done the White Sox is down here and trying to win the first 2 games on their merits so it looks like the serious would not be forfeited after all.

Most of the experts went to the 2 different managers to try and learn who was going to pitch the opening game. So to be different from the rest of them as usual, I passed up the two managers and went to the umpires. The first one I seen was Cy Rigler and I have known him all my life. "Who is going to win, Cy?" I asked. "I don't know," was his ample reply. You can take that tip or leave it. Personally I am betting on his word. He will give them the best of it if possible.

The next umpire I seen was Quigley. "My system," he said, "is to call everybody out."

The 2 American league umpires could not be seen as they was both up writing their stuff, but you can be sure that neither of them will give anybody the best of it. So all and all, it looks like a even break in the umpireing.

That brings us to the hotel accommodations. A large Chicago newspaper has got the prize rm. of the lot, namely, the smoking rm. off the ball rm. in the Gibson. This means that if anybody wakes up at 3 in the morning and wants to smoke why they can do so without moving out of their rm. And if they want to dance why all as they have to do is go in the next rm. And look for a pardner.

A great many people has written in to this hotel to ask how I am going to bet so they can do the opposite and make big money.

Well gents I might as well tell you where I stand. I dont believe either club can win as neither 1 of them has got a manager. But I do know both of the socalled managers personally and I have asked them who is going to pitch the opening game and they both say everybody on the staff so it looks like a free hitting game with Gerner and Mayer in there at the start and Mitchell and Lowdermilk to relieve them, but neither has made any provisions in regards to who is going to relieve us newspapers guys.

The other day as you may remember, I tried to make a comparison of the 2 clubs man for man and when I come to the shortstops why I said the logical thing, which is that no shortstops can win the serious as nobody ever hits to the shortstops in a big event like this. But thousands of birds wrote in personal letters to know what I thought of the 2 shortstops any way so I suppose I have got to tell them.

Well of the 2 shortstops mentioned Risberg and Kopf will be in there at the start of the serious but they will both be took out before the serious is 9 games old.

Compareing the both of them, Risberg is a Swede, but on the other hand Kopf hits from both sides of the plate. Both of them is tricky and is libel to throw a ball to a different base than expected. Kopf is the better looking but Risberg is the tallest and if they ever try to drive a high line drive over his head they will get fooled.

The 2 stars of the comeing serious has both been overlooked by the experts and I refer to Sherwood Magee and John Collins whom a lot of you think wont be in there. Even if they are not they are both good fellows.

Another question the public keeps asking we experts is who gets the advantage of having the serious 9 games in the stead of 7. Well gents all as I can say is it isnt the newspaper men. Further and more I wouldnt be surprised if neither ball club liked the new regime as I have nicknamed it as it looks to me like both mgrs. would use up all the pitchers they have got tomorrow and wouldn't know what to do next.

All together it looks like a long serious, and whoever made it 9 games had it in for us.

A Polecat in the Hotel
Major Leaguers Fail to Drop Color Bar

FRANK A. YOUNG

Chicago Defender December 12, 1942

The National and American League owners and managers quietly and superbly sidestepped the question of admitting Negroes into the big leagues at the annual meeting of the two leagues at the Palmer House, which was a busy place last week.

They discussed every other angle—transportation, trades, spring training dates and everything else relating to the game. But when the Negro newspaper man made his appearance, things changed in a hurry.

Mr. So and So, president of this or that club, could not be reached even by phone. One or two who were collared "had nothing to say," at this time. Anybody would have thought a polecat had come into the hotel.

One newspaperman ventured to confidentially tell us just what the trouble was but only on the promise that his name would not be used.

He believed the time was ripe for Negroes to get in major league baseball but that those behind the move had gone about it in the wrong way. First, he said, there are owners, who, like Clark Griffith of the Washington Senators, believe the two Negro leagues ought to clean themselves up. By that he said it was generally known that there are men connected with both leagues who couldn't stand to have light shed on their businesses. He said major league baseball had no place for such operatives.

The general impression was that the Communists were behind the move. Asked how the Chicago Defender and millions of baseball fans of color could be classed as Reds simply because they demanded a fair deal for all, this informant said he knew but was telling us what others thought.

On Thursday afternoon, a committee of 19 members of the CIO was balked in its efforts to place the matter of discrimination against Negro ballplayers before Judge Landis and the joint committee of the National and American Leagues, which was in session at the Ambassador East hotel on the North Side. The committee desired to present its case but was met at the door by Les O'Connor, secretary to Judge Landis, and told that the committee would be given a hearing if a place could be found on the program.

After a long wait, the committee told O'Connor that if the committee was not given a hearing that the matter of Negroes being employed in the major leagues would be taken up with the Fair Employment Practices Committee. This riled O'Connor who went back in to the joint meeting and returned with Landis' "No," with regard to any hearing.

The time was ripe last summer to inject Negroes into major leagues when a wide amount of publicity was given Larry MacPhail, then president of the Brooklyn Dodgers but now an officer in the Army, and President William Benswanger of the Pittsburgh Pirates who made a statement that Pittsburgh would give three or four a tryout at the end of the season.

What the end of the season meant no one but Mr. Benswanger knows as no Negro players even got a chance to appear with the Pittsburgh club in a workout.

The whole question died down with the coming of the World Series although it is reported that it came up in New York at a meeting and things waxed so warm that the phonograph record of the meeting was ordered smashed.

The following telegram was sent to the Pittsburgh club president by the Chicago Defender:

William Benswanger
President, Pittsburgh Pirates
Palmer House
Chicago, Ill.

Last summer the Chicago Defender was among the first to congratulate you on your decision to give tryouts to four Negro baseball players. We again want to congratulate you on your stand for fair play to all races in the major leagues. However, we believe that the question of Negroes in big league baseball must be before the major leagues meeting now in the Palmer Hotel. In the interest of national unity and morale in these crucial war days, we believe that you should act to place this important question before the current meeting by insisting that it be placed on the league agenda. You will be making a major contribution to our war effort through this action, which will go a long way towards breaking that racial barrier holding back the all-out prosecution of the war against the race-hating axis.

John Sengstacke
General Manager
Metz T.P. Lochard
Editor
The Chicago Defender

The Game of the Century

ARCH WARD

Chicago Tribune July 6, 1933

The Game of the Century at Comiskey Park this afternoon is the answer to oft-repeated statements that major league baseball is a stenciled, unvarying procedure that shuns extraneous innovation.

Scores of fans have written to this department since the game was announced venturing the opinion that eloquent persuasion must have been required to win approval of the league presidents and club owners.

There is no better time to make known that the proposal was received enthusiastically right from the start by nearly every man connected with the game. Save for a few minor details the game will be played exactly as outlined in the original suggestion.

The first person to whom we mentioned the idea was William Harridge, president of the American League. Our selling points were these:

1—Baseball needed an opportunity to show it was not in a state of decadence.

2—A Century of Progress Exposition was an ideal setting for baseball to display its wares.

3—All profits of the game would be donated to the Baseball Players' Charity fund.

4—THE CHICAGO TRIBUNE guaranteed all expenses in case the game was rained out.

5—The fans of the nation would be invited to help pick the all-star teams.

We asked Mr. Harridge for his candid reaction. He answered as follows:

"I am all for it. While there has never been anything like it, I know no reason why it is impossible."

This was on April 20. Harridge promised that if we could interest the National League in the proposal he would submit the idea to the American league club owners at their meeting in Cleveland May 9.

The next day we called upon William Veeck, president of the Cubs. He said it was just the tonic baseball needed and offered to help interest other National League clubs.

Fortified with the endorsement, we wrote President John Heydler of the National League. His immediate reply was strong personal support and a promise to take a mail vote of the club owners.

There was nothing to do then but to wait. The American League at its meeting May 9 officially approved the game and instructed President Harridge to make necessary changes in the schedule to clear the way. From a National League owner we learned the vote was progressing satisfactorily in that organization.

On May 15 when it looked as if everything was set we received a wire from Mr. Heydler stating that the National League would be unable to accept the invitation, due to the objection of a few of the club owners.

The objections, we learned, came from St. Louis, Boston, and New York. St. Louis feared precedent, but said it would not take the responsibility of blocking the game. The complication involving New York and Boston was a doubleheader scheduled between those teams at Boston July 5, the day before the game in Chicago. It is impossible to play even a single game in Boston and be in Chicago the next day.

The Giants were playing the Cubs at Wrigley Field at the time, so we called upon Secretary Jim Tierney. He said New York would have no objection to the interleague contest if it could get out of the twin bill at Boston. That left the Boston club the last obstacle in the way of the big game. A telephone call to Charles Adams, owner of the Braves, brought the information that they would make no protest if President Heydler ordered the doubleheader shifted to another date.

Mr. Heydler came to Chicago the next day. When he learned St. Louis, New York, and Boston were willing to take part, he immediately gave official approval and the game was on.

THE TRIBUNE then invited 55 newspapers in all sections of the United States to cooperate in conducting a poll of the fans to determine their idea of the strongest teams that could be recruited. All 55 papers accepted and 500,000 fans participated in the voting.

This is truly America's game. Never have so many people had a hand in the arrangement of a sports event.

The first All-Star Game was a great success, drawing 47,595 fans to Comiskey Park and featuring a home run by Babe Ruth as the American League won, 4–2. The game quickly became a highlight of the baseball season.

George Halas
"I Always Liked the Tough Ones"
JACK GRIFFIN

Chicago Sun-Times August 16, 1972

RENSSELAER, Indiana—The old man was scurrying about in his golf cart machines, admiring the texture and the deep green of the pasture on which the Bears gambol at practice.

"Beautiful stuff," said George Halas. "Planted it myself, a blade at a time. My own special formula. Did you know that?"

An old friend nodded. He had been there, at the birth of this wonder, and he would not forget it. He told Halas he had stayed up most of one night in Houston with Tank Younger.

"A fine young fellow," Halas said. "I hope you remembered to give him my regards. I always thought highly of Tank."

The old friend said Tank had told him about the afternoon he had laid out Johnny Lujack, and Halas had screamed from the sidelines that Younger had better start notifying his next of kin.

After the game, Tank had recalled, he thought Halas was going to mug him with a set of tire chains. Instead, George threw an arm around his shoulder and said he wished Tank would go to work for him.

A misty look came on George's face as he remembered the afternoon. "That's the way it went," he said. "I always liked the tough ones. And I wanted them on my side. How the hell do you think I got this team started, anyway? Did I ever tell you about Ed Healey, about how I got him?"

As a matter of fact, the old friend did know the Ed Healey story. But what the hell, one more time wasn't going to destroy anything. Tell the Ed Healey story.

"Well, Ed was with Rockford then," Halas said, "and he was as mean a tackle as I ever knew, and one game he laid me down on the ground with a pretty good thump."

There he was, Halas said, semi-conscious on the hard ground, and Healey was thoughtfully engaged in trying to twist off his head. George was ecstatic with the memory of such a delightful afternoon.

"It was due only to my marvelous agility that I was able to escape with my life," he said. "Right then I figured anyone mean enough to do that to anyone as devious as me should be playing on our side. After the game, I hired him away from Rockford. I think I gave him a $100 bonus."

All about there was the sound and the fury of football practice ringing across the prairies. The ground trembled from it, and the cornfields swayed under the late afternoon humidity.

Ronnie Smith, who wasn't really doing anything wrong, was beginning to wonder just what in the bloody blazes he was going to have to do to get a kind word out of one of the coaches.

A defensive back played his man a shade too loosely, and Abe Gibron roared, "Hit him. For God's sakes, what do you think this game is all about? Until that ball goes in the air you can hit him, and I don't mean kiss him, either."

Bill George was prowling about snarling at everyone. "I am getting exasperated," he said. "I am about to abandon my sweet Hitler mood and really get mean." By and by, Larry Horton and Glen Holloway took private exception to each other, Holloway buried a fist in Horton's nose, and Larry responded to trying to detach one of Glen's ears.

Whitey Dovell got in between them, and for a few moments it seemed the Bears offensive line coach might have to come to work in a bucket. Ronnie Smith was gleefully hopping up and down on the sidelines, screaming, "Let 'em go, let 'em go. Don't spoil the fun."

Gibron watched approvingly for a bit, then told them to break it up because he didn't want any of the merchandise scarred. He congratulated them, however, on their enterprise, and suggested they retain some of that energy for the Sunday game with New England.

"Beautiful," Halas said. "Very spirited practice, don't you think?" The old friend said he hadn't seen anything to compare with it since he used to go on patrol with the Infantry in Korea.

Then it was five o'clock and Abe said they'd had enough fun for one day.

George Halas died in 1983 at the age of eighty-eight. As founder, owner, player, and coach, he spent more than sixty years with the Chicago Bears.

Ray Meyer
The Name of the Game Is Loyalty

DAVID CONDON

Chicago Tribune March 20, 1979

A basketball takes some funny bounces.

It certainly has for Ray Meyer, a longtime sidekick who was chauffeur on my honeymoon and who Monday confirmed that he will return next season for his 38th campaign as coach of DePaul's Blue Demons, 1979 NCAA semifinalist.

Ray Meyer is DePaul athletics. DePaul athletics are Ray Meyer, the kindest man I've known in sports. Yet, once there was no George Mikan or Dave Corzine or Mark Aguirre, not even a DePaul, in Ray Meyer's future. That was when Ray was the regular handball opponent for a new Notre Dame football coach named Frank Leahy. We honchos at Notre Dame's Rockne Fieldhouse sensed that Leahy and Meyer would be coaching wizards in their chosen sports.

We were wrong, though, in guessing that Meyer's success like Leahy's would come at the alma mater. The heir apparent to Notre Dame's top basketball job took DePaul's coaching post at $1,800 a year. The contract was negotiated by Meyer's ailing Notre Dame boss, George Keogan, who died a few months later—in midseason—to leave open for Ed "Moose" Krause the job for which Meyer had been groomed.

At DePaul, though, young Meyer took fate into his own hands. His tool was George Mikan, an awkward giant from Joliet.

While others saw Big George as a Goliath who might make a crowd-attracting drum major for some American Legion drum and bugle corps, Meyer saw Mikan as a potential superstar.

With the patience for which he has become renowned, Meyer developed George Mikan into an athlete to be voted basketball's outstanding player of this century's first five decades. Mikan led DePaul to the 1945 National Invitation Tournament championship.

But after Mikan, the fates seemed to mock Meyer's relentless efforts to add more championships. The DePaul coach became known both as the coach who always was available to give his time to your charity, lodge, or church of any denomination, and as the coach who always came up a player short when the big tournament competition began.

Meyer didn't have to remain at DePaul, of course. There were other coaching offers, including the chance to return to Notre Dame.

No offer, though, was attractive enough to tempt Ray to pull up roots. Those Chicago roots were deep. Ray had led St. Patrick Academy to the national Catholic High School championship. He was a hero in Chicago as a two-season captain at Notre Dame. He had starred in the Catholic Youth Organization and Knights of Columbus League when those were the most physical basketball circuits in America. Ray also had been captain of the La Salle Cavaliers in the standout National AAU League. He helped coach the pro Chicago American Gears, and the Harlem Globe Trotters.

Beyond those roots was a loyalty to DePaul. Loyalty isn't such a prized value in these days, but early in Meyer's coaching career it was a fine quality in a man.

Sometimes I've wondered how he has done it, because coaching basketball at DePaul isn't like coaching basketball at UCLA, training Muhammad Ali or managing the New York Yankees. It has been watching the budget and searching the discards for talent. It has been contesting with coaches less honorable in recruiting tactics.

Before the basketball fix scandals of the 1950s, a New York gambler invaded Meyer's hotel room and suggested it would be worthwhile for DePaul to shave points in a Madison Square Garden game. Meyer later laughed when recalling how naive he was.

"Gee whiz," he said. "I'd never heard of such a thing. I thought the guy was kidding. So I chased him from my room and forgot the joke—until the scandals broke. Another time I was at lunch at Henrici's. A guy began talking about DePaul's players. I thought he was a fan and was flattered that he knew everything about our team. I invited him to watch practice, and I nearly fell over when he said, 'You don't want me around. I'm one of America's biggest basketball gamblers.'"

It only could have happened to a coach who sees only the good.

Sometimes at DePaul, though, it must have been a horrible strain to see the good. Once Meyer converted a basement into sleeping quarters for a couple of athletes he recruited to the bus stop-elevated line campus on our North Side. A priest appropriated the quarters.

I was in Ft. Wayne for an NCAA sectional tournament that drew both Notre Dame and DePaul. After the first evening's games, Notre Dame opened a big press room with steaks and refreshments for the media and the coaches. In DePaul's quarters the padres and coaches were chipping in for cheeseburgers.

Meyer made DePaul the host team and headliner at the Chicago Stadium double-headers promoted by the late Arthur Morse. DePaul's players had to get to the Stadium on their own. The sparse school budget needed DePaul's share of the gate. In a rare moment, Meyer said to me, "Just once I wish Art would give the boys on the host team a big meal after the game."

Last year, when DePaul made a big splash in the NCAA playoffs, Meyer held his counsel while another member of the athletic department was almost canonized for giving a great boost to the Blue Demon program. The guy is no longer there, so perhaps now they'll finally give Ray Meyer the long overdue accolades for dedication.

Ray Meyer coached at DePaul for forty-two seasons before retiring in 1984. He died in 2006 at the age of ninety-two.

Bill Veeck
A Man for All Seasons

JEROME HOLTZMAN

Chicago Tribune January 5, 1986

Bill Veeck was living in Easton, Md., when President John F. Kennedy was assassinated in 1963. Easton is an hour's drive from Washington and Veeck and his son, Mike, drove to the Capitol building where the body was lying in state at the Rotunda. It was a damp, cold night. Tens of thousands of people had gathered. A security guard recognized Veeck and told him: "C'mon this way. There's a VIP entrance."

Veeck, who had one leg, declined, and for seven hours he and Michael waited in line. Bill Veeck had come to pay his respects as a citizen, not as a celebrity.

"I've been thinking about Bill," said Andrew McKenna, who has been chairman of the board of both the Cubs and the White Sox. "I've been thinking he would be my ideal guy if I went on a round-the-world trip. He was truly a man for all seasons, and not just the baseball season but for all four seasons: winter, spring, summer and fall."

McKenna told of the night he and his wife, Joan, invited Veeck to a formal dinner party at their North Shore home. "I sat him next to an older woman, a dowager," McKenna recalled. "She eyed me with apprehension, as if to say, 'Who is this ill-mannered man without a necktie?' Later, after dinner, she said: 'What a fascinating young man. He can talk about everything.'"

Nick Kladis, a South Side grocer, was among Veeck's friends: "The last year or so, we had breakfast almost every day. The year before, it was lunch. We'd talk about everything: sports, business, his health. He was my psychiatrist, my father, my friend.

"One day I'm driving along and I see Bill sitting on the grass in Hyde Park, reading a book. He had taken his leg off. He used to paint it and put it on a bench, leave it out to dry. I threw the leg in my car, and as I'm driving away, I rolled the window down and yelled, 'Get home on your own.'"

John P. Carmichael, the retired columnist for the Daily News remembers Veeck when his father ran the Cubs and he was just a boy selling peanuts.

"I remember the '48 series when he had the Indians," Carmichael said. "They started Bob Feller—I think it was the fourth game—and Boston treated him rather rudely, knocked him out of the box. That night, in the press room, Bill was there and lots of other guys. In comes Toots Shor, the New York restaurant guy. Toots, who must have lost a bundle, looked at Veeck and said, 'Why don't you buy some ballplayers?' Then he threw a $100 bill at Bill and says 'Here, buy someone to relieve Feller.' Bill wasn't in a mood to be funny. He picked up the $100, tore it into a million pieces and dropped it in Toots' drink."

"His nine lives have run out," said Hall of Fame slugger Hank Greenberg, probably Veeck's closest friend. "He lasted a long time for a guy who underwent the knife as often as he did. His spirit was fantastic. He never complained. Even when he was in the hospital. You'd come to visit him and he made you feel great. He always had a feeling for the underdog. I learned a lot about life from him. I'm going to miss the hell out of him."

Veeck sold his White Sox holdings in the summer of 1961. In poor health, he moved with his family to Easton, Md., and they remained there for 14 years in a two-story farmhouse, an idyllic setting. Their neighbors were mostly the landed gentry, fiercely opposed to integration. After settling in, Veeck and his wife, Mary Frances, had a dinner party for their neighbors.

By coincidence, Minnie Minoso, who had played for both Cleveland and the White Sox, had arrived for a visit. As cocktails were being served, Veeck announced, "A special guest from Chicago will be joining us for dinner." In walked Minoso, a coal-black Cuban. "What was really wonderful," Veeck said later, "was that Minnie had them enthralled. He was the star of the evening."

Veeck's right leg was amputated below the knee in 1946 the result of a wound suffered on Bougainville during World War II. In the years since, he underwent 32 more operations, most of them on this same leg, and eventually, he lost the knee. Seven years ago, he shattered his only knee in a fall while fulfilling a speaking engagement at Tilden Tech High School. In the summer of '84, he fell again.

"I was sitting in my office when Bill called," said Dr. Sid Shafer. "He said: 'I'm on Roosevelt Road, in a grocery store. I either broke or dislocated my hip. If you're going to be in your office, I'll come right in.' He took a cab and came up to my office on the 17th floor of the Pittsfield Building. He had fractured his hip, on the same side as the amputation.

"Bill Veeck had more physical courage than anyone I've known. I never heard him complain. Two weeks ago I was in the hospital and he called me every day to cheer me up."

To Veeck, all men were created equal—until proven otherwise. The mass held for him Saturday at the Church of St. Thomas the Apostle began, appropriately, with Aaron Copland's "Fanfare for the Common Man."

The Rev. Thomas J. Fitzgerald, the celebrant, told of the time in the summer of 1984 when he gave Veeck the sacraments of the church. It was the day before Veeck underwent surgery for lung cancer.

"While I was with him, he called Mary Frances," Father Fitzgerald said. "And he said to her: 'Mary Frances, Father Fitzgerald is here with me. Now, everything's kosher.'"

Double Duty Radcliffe
The One and Only

DAVE HOEKSTRA

Chicago Sun-Times August 12, 2005

With a name like Theodore Roosevelt "Double Duty" Radcliffe, the son of a shipyard carpenter had to be destined for adventure. The Negro League baseball legend died Thursday in his Chicago home of complications from cancer. He was 103. Mr. Radcliffe was thought to be the oldest professional baseball player.

Mr. Radcliffe was born in Mobile, Ala., a baseball port that also would deliver Henry Aaron and Satchel Paige. He was one of 10 children who played baseball with his brothers by making taped balls of rags.

As a teenager, Mr. Radcliffe and his brother Alec embarked on a two-week hitchhiking trip to Chicago. They settled near old Comiskey Park, a legendary mecca for Negro League baseball. He threw his first pitch in

Chicago for the Scrub Packing Co. in a game against the Armour Stockyard Co.

Mr. Radcliffe entered the Negro National League in 1928 with the Detroit Stars. He went on to play for the Chicago American Giants, Homestead Grays, Brooklyn Eagles and made other stops in the Negro Leagues. In his prime, Mr. Radcliffe stood 5–9 and weighed 210 pounds. He was built like a boxcar and had the heart of a steam engine.

Mr. Radcliffe was given the nickname "Double Duty" by New York sportswriter Damon Runyon in the 1932 Negro League World Series when he played both games of a doubleheader for the Pittsburgh Crawfords. In the first game, he caught a Paige shutout; in the second, he pitched a 6–0 shutout.

"There were 46,000 people in Yankee Stadium," Mr. Radcliffe told me in 1991. "It was the first recognized Negro League World Series against the Lincoln New York Giants. Satchel pitched a three-hitter in the first game. I caught him and hit a home run with two men on base. After resting 20 minutes, I pitched, shut them out and hit a bases-loaded double."

Negro League statistics are sketchy, but Mr. Radcliffe played for or coached 30 teams in his career, recorded an estimated 4,000 hits and 400 home runs and won 500 games with 4,000 strikeouts as a pitcher. What is undisputed is that he appeared in six East-West All-Star Games, pitching in three and catching in three. He compiled a 13–5 record for the 1932 Crawfords, which included future Hall of Famers Josh Gibson, Oscar Charleston and James "Cool Papa" Bell. Mr. Radcliffe was best man at Bell's 1928 wedding.

"The most I ever made was $1,000 a month," Mr. Radcliffe said. "And I was the catcher, a pitcher, one of the best hitters, the secretary and the bus driver. I even changed the tires."

Even late in life, Mr. Radcliffe's fingers were short, thick and as hard as tree trunks. He shook hands as if you were coming instead of going. In 1937, Mr. Radcliffe managed John "Buck" O'Neil for the Memphis Red Sox. O'Neil, 93, is board chairman of the Negro Leagues Baseball Museum in Kansas City, Mo.

"He had a good baseball mind," O'Neil said Thursday from Kansas City. "As a catcher, he knew how to run a ball club."

While playing with the Kansas City Monarchs in 1945, Mr. Radcliffe roomed with Jackie Robinson and later was credited with integrating two semipro leagues. Ty Cobb liked to tell people that as a catcher Mr. Radcliffe wore a chest protector that said, "Thou shalt not steal." In 1994, Kyle McNary and Mr. Radcliffe self-published the biography *Ted "Double Duty" Radcliffe: 36 Years of Pitching and Catching in Baseball's Negro Leagues*.

It was Mr. Radcliffe's dream to be elected to the Baseball Hall of Fame. When the Hall of Fame Veterans Committee met in March, Elston Howard, Minnie Minoso and Mr. Radcliffe were among those on the ballot. No one was voted in.

"He should be in the Hall," said O'Neil, a member of the Veterans Committee from 1983 to 2001, when the rules were changed to include only living Hall of Famers on the committee. "Double Duty was good enough. He was a good hitter, and he had hard stuff as a pitcher. He didn't have a slider; we called it a nickel curveball. A curveball was a drop. He threw it overhanded."

At 96, Mr. Radcliffe became the oldest man to appear in a professional game when he threw a single pitch for the Schaumburg Flyers of the independent Northern League. His pitch counted in the game, and Mr. Radcliffe appears on the Flyers' all-time roster. Former White Sox slugger Ron Kittle was the Flyers' manager.

"He walked out with his cane," Kittle recalled Thursday. "The umpire said, 'You can't use the cane.' I said, 'Hell, he can't.' And he did. He tried to wind up and throw the ball. He got his arm up to where it was sideways and the ball bounced in.

"I escorted him out there on my arm, and I took him out arm-in-arm. It meant the world to him. I was his last manager–how cool is that?"

Every year since his 99th birthday (including his 103rd birthday July 7), Mr. Radcliffe threw a ceremonial first pitch for the Sox at U.S. Cellular Field.

"Double Duty shared such a love for baseball and a passion for life," Sox chairman Jerry Reinsdorf said in a statement. "We all loved to listen to his stories and share in his laughter. He leaves such a great legacy after experiencing so much history and change during his long life."

LEGENDS AND HEROES

They are the players and coaches who, through the decades, gave faces and voices to the yearnings of Chicago sports fans. When the roll is called, the greatest of them need no first name. Payton. Banks. Jordan. Hull. Fox. Jenkins. Sayers. Ditka. Durocher. Butkus. Mikita. Pierce. And so many more.

We meet some of them here at various stages of their lives and careers. Ernie Banks and Ryne Sandberg at the top of their games. Walter Payton and Nellie Fox at the end of theirs. Bobby Hull and Gale Sayers saying goodbye. Minnie Minoso trying for one more summer in uniform. Mike Ditka waiting for the phone to ring. Ron Santo and Chico Carrasquel playing the hands they were dealt. Dick Butkus and Tony Zale being described by some of the people who knew them best. Phil Cavarretta, Andy Pafko, and Leo Durocher wandering down memory lane.

Harry Caray, who, Skip Bayless reminds us in a column written shortly after his death, was a phenomenon long before he came to Chicago, belongs in this pantheon, too, I believe. In a sense, he stands for all the announcers who have shepherded the city's fans from one game to the next, one sport to the next, one season to the next, one generation to the next. Jack Brickhouse, Bob Elson, Lloyd Pettit, Lou Boudreau, Vince Lloyd, Jimmy Piersall, Jim Durham, Johnny Kerr, Irv Kupcinet, Pat Foley, Lorn Brown, Pat Hughes, Steve Stone, Ken Harrelson, Santo and others. They were, when you get right down to it, the soundtrack of our lives.

It's a Beautiful Day for Mr. Cub

DAVID CONDON

Chicago Tribune May 13, 1970

After you've mentioned the name of Ernie Banks to a Chicago Cubs' fan, there's nothing left to be said. No other names to be dropped, Ernie Banks is the all-time name of the game.

Ernie Banks is more than the name of the game. Ernie has more than the charisma of Ron Santo or the pride and humility of Billy Williams. Ernie Banks is soul.

He has made the worshipping Wrigley Field throngs forget Rogers Hornsby, Gabby Hartnett, Bill Nicholson, Hank Sauer, and others once set up as house heroes by the most fanatic band of fans in sport.

This was emphasized yesterday by the uproar greeting Ernie's 500th home run. No other player has hit even half as many homers while wearing a Cub uniform. Not the Rajah. Not Gabby. Not Swish Nicholson. Not even Hank Sauer, the once-revered "Mayor of Wrigley Field."

No other accomplishment by an athlete ever pleased me so much as yesterday's 500 milestone home run by Ernie, I'd venture that several hundred thousand of you say the same. And we'd all probably agree that it seems like just the day before yesterday that Ernie arrived on the scene.

Perhaps half a dozen times within the past decade, managers and writers have tacked a "has been" label on Ernie. Today, though, at the age of 39, Ernie indicates he'll still be going strong even after Ol' Man River has quit rollin' along.

Ernie was born on Jan. 31, 1931. Three other baseball greats—Willie Mays, Mickey Mantle, and Eddie Mathews—were born the same year. Now all four are in the 500-homer club, as they're certain to someday be teammates in the Hall of Fame.

Banks is the only one of the quartet who hasn't played in a World Series, and he may get about that business this fall.

It's unfortunate that outside Chicagoland, Mr. Cub is the least famous of the four. But from yesterday, and forevermore, no baseball fan need be afraid to mention Ernie Banks in the same breath with Mays, Mantle, and Mathews.

I've shared a few of Ernie's wonderful moments in baseball. All of us Southsiders neighbor considerably, and one afternoon in November of 1958 I dropped around Ernie's apartment, where the welcome sign was always out. I'll never forget that day.

All of us were nervously listening to a radio as the 5 p.m. newscast neared. My watch reached 5, and a minute past, but after what seemed an eternity, the news announcer said: "Ernie Banks of the last-place Chicago Cubs today was named the National League's Most Valuable Player for 1958. Banks, who hit 47 homers this season, received 283 of a possible 336 points. Willie Mays was a distant second, and Hank Aaron third."

Ernie shook his head in disbelief. He had known his chances were good, but it seemed too good to be true for the kid who even had helped drive the team bus in one of the lowest of the old Negro leagues.

For years now, Ernie's first greeting when you meet him at Wrigley Field is, "This is a wonderful day for a baseball game. I wish we were playing two double headers." A year or so ago, when Ernie went to entertain troops in Viet Nam, Bob Elson cautioned him: "Now don't get up some morning and tell those soldiers it's such a wonderful day you wish we had two wars."

I have to laugh, remembering two years ago when Ernie told me, "I can't be certain I won't be traded some day, too." Well, Phil Wrigley will be selling Dentyne at the corner cigar store before Banks is traded from the Cubs.

I thrill to Ernie's ability. Moose Moryn summed up Ernie's talent once by saying, "Batting behind Banks is like being a leadoff man. I'm a clean-up hitter with nothing left to clean-up."

Even as a member of the St. Louis Browns' fan club, I'm happy Ernie didn't wind up with the Browns. He could have if Bill Veeck hadn't been almost bankrupt. Veeck was the first to spot Ernie in the Negro leagues and tried to buy him on credit. The guy owning Ernie's contract said, "I'm as broke as you—a jump ahead of the sheriff." So Veeck routed Ernie to the Cubs "to keep him out of the American League."

A few years ago, after a game in Wrigley Field, I was headed for a steak dinner with my two all-time Cub favorites. As usual, Ernie was mobbed by young autograph hounds and obliged graciously. The old-timer with us stood in the background while Banks was being mobbed.

I grabbed a couple of the kids and said: "Get that guy's autograph, too. That's Rogers Hornsby, the greatest right handed hitter who ever lived."

"Who's Rogers Hornsby?" snorted a punk.

I know that Ernie Banks suddenly was filled with sadness about Hornsby. That Banks, he's beautiful. That Ernie Banks, he's a soul.

Walter Payton
Records Are Like Dreams
BERNIE LINCICOME

Chicago Tribune November 2, 1999
WALTER PAYTON, 1954–1999.
Walter Payton always got up. Always.

For 13 years with the Bears he took every hit, survived every collision, confronted every menace, shook off every tackle, always gave better than he got. Walter Payton always got the extra yard. Always.

He was the rock of the Bears, the one to take the ball every time anyone wanted to hand it to him, and he outlasted a full dozen Bears quarterbacks, any one of whom can claim no higher accomplishment than having handed the football to Walter Payton.

Gary Huff. Bob Avellini. Bobby Douglass. Mike Phipps. Vince Evans. Rusty Lisch. Why would Rusty Lisch ever be recalled except in connection to Payton? Jim McMahon. Steve Fuller. Greg Landry. Mike Tomczak. Doug Flutie. Jim Harbaugh.

Fuller once told me, "Sometime in the future the thing everyone in this locker room will be telling their grandchildren is that they played on the same team as No. 34."

The Bears' quarterbacks were the page-turners at the grand piano and Payton was the maestro, a football virtuoso. Payton played the sweetest music. Always.

He could throw the football and he could catch it. And when it was someone else's turn, he could block. Payton loved to block. One of Payton's fondest memories was picking up Lawrence Taylor on the blitz. Jim Brown never blocked. Never.

Payton's most vital contemporary, Franco Harris of the Steelers, saved himself by running out of bounds. Payton never ran out of bounds. Never.

Payton was the toughest Bear, tougher than Butkus or Ditka or Hampton. Payton has more records than any Bear, is held in more hearts than any Bear. Forever.

"Records," Payton once said, "are like dreams. They're good when you're having them, but when you wake up, you've forgotten what you were dreaming about."

The day he ran for 275 yards, breaking O.J. Simpson's single-game mark by two, the Bears won the game only 10–7. It was typical of Payton's lot. Not just that he was so ill with the flu that he wasn't sure he would make it through introductions, that he sucked it up and excelled, it was that Payton worked by accumulation, not by inspiration.

And even when he left football as the greatest rusher ever, his numbers were dismissed in favor of Simpson's verve, or Brown's power or Gale Sayers' electric legs.

Payton led the NFL in rushing only once, in 1977 with 1,852 yards, but he had more than 1,000 yards for 10 seasons in a row. He lacked that extra gear, the one that would have ended all arguments about the greatest running back ever. But which is more impressive, to outrun a defender or to drag him the last 15 yards into the end zone?

Someone always seemed able to find a back better at one thing than Payton, but no one ever has found a back better at everything than Payton. Ever.

Payton did not play football until the 11th grade in Columbia, Miss. He liked music and preferred the band. The first time he carried the ball, he ran 60 yards for a touchdown. Music never missed Payton and football was blessed to have him.

Payton was the cause of my initial fallout with Mike Ditka. I accused Ditka of indulging Payton in the only loss of the Super Bowl season, giving Payton the ball in order to get some record or other—consecutive 100-yard games, I think—and not only did Ditka not deny it, he reveled in it.

"I enjoyed giving Walter the ball," Ditka said. "I enjoyed it very much."

Ditka did not give Payton the ball in the Super Bowl to get an easy touchdown. He gave it instead to William Perry. In one of the few times Payton hinted at any selfishness, he admitted he was disappointed.

"I don't mind being a rabbit," Payton said.

But of course he did. And that's the way he finished with the Bears, a bad fit in a backfield with Neal Anderson. His diminished status didn't bother him as much as the thought that maybe he was hurting the Bears by taking up a roster spot out of sympathy.

No one ever needed to feel sorry for Walter Payton. Not then, not even when his ominous health condition was revealed. Prayers were welcome, pity was not. Payton died with the same great dignity with which he lived, as if he could have done anything else.

Never the optimist, Payton was a realist. Tomorrow is promised to no one, he said.

And though he was talking about all the hits and all the risks of running the football when he said it, this thought chills the heart today.

"It's just a matter of time," Payton said. "The law of averages will catch up with you."

What a cruel law.

The Compelling Absence of Bobby Hull

DAVID ISRAEL

Chicago Tribune November 2, 1978

The cheer would start in the second balcony and wash down through the stands of Chicago Stadium, a great tidal wave of excitement and anticipation.

Bobby Hull had picked up the puck now and was gathering himself for a rush up left wing. He would accelerate effortlessly, with the grace and ease of a cheetah eluding its hunter. He would deke and speed ahead, leaving defenders fumbling and helpless behind him. He would race across the blue line and wind up and fire the slap shot, the most savage of all the shots in the history of hockey.

And it did not matter at all whether Bobby Hull scored or he missed. For watching Bobby Hull rush the length of the ice to a shot was watching a master artist at work. It was watching Baryshnikov or Nureyev dance. It was listening to Casals or Rubenstein. A rush up ice by Bobby Hull was a brilliant aesthetic achievement, regardless of the result.

Gordie Howe is the hockey player who has endured the longest. Bobby Orr is the most gifted player ever to have performed. But Bobby Hull was the most exciting, the most thrilling.

And now Bobby Hull says he will never play again. Wednesday evening at a press conference in Winnipeg, Bobby Hull announced that he was retiring from the game at the age of 39. Now the hockey greatness of Bobby Hull will be something seen only in memories.

Of course, in Chicago, that has long been the case. For 15 winters, Bobby Hull played here. For 15 winters and 604 goals and a million exciting moments.

But then, in 1972, some rich men came together and decided they wanted to start a new hockey league, one called the World Hockey Association. They knew that right at the beginning they had to establish their credibility. They called up Bobby Hull. They said they heard he was in need of a new contract. They said they wanted to set him up for life, that they wanted to make him a wealthy man.

Bobby Hull said that sounded nice, but that he was a man of strong loyalties. He said he had to talk to his employers. It hardly occurred to him that his employers would not match the offer.

But William Wirtz, operating with the arrogance of a man born into wealth who has never looked for a job, determined that something called the Chicago Black Hawks was bigger than Bobby Hull. William Wirtz said he was not going to upset his pay scale on the account of one left wing.

So Bobby Hull jumped. He took the money from the men in Winnipeg. And he changed the pay scale of every team in professional hockey. After he went to work, the owners of the other teams in the National Hockey League started locking up their players with lucrative, long-term contracts. Bobby Hull made many more players than Bobby Hull wealthy.

In other sports, men have tried similar endeavors as the WHA. They tried the American Basketball Association. They tried the World Football League. They tried, but they could never succeed. And that was because there was no Bobby Hull to sign. There have been other players in sports as famous and others as talented, but there has never been a player as appealing as Bobby Hull. Besides, perhaps, Pele, there has never been a player in any team sport whose accomplishments were so vivid, whose strength and speed were so obvious, whose presence was as exciting as Bobby Hull's.

Even the other players felt it on the ice. Chico Maki, who centered Hull's line for years, came to regard Hull as a Rolls-Royce. Maki said you would be doing your job on the ice, carrying the puck, and then you would hear this Rolls-Royce purring and moving along, and you would give him the puck and get out of the way and let him conduct his business, which was scoring goals.

And his absence was just as compelling. For the Black Hawks, it created an emptiness that still has not been filled.

He has been gone since 1972, but still they bring him back here to do television advertisements for a bank. He has been gone since 1972, but still the Hawks have never recovered the fans who felt betrayed by their owners.

When Bobby Hull played for Chicago, the Hawks were the drawing card, and the Stadium was always filled. They came because they knew he would thrill them, because they never knew when he would score a hat trick or start a 10-game streak. On the night when Bobby Hull announced his retirement from hockey, the Hawks were playing the Vancouver Canucks and the Stadium was half empty. Since he has been gone, the Stadium has been filled only when the opposition warranted it, when it was Montreal or Boston or Philadelphia.

His absence has been so compelling that even the imperial boss, Billy Wirtz, came to admit that he had made a mistake, that he had erred, that he should have signed Bobby Hull.

Finally, of course, Billy Wirtz tried to atone for his family's sins. He went out and signed Bobby Orr, who had been to Boston what Bobby Hull is to Chicago, to play for the Black Hawks.

And on the day when he wanted to inform everyone of this great accomplishment, Billy Wirtz called a press conference at the Bismarck Theater.

Wirtz took the microphone in this moment of personal triumph and started talking.

"It's my pleasure to introduce the greatest hockey player ever, the newest Black Hawk," Billy Wirtz said, "Bobby Hull, er, Orr."

The place broke up. There was a roar of cheering and laughter. It was almost as if the noise had started building in the second balcony and had tumbled down here, to the ice, where it was giving Bobby Hull energy.

In 1986, the Chicago Black Hawks changed their names to the Chicago Blackhawks. Readers will encounter both designations in the pages ahead.

---

36 A Whale of a Tale about Tony Zale

JOHN SCHULIAN

Chicago Sun-Times April 30, 1984

So the champion's people rolled into the gym and what they saw was not the Tony Zale who would wage such unforgettable wars against Rocky Graziano, who would become the first middleweight since Stanley Ketchel to win the world title twice, who would one day hear Frank Sinatra praising him from a Las Vegas stage. What the champion's people saw, rather, was a boxer who bore a much closer resemblance to Anthony Florian Zaleski, the mill worker from Gary who could change his name but not the fact that he once lost three straight fights to guys you never heard of.

He was on the road to nowhere in 1940, and he was getting there fast. "A durable opponent, that's what he was becoming," says his old friend, Ben Bentley. Opponent is boxing's way of describing someone who isn't supposed to have any more future than a filet mignon in a logging camp.

To watch Zale in the gym even in his glory days was to wonder how he ever won a round, much less a fight. His lack of elegance had nothing to do with deception or sloth or anything else. It was just one of those things. And the champion's people didn't take that into account when someone suggested that their man, Al Hostak, could get some useful, non-title exercise against Zale. "This is what they said," Ben Bentley remembers. "They said, 'Do you think the commission would approve it?'"

Bentley looks at Tony Zale, sitting there listening in a stuffy room in a South Side gym, and then he looks at Zale's wife, Philomena. "Am I telling the truth?" he asks. "Is this a true story?" Zale nods his agreement. Philomena starts to say something.

But Bentley is already talking again. "Lemme finish the story," he says, because he was the publicity man at the Stadium and Marigold Gardens when boxing was something in Chicago and Tony Zale was establishing himself as somebody. He was there when Zale won a 10-round decision over Hostak and the champion's people demanded a rematch, for the title, on their turf in Seattle. "It was a fatal mistake," Bentley says. Zale, suddenly aware of the potential in his fists, didn't risk waiting for any out-of-town judges to put the National Boxing Association crown on his head. He knocked out Hostak in the 13th round.

"So they're on the plane back from Seattle, right?" Bentley says. "And they run into this terrible storm. The baggage is flying around, and people are heaving, and Art Winch, who was one of Tony's managers, he's down on the floor with his crucifix, praying. He figures it's all over, and he looks back behind him and there's Tony doing the crossword puzzle. If I'm lying, I'm dying. That right, Tony?"

"I look at it this way," Zale says, smiling as serenely as anyone can after 90 fights. "God's will be done."

There is a beauty about that philosophy that belies the savagery of the way Tony Zale hammered out his reputation. Though he dealt in pain— former champion Billy Soose always said Zale's body shots were "like having a hot poker stuck in you"—he tempered the deeds that put him on pages 659 and 660 of The Ring Record Book with a beguiling sense of decency. Never is it more apparent, in fact, than in the tale behind his latest honor.

When the 70-year-old Zale is inducted into the Chicago Sports Hall of Fame Thursday night, inducted with hors d'oeuvres and high-flown oratory at the Conrad Hilton Hotel, he will have gotten there the way he wanted to. "The right way," says Philomena Zale. The wrong way, as far as her husband is concerned, would have been to go in the hall when it was sponsored by a beer company. For he was never a drinker and be always told the kids he trained to lay off alcohol and he was damned if he was going to be a hypocrite just to get his name on another plaque.

Why, when they put Tony in the Boxing Hall of Fame, he had movie stars there," his wife says. "He's in the Polish Hall of Fame too, and one up in Canada and another one in New York and they're trying to get him in New Jersey. But to be in all the other hall of fames and not the one in Chicago was not flattering. He had to stick up for what he believed, though. If he had gone chasing after it, it wouldn't have been of no value."

Now Tony Zale has two kinds of satisfaction. First, he can sleep nights knowing that he is being honored by the Chicago Park District, which still employs him as a boxing instructor. Second, he can take pride in knowing he has been honored at last by the city where he fought his first amateur fight, and tried out for the 1932 Olympic team, and lit the sky with his part in the most glorious series of battles the Sweet Science saw in the 1940s.

Oddly, the only fight Zale lost in his three world title bouts with Rocky Graziano was the one they had in Chicago. It came after Zale had knocked the Rock kicking in New York, and it ended with Graziano raging because he thought his bleeding purple balloon of a right eye had forced the referee to stop the festivities in the sixth round. When he finally realized he had been declared the winner by technical knockout, Graziano celebrated with a unique turn of phrase: "I like Chicago. They trut me good."

Zale, of course, had plans for treating Rocky another way—bad. "Somebody asked me right away if I wanted a rematch," he recalls, "and I said, 'Sure, I'll knock him out in three.'" Zale did, too. He starched Graziano in Newark, N.J., and secured his place in boxing history by regaining his championship. He made a friend out of Graziano as well. "Oh yes," Philomena Zale says. "Rocky still calls, and when they do appearances anywhere together, Rocky makes sure Tony gets the same price he does."

It is a compliment, but to hear Zale talk about a chance encounter he had with Sugar Ray Robinson is to wonder if everything must bear a pricetag. The year was 1950, Zale was retired, and there was Sugar Ray, pompadoured, preening and seemingly primed for action. "He saw me," Zale recalls, "and he said, 'Hey, Tony, they offered me a lot of money to fight you. Thank God I didn't take it.'"

"You would have destroyed him," Philomena says.

And Tony Zale, who has always relied on God's will, just smiles.

Tony Zale died in 1997 in a nursing home in Portage, Indiana, at the age of eighty-three.

Gale Sayers
Curtain Call for a Legend

RAY SONS

Chicago Daily News September 11, 1972

He has limped off his last playing field. Gale Sayers. The most exciting athlete I've ever seen. Through at 29.

And it's a damn shame.

As I write this, Joe Moore lies on an operating table and the knife slices into another football knee and the endless toll cries out for a remedy.

Somehow, the solution must be found, for the sport is devouring its best young men, the quicksilver running backs who kindle the excitement.

Gale was somber when I talked to him late Sunday night after the day that had rung down the curtain. In the morning he had told George Halas he was retiring.

"It made me very unhappy to tell him," he said.

Halas, the old curmudgeon of football, has been like a second father to this quiet, withdrawn young man since Gale came out of a poor neighborhood in Omaha, Neb., only seven years ago.

Halas, in fact, was the reason Gale tried to come back this year, on knees that had taken too many hits and would never be the same again.

"I owed the old man one more year," Gale said. "He's been very good to me, and I haven't been able to do much for him the last two seasons."

So he went into Busch Stadium in St. Louis Saturday night, and carried the ball three times. Once he tripped over Don Shy's feet. Twice he fumbled and gave the Cardinals cheap touchdowns.

What a sad curtain call for a legend!

Had he really felt that he could come back this year?

"Yes, I'd always had the feeling I could do it," he replied. "I thought I ran well, but the pounding from the AstroTurf and from getting hit were too much. My knee was so sore."

So he came to realize Sunday morning that it could only be another season in which he'd be "in and out of the training room all the time, and not able to play every game."

A few minutes earlier, he had told his friend, Johnny Morris, on television: "I know I can't go on . . . I'm just getting myself into condition to walk right, not run."

This is a man who once could run like a wind-swept ghost.

I covered every league game he played as a Bear, except the first two, and I don't expect ever to see his equal.

There is no runner in football today who can approach him. In his prime, he could flit through a whole team with hardly a hand being laid on him.

He had the grace of a ballerina, the unpredictable moves of a tumbleweed in a tornado.

This was the man who was now looking me in the eye and saying: "I walk with a limp. I want to work that out. I was pressing too hard to get ready to play. Now I don't have to press. I can take my time."

And he moves on, at 29, to do something else.

Someday they'll put him on a pedestal in the Hall of Fame, with Thorpe and Grange and Jim Brown.

In that company, he'll run forever—without a limp.

Nellie Fox
The Mighty Mite Battles On

I ast yuh, what kind of team is it with players named Nellie and Minnie, maybe the Bloomer Girls? Well, it's a team what drives my Yankee champeens crazy.— Casey Stengel, as Yankee manager

DAVID CONDON

Chicago Tribune November 8, 1975

They called him "The Mighty Mite" when he was the American League's Most Valuable Player. He was better than that. Even today—battling cancer—he is Dynamite.

Fans called him "Little Nell." Or, in Minnie Minoso's words, "Little Bit." But he was The Big Man with the White Sox in their glorious Go-Go decade.

Connie Mack said "he's got baseball in his blood." Ted Williams said "he's a fielding pest who drives hitters into retirement." Rogers Hornsby said "except for Ted Williams, he has the best hitting eye in the game."

White Sox Manager Al Lopez declared that the Little Looey (Aparicio)–Little Nell tandem was the greatest all around shortstop–second base combination he ever had seen.

Any way you look at it, if they put people in the Hall of Fame for being self-made baseball stars, Jacob Nelson Fox would have arrived at Cooperstown ahead of Babe Ruth and Ty Cobb.

He was one great competitor. Perhaps the only 5-foot-8-inch giant I've known.

Little Nell tried to make us believe he was 5–9. Just as he tried to convince everyone that he weighed close to 160. I once saw Little Nell hit the scale, and it showed 152 pounds. They must have weighed him without his heart.

Nellie Fox was and is my kind of competitor. Even at this late hour I make Little Nellie 1 to 5 favorite in his battle against a dreaded disease.

The record books show that Nellie Fox, a Christmas present for all the baseball world in 1927, had a lifetime 19-season batting average of .288. He played 2,295 games at second base and had 2,663 career hits.

In 19 seasons, Nellie struck out only 216 times. (Mickey Mantle had 1,710 strikeouts in 18 seasons.)

But statistics and measurements are uninspiring unless you are running the tape measure around and about at the Miss America pageant. Statistics offer only a superficial picture of Little Nell's greatness.

The tobaccy-chawin bantam just had to be something to be so idolized by the fans.

How many remember Nellie Fox Day in the White Sox pennant year of 1959? Mayor Daley does.

Mayor Daley was there to see fans give Nellie t-w-o (2) automobiles, a power sailboat, groceries, vacation trips, furs for the Mrs., other gifts galore.

White Sox mates gave a fancy shotgun to the pepper pot who wintered in the Pennsylvania hunting fields. His eye with the shotgun was as keen as his eye with the bat.

And Little Nell's eye with the bat was super keen. The great Hornsby once said:

"You can get the whole message by looking at Little Nell's bat. He has such a true swing that one part of the bat is practically flattened by contact with the ball."

Pitcher Gaylord Perry also can tell you about Nellie's bat. When Nellie was tail-ending it in the National League, he got a crucial hit to beat Perry. The infuriated pitcher rushed to the plate and busted Fox's bat.

That cost Gaylord the price of a new Louisville stick, then $3.98.

Nellie Fox was a high school sophomore in St. Thomas, Pa., in the wartime spring of 1941. He was no larger than the diamond in a $23 engagement ring, but his baseball hopes were big.

He begged his father to take him to the Philadelphia Athletics training camp—the big stuff, not a tryout camp—at nearby Frederick, Md. Papa Fox loaded the kid and his glove in a pickup truck and off they went.

It must have been something to see the 16-year-old Mighty Mite talking to Connie Mack, 82-year-old Athletics' manager. Mr. Mack offered little encouragement.

Once he saw Nell's hustle, though, Mr. Mack told the elder Fox: "Leave your boy with me."

Nellie apprenticed in the minors and eventually wound up with the parent Athletics. They traded him to the White Sox for catcher Joe Tipton on Oct. 19, 1949.

Fox played in 130 White Sox games in 1950, getting the big shot after All-Star second baseman Cass Michaels was traded. He batted only .247. So the Sox brought in Joe Gordon to teach Nellie hitting. Doc Cramer improved Fox's fielding. Richards was Nellie's bunting instructor. From then on, all systems were Go-Go.

Nellie Fox was a winner then and we hope he's a winner again.

Nellie Fox died of skin cancer on December 1, 1975, at the age of forty-seven. He was inducted into the Hall of Fame in 1997.

Da Ex-Coach Hasn't Mellowed One Bit

RICK TELANDER

Chicago Sun-Times September 3, 1995

The wounded bear is restless.

He grumbles and fidgets in his lair, which for now is a well-appointed bedroom at his north suburban cave—excuse us—house.

Mike Ditka, the closest living creature we have to a real, honest-to-God, old-fashioned, rub-some-dirt-on-it-and-get-back-in-there-and-kill-somebody Chicago Bear, raises the leg rest on his reclining chair and shifts his weight.

Again.

It's not easy having a right hip that's more battered than a ham hock in a dog kennel. But that's what he's got.

He had surgery to replace his left hip years ago, then he had the right one redone a month ago. And that right hip came apart just eight days later, because of (choose one): natural causes, patient irresponsibility.

So he had more surgery, and now he's got a room full of canes and crutches, with a urine bottle hanging on the edge of the bed.

He has a tube in his chest, into which he shoots antibiotics twice a day. And he has wife-nurse Diana sitting at the foot of the bed, griping that her big, muttering patient is putting a serious cramp in her golf game.

"Go on. Play golf," growls the Bear.

But she only smiles. She's more devoted to the big lunk than ever.

The only coach who ever led the Bears to a Super Bowl title clicks his TV changer.

U.S. Open tennis is on. Women playing. Ditka loves it.

"I love all games," he states. Except baseball now. Because of last year's greedy strike and the cancellation of the World Series.

There is no dignity in that, he says.

"How high is high?" he asks. "What's enough?"

He lowers the leg rest, fidgets, changes channels.

Nice Super Bowl ring on his finger.

"It's the Hall of Fame ring," he corrects. "The Super Bowl was a great thing. But I took the ring off because we weren't champs anymore."

Back to ESPN.

Ditka doesn't want to talk about the 1985 championship Bears or owner Mike McCaskey, who fired him, or whether he has been blackballed from coaching in the NFL.

"I can't win talking about that stuff," he sighs.

OK, does he want to coach again.

"No," he fires back.

Then he looks at his guest with those fiery, deep-set, attacking-animal eyes.

"Could I coach?" he growls. "Yes. My way? Yes. Could I win? Yes."

"If he had an owner who had the same attitude as his," chimes in Diana, making it clear that she and hubby maybe have discussed this before.

Well, let's check McCaskey off that short list, then.

Still, Ditka's out there. He's on TV. He may be crippled, but he's only 55. Some owner must want to win, Ditka-style, no?

"Ah, they set their goals to be competitive," he grimaces. Competitive sucks.

Why is his old assistant Buddy Ryan still in vogue then?

"Because he's great!" the ex-coach snaps.

How did Buddy get former Arizona Cardinals head coach Joe Bugel's job, anyway?

"Buddy called down there and made a sales pitch," Ditka says. "One fat guy sold himself to another fat guy."

Shall we check Cardinals owner Bill Bidwell off the list?

A wine salesman enters the room.

He and the Ditkas discuss fine merlots.

Isn't Da Coach supposed to be off wine and cigars and all that stuff since his heart attack way back when?

Haven't had a cigar or a drink in a month, Ditka says.

Well, sure, he's been laid up that long, too.

And that hip, that didn't just fall out on its own, did it?

Ditka swears it came out after surgery when he was riding in a golf cart, watching son Mike Jr. play a big-money game in Aurora.

He swears he was not actually swinging a club.

"When I moved on the cart, it moved tremendously," he defends. "So I had a friend of mine pull it back into the socket."

When he was playing for the Bears back in 1964, Ditka dislocated his left shoulder and two doctors stood on him and yanked like crazy to get the limb back into place.

"Had a foot on my chest, one here, and one on my neck," Ditka recalls. "I thought they broke my neck."

It's just pain, anyhow. Nuisance. Nothing.

He'll be up and about soon, he says. All that ever remains are the memories.

His epitaph with the Bears? "I came. I saw. I did what I had to do," he says. "I'm gone."

Summer Love
Harry Caray, a Radio, and Baseball
SKIP BAYLESS

Chicago Tribune April 2, 1998

Forgive me, but I prefer to remember the old Harry.

The St. Louis Harry. The Harry who was heard but rarely seen. The Hall of Fame Harry who described baseball as sharply and dominantly as Bob Gibson pitched. The Harry Caray who made summers so magical and memorable for so many millions in so many Middle American states.

The old Harry was the best baseball broadcaster I ever heard, and that includes Vin Scully and Mel Allen. If you never heard that Harry, I feel for you. I enjoyed the Chicago Harry too, but he had spoiled me too much to embrace him the way Cubs fans did.

To me and many of my boyhood friends, the Cubs Harry turned himself into a lovably goofy sideshow for a franchise that had little else to offer its faithful. Harry Caricature, we called him.

The one thing he couldn't do with his voice was sing. Yet Cubs fans stayed until the seventh inning just to watch him lean out of the press box and lead them through "Take Me Out to the Ball Game."

The St. Louis Harry took me out to the ballgame via radio, and I never wanted to miss the eighth and ninth. That Harry was so good he ruined the first big-league game I saw in St. Louis. It didn't quite measure up to the ones Harry had brought to Technicolor life for me as I lay in bed with the lights out.

As the home opener approaches, allow me to pay my last respects to that Harry, who died less than two months ago. Holy cow, was he talented.

That Harry was known and cherished by millions from North Dakota to south Texas. That Harry did games for 50,000-watt KMOX out of St. Louis, along with affiliate stations from here to Petticoat Junction. For all I know, Harry willed his voice into homes and cars from the halls of Montezuma to the shores of Tripoli.

I've heard from people who had "Twilight Zone"–like Harry experiences while driving alone on a late summer night down some lonesome road in, say, Georgia or New Mexico. One minute, they were listening to Mel Tillis on KCOW; the next, Harry was saying, "Two-two to Cepeda. McCarver would be next."

Some nights, Harry so electrified games that he probably interrupted signals up and down the dial. Oh, did I love hearing him say something as trivial as "two-two." Harry hit the "ts" so hard that he made "two-two" sound more dramatic than "Four score and seven years ago . . ."

Harry didn't just say words; he fired them at you like rising fastballs, emphasizing odd and unpredictable syllables. "Ho-LEE cow!" he might say.

During our teenage years, Harry was to my buddies and me what Wolfman Jack was to "American Graffiti." Harry's voice was omnipresent on hot nights in Oklahoma City. You ate dinner and did your homework to Harry. You cruised for "chicks" with Harry on the radio of your 65 Mustang or 67 Camaro. Girls wouldn't go out with you a second time because you wouldn't let them change the station. Who needed the Beatles or Stones when you could listen to Harry rock and fire?

The St. Louis Harry did not mispronounce names. A stroke hadn't yet robbed him of his diction. He was not yet Everyfan, broadcasting from the bleachers, drinking beer and getting a little crazy with the Toms, Dicks and Harrys. We didn't want the St. Louis Harry to be one of us.

We considered him a higher authority. Harry knew the game and he wasn't afraid to constructively criticize those who played it. It was almost as if you were listening to the Cardinals manager, supplying you with his clever, unedited insight.

Harry was not as eloquent as Scully or as folksy as Allen, but he could tell stories as effectively as either. For my money, he was more consistently entertaining than Scully or Allen because he was more passionate. Harry's voice conveyed drama the way wire does current. Harry could jolt you out of a backseat kiss.

Of course, through the 60s, Harry was fortunate enough to describe many classic moments. If the Cardinals hadn't played in three World Series, maybe Harry wouldn't have sounded quite so great. But I believe I would have listened to the 60s Harry if he had been doing the Toledo Mud Hens.

That Harry didn't yet wear cartoon-size glasses. That Harry wasn't yet a "Cub fan and a Bud man" or the Mayor of Rush Street. That Harry didn't yet cultivate the image of the broadcaster who could outdrink anyone in the sports bar. For me, watching the Cubs Harry was sometimes like watching Olivier do vaudeville.

I sometimes wondered if Harry, in effect, died for the Cubs cause—if he sacrificed some of his credibility for the good of so many bad teams. If possible, Harry became a bigger attraction than Wrigley Field itself—bigger than the ivy. He once said that a full house would show up just to sing "Take Me Out to the Ball Game" with him. That was sadly true.

But not nearly as sad as this: "Saturday Night Live" began doing skits of Harry as a babbling, mush-mouthed talk-show host. To me, this was appalling. This was supposed to be my Harry, the greatest ever. Oh, take me back to the ballgame, Harry.

I loved him as much as Cubs fans did, but I prefer to hold on to earlier memories. Summer hasn't been quite the same without him. On clear nights, maybe, you can still hear him on some lonesome two-lane: "Two-two to Cepeda . . ."

Back to the Bush Leagues with Minnie Minoso

TOM FITZPATRICK

Chicago Sun-Times

I met Minnie Minoso one day in his room in Chicago's Southmoor Hotel, where he was staying for a few days before leaving for Guadalajara to join his team, Charros de Jalisco. After fourteen seasons as a major-league star, he was going back to the bushes. Only this time Minnie was admitting to being forty-two or forty-three years old. Why did he do it?

"This is the one profession God gave me," Minnie said as he leaned forward in his chair. "I'm going to do it until He tells me I can't do it any more. I slow down sure, maybe one foot, no more. My eyes are the same. I hit. I keep playing because i want to find out for myself if I can do these things without hurting myself—without getting on the rubbing table every day."

Minnie smiled as he recalled the reaction of Mexican fans to his brand of play, which has often been described as eccentric, but never demeaned as being dull.

"Every city in Mexico I go to," he said, "writers and radiomen come to me. They ask me, 'Minnie, how come you are here? You can still play in the big leagues.' Sometimes they even ask: 'Did you do something wrong that you must be here?' I still tell them that I did nothing wrong except to run into a wall for a fly ball or to get hit on the head with a pitch."

Minnie sat quietly, fingering a World Series ring on his left hand. Minnie never played in a World Series game, but the ring was given to him as a gesture of friendship by Bill Veeck after the White Sox won the pennant in 1959. Minnie was with the Cleveland Indians in 1959 but was traded to the White Sox for the 1960 season.

"I know I can still play in the major leagues," he said, "but I guess they want young men that have years to play. Maybe I have one year. The only future I have is to hang up my glove. I have great respect for my profession and for the fans who come to see me play. I would not want to play if I would make the fans ashamed because I would not do a bad thing . . . not to be able to do the things I did before."

Veeck is still one of Minnie's greatest admirers. Once he advised Minnie to go to a big-league camp without a contract and ask for a tryout. Minnie, his eyes flashing, recalled his answer:

"'Veeck,' I told him. 'I'm just like you. I believe I die before I go down on my knees to beg. I have pride. Perhaps it is too much pride. But that is the way I am.'"

Minnie stopped talking then. He stared straight ahead at a picture on the wall through shining eyes. He swallowed hard several times but there were no more words to come.

Ryne Sandberg
Every Day Was a Battle

BARRY ROZNER

Arlington Daily Herald January 5, 2005

Most days, finding the good in pro sports is akin to looking for a needle in a stack of needles.

But on a rare day like Tuesday, the good washes over you like a warm bath after a frigid day in the snow.

Ryne Sandberg, who did it all the right way, got what he richly deserved Tuesday, a perfect trip to baseball's Mecca.

The long journey to Cooperstown, which began in a tiny Montana garage converted into an apartment 27 years ago, will conclude July 31 with the greatest honor baseball can bestow.

Sandberg is officially what we've all known for a long time: He is a Hall of Famer.

He got there by defeating complacency, by refusing its temptation and with a silent fire few understood.

Even Tuesday, on one of the greatest days of his life, Sandberg refused to travel off the road of humility that led him to immortality.

"I don't know what it feels like to be considered among the greatest who ever lived and I don't know if I ever will," Sandberg said, phoning from his cell phone as he scurried for the airport and a flight to Chicago. "I have too much respect for the game and for the players who played it before me to think anything like that."

In stark contrast to those who campaign for it and even assume induction, Sandberg seemed in disbelief Tuesday.

At 11:30 a.m., Sandberg got the call 90 minutes before the announcement was made, learning that out of 516 ballots cast, he received 393 votes—or a mere six more than necessary in his third year of eligibility.

"Total elation was the first thing I felt, after a lot of butterflies," Sandberg said. "You think of so many people at that moment, too many to mention. So many people in your family and on all those teams make this happen. You don't do this yourself."

Sandberg can't forget the effort that went into being a 10-time all-star and nine-time Gold Glover, so he didn't need a bust or a plaque to validate his work.

"No, I didn't need it, but it sure is an honor and I think the greatest honor there is in sports. It's one of a kind," Sandberg said. "It's really something that lasts forever. When you think about that, it's overwhelming.

"It's one thing to be thought of as an excellent player, but this takes it to another level."

Perhaps the reason you feel so good about it today is that Sandberg never let himself believe he was a star.

He started at the very bottom of the minors and worked his way to the majors, never asking anyone for anything but a chance to play.

He had to struggle to get past highly touted draft picks in the Phillies organization, usually without the support of execs who didn't see his major-league potential.

He had to fight to be noticed, and he did that only on the field. Off the field, he believed what he was taught by the veterans: Be seen and not heard.

He did it with a work ethic that was unmatched in a Philadelphia organization that insisted on nothing less than ferocity.

"Ryne Sandberg worked harder than any player I've ever seen," Pete Rose said in 1994. "A lot of guys with his athletic ability get by on that and have a nice career. Sandberg worked his (butt) off because he knew it was wrong not to."

That helped him survive his early career struggles, and when he became a superstar in 1984, Sandberg knew exactly how to handle it:

Work harder.

"Basically, I was afraid to let anyone down," Sandberg said. "Dallas Green and Jim Frey and Don Zimmer and my teammates and the fans and my family. Everyone expected a certain level of play and I didn't want to disappoint anyone.

"I didn't want to let myself down. I was terrified. The best way I knew how to do that was to work at it."

So Sandberg never took much time off in the winter, and each spring he reported with pitchers and catchers, no matter the success he had the season before.

"That's what I thought I had to do," Sandberg said. "I went into every spring convincing myself I had to make the team."

There was nothing as reassuring as seeing Sandberg on the field 45 minutes before the rest of the team at Fitch Park, taking an extra 45 groundballs.

The best fielder in the history of his position never took a hop for granted, so before some guys were awake, he'd take 15 grounders right at him, 15 to his left, and 15 more to his right, each time completing the throw to first as though it really counted.

"Every day was a struggle," Sandberg said. "Every day was a battle. It didn't come easy to me and I never treated it like it did."

So he did it the right way, never taking anything for granted, never campaigning for awards or all-star teams, and he refused to beg for Hall of Fame votes.

Sandberg truly believed that would take away the exhilaration and satisfaction of winning election if it ever happened.

He did not play to the suggestions that someone is or isn't a "first-ballot Hall of Famer." You can't be a second- or third-ballot Hall of Famer any more than you can be sorta-pregnant. You are or you're not.

But Sandberg didn't let those who passed him by the first two years compromise his integrity. He would not start pandering now.

During his playing days, he didn't do back flips. He didn't mug for the cameras. He didn't blow kisses to the fans, self-promote or take as much human growth hormone as you can stuff in a cash-filled paper bag.

He just played the game the right way on the field, and off it he could only be himself. And while that wasn't good enough for many, he was true to himself, and that meant more to him than a few more votes or a few endorsement dollars.

One of the most misunderstood athletes in Chicago's history, most media never spent more than 30 seconds at a time near Sandberg's locker, but their perception that he had nothing to say was OK with him, because it meant fewer interested parties, less time answering questions and more time for what he considered important: game preparation and time at home.

In the 1980s and '90s, Sandberg was all that was good about a great game, a throwback to an earlier generation that believed in hard work and the rewards it brought. That is how he got to this day.

Ryne Sandberg, Hall of Fame, Class of 2005.

"It lasts forever," Sandberg said, his voice cracking. "That's the part that's kind of shocking. It's forever."

He's part of history now, never to be forgotten. Inhale, drink it in and enjoy the feeling. We don't get many chances to remember what used to be.

Thanks, Ryno, for one last thrill.

Just One Word for Terror
Butkus

DON PIERSON

Chicago Tribune February 4, 1979

He never needed a first name. Nor an aptitude test. Like the middle linebackers before him—George, Schmidt, Nitschke—a first name seemed superfluous.

And their profession was as subtle as the sound of their last names. "Tackle by Barry Manilow" never would have seemed quite right.

Butkus. He was as Chicago as Daley, as Illinois as Grange. Some people are born to play football. Football was born for Dick Butkus. Some people name their children after their heroes. In Chicago, people name their dogs after Butkus—out of respect. He symbolizes the ferocity of his sport. He is in the Hall of Fame now, and a thousand NFL players are oh so glad he's there and not still on the field.

These include some of his former teammates, who used to be terrorized in their training-camp dormitories, much as running backs were terrorized on Sunday afternoons.

Doug Buffone and Ross Brubacher, outside linebackers who flanked Butkus through much of his career, still insisted he set their door on fire one night. They didn't see him do it, but they heard the chuckle, the same fiendish chuckle he laid on running backs when they were on their backs.

"He was so diabolical," said Buffone. "You could catch him red-handed doing something and he'd deny everything. 'Whaddaya talking about?' he'd ask."

"He blamed (Bobby) Douglass for setting our door on fire, but Douglass was so drunk he couldn't have formed the intent to do it," said Brubacher, who talks like a trial lawyer, which he is. "Butkus even had the motive. A half-hour earlier, he was in our room chewing tobacco and spitting it on the: floor. We chased him out.

"I have nothing to confess," Butkus said. "Circumstantial evidence. It all leads up to me, but I've got witnesses. And they've never called me on my offer to take a polygraph test. I just figured it was Douglass, because Douglass' sheet had throw-up on it and that was the sheet that started the fire.

"They just thought it was me because I used to hang around with Mirro Roder (former placekicker), and Mirro would do anything I told him to. One night I was going around spraying lighter fluid on the doors, and Mirro was following me dropping matches."

Butkus got blamed for everything.

At the University of Illinois, he was blamed by school officials for telling a writer he came to Illinois to play football instead of to become a nuclear physicist or a public relations expert.

"Well, it was the truth," said Butkus.

He was blamed for biting a referee during an exhibition

"I never said he bit me," said Ralph Morcroft, the referee. "There were a lot of fights and I was trying to break up one. Butkus was involved. I was throwing people out of the game and Abe Gibron asked me why. I said, 'Look at the blood on my hand. I have to throw out someone.' Next thing I know Butkus is denying in the paper that he bit me. I still don't know how it happened."

He was blamed for being a dirty player. "Oh, yeah," said Ed Flanagan, former Detroit Lions' center who was Butkus' arch-enemy from his college days at Purdue. "He'd kick, spit, grab my face-mask, anything to get to the ball-carrier. He bit me once in a pileup. In the leg. He was just nasty."

"The Lions are the only team that ever called me dirty," said Butkus.

Butkus never bit Mick Tingelhoff. "But once he untied my shoe in a pileup," said Tingelhoff, Minnesota center who roomed with Butkus at the College All-Star game in 1965.

53

"How could he bite anyone through his facemask?" asked Brubacher, ever the attorney.

"I don't think he ever bit anyone," said Ed O'Bradovich, former defensive end who was Butkus' closest friend on the Bears. "I wouldn't put it past him, though. Maybe if someone stuck their fingers through his facemask . . . If he did bite anyone, I'm sure he did a good job of it."

He was blamed for punching Detroit runners Mel Farr and Altie Taylor on a Monday night television game.

"I don't know if there was some unwritten rule that you couldn't go for the ball when you made a tackle," said Butkus. "I was drawing my hand out, and I looked like I was punching them. I never could understand why players would wait until the last 20 seconds of the game before going for the ball when you could do it the whole game."

He was blamed for flooding the bathroom at the Bears' old Rensselaer, Ind., training site.

"Someone took the nut and bolt out of the toilet, and water was streaming across the floor," said Butkus. "It started dripping through the ceilings, so we tried to screw the nut in, but the pressure blew it into the toilet.

"I didn't do it, but then guys started making fun of me, saying the next thing they'd see me do was stringing two wires from the dorm to blow them up."

"We thought we'd see him out on the lawn pushing the dynamite plunger," said Buffone.

"You know how these stories get started," said O'Bradovich. "Pretty soon, he's committed murder."

Mayhem, maybe.

He used to call time out in the final seconds, even with the Bears hopelessly behind, just to "get another shot" at a center.

"He'd spit on the ball, insult me, my mother—we had a real resentment going," said Flanagan. "He used to love me on punts. He'd take three steps back and try to kill me."

The intimidation would start before the game.

"Once we came to Soldier Field and it was cold," said Flanagan. "I was centering for punts in the pregame drill, and I took my warmup jacket off. I looked up and there was Butkus wiping his feet on it."

"I was centering in warmups once, and I felt something wet on my hands," said Tingelhoff. "I couldn't figure out what it was because the sun was shining. I looked up and Butkus was standing there spitting on me. True story."

It might be difficult for anyone except a football player to understand, but Flanagan is as sincere in his praise of Butkus as he is in his dislike.

"He played on some of the worst teams the Bears ever had," said O'Bradovich. "If he had been playing for Oakland or Miami, they'd have barred him from the league."

"He was rough and rugged, and you had to respect a guy like that," said Tingelhoff. "He said some bad things about my holding. Said he'd recognize me if the lights went out by the feel of my hands. He would accuse me of clipping, and I'd try to step on his hands.

"I enjoyed it a lot."

Andy Pafko and the Cubs
How Do You Explain a Love Affair?

STEVE DALEY

Chicago Tribune May 1, 1984

Pick any year in the long and blissfully melancholy history of the Chicago Cubs and you'll discover that 1948 was as grim as any of the rest.

Three short summers after losing the World Series to Detroit, Charlie Grimm's Cubbies were on their way to a 64–90 record and eighth place.

As it happened, both Chicago baseball teams were ticketed for the wine cellar that season. The Sox would finish an unspeakable 51–101 under Ted Lyons, and one Chicago paper did its bit for civic esteem by printing the baseball standings upside down.

Still, then and now, no bespectacled European philosopher or Asian guru can best a Cubs fan when there is anxiety to be confronted and explained away.

A Cubs fan sees diamonds where others see broken glass. Give the man or woman in the bleachers the genuine article—a Banks, a Williams, a Buckner—and they'll follow you anywhere.

In 1948, the Wrigley Field love affair with Andy Pafko was in full flower.

It was his fifth full season in Chicago, and the years spent patrolling center field for the wartime Cubs were kind for all concerned. Futile in a baseball sense, of course, but kind.

Sure, a series of dismal events had made a third baseman of Pafko in '48, against his will and his better judgment.

Playing out of position next to the semi-legendary shortstop Roy Smalley, Pafko had 29 errors while Smalley made 34 at short. The good news was that Pafko also hit .312, with 26 home runs and 101 runs batted in. In his fifth full year with the Cubs, the kid from Boyceville, Wis., was everybody's darling.

"I don't know why it is," Pafko said one day last week. "Cub fans do seem to kind of pick out one guy they like and stick with him.

"You go to other parks and maybe they make every guy on the club a hero. It's a pattern you don't see in other ballparks. Cub fans always seem to have a soft spot for certain players, I guess. Ernie Banks was one, of course, and Bill Buckner, I guess. I was lucky enough to be one of them."

Three summers later, in 1951, after hitting 36 home runs for a seventh-place club, Pafko would be traded to Brooklyn in an eight-player deal that would set the standard for Cubs' front-office ineptitude right up until Lou Brock left town and Ernie Broglio arrived.

"Thirty years later, people still talk to me about that trade," said Pafko, who, not long after arriving in Brooklyn, watched Bobby Thomson's historic home run sail over his head in left field. "We were playing a three-game set in June with the Dodgers in Wrigley, and (Brooklyn pitcher) Don Newcombe came up and told me I was going to Brooklyn.

"I came home to have dinner after the first game of that series, and the Cubs called me to tell me I'd be playing for Brooklyn the next day. I was, and hit a home run, in fact. They booed me in Wrigley. First time that ever happened.

"You know, people say to me, 'The Cubs never won another pennant after they traded you, Andy.' And they never had a center fielder, either, when you stop to think about it."

Pafko spent seven years in the Braves' organization as a player, did some scouting and managed in the minor leagues before leaving the game in the early 1960s. These days, he lives in suburban Mt. Prospect and works as a starter at a local golf club.

Pafko makes infrequent trips to Wrigley Field and gets together with old friends at events like the Cracker Jack Old-Timers game in Washington.

"Old ballplayers," he said, "we sit around and talk about the money these young guys make and about who ought to be in the Hall of Fame."

In conversation, Pafko carries traces of a middle European accent and a farm-boy dignity into his 63rd year.

"People still remember," he said, smiling. "I was driving down in Georgia a couple of years ago, and I stopped to get gas. I gave the guy in the station my credit card to pay for it, and he just stared at the card.

'It can't be,' the guys says to me. 'Andy Pafko. It can't be.' Kind of nice when they remember."

This week, a part of his town will remember when Pafko is inducted into the Chicago Sports Hall of Fame. He'll sign on Thursday along with the likes of Tony Zale, Alex Agase, Keith Magnuson, Minnie Minoso and a dozen other worthies.

Pafko likes the company and likes the shock of recognition that comes with the mention of a vintage Cub name.

"It's funny," he said. "I always think of myself as a Cub and a Cub fan, even though I played more years with the Braves' organization.

"I met my wife in Chicago and kept my home here since '43, since my first season with the Cubs."

There's a World Series ring on Pafko's left hand, circa 1945, and no one is more aware of the scarcity of that particular item than the bearer.

"It's the last one, you know," Pafko said. "I never imagined the team would go so long without a pennant. I mean, I thought they might accidentally win one."

What's Up with Phil Cavarretta

JOE GODDARD

Chicago Sun-Times September 29, 2002

AGE: 86.

HOME: Villa Rica, Ga.

FAMILY: Wife Lorayne, daughters Diane, Patti Jo, Cheryl Jean and Lori, son Philip Jr.

OCCUPATION: Retired. After playing for 22 seasons, he coached and scouted for the Detroit Tigers and was a hitting instructor for the New York Mets.

POSITIONS: First base, left field.

NICKNAME: Cavvy, Philabuck.

BASEBALL BACKGROUND: One of the most popular players in Cubs history, Cavarretta went from Lane Tech in 1934 to starter for the National League champion Cubs in 1935. Playing 20 seasons with the Cubs (1934–53) and two with the White Sox (1954–55), Cavarretta hit .293 and took part in three World Series. He reached base a record five consecutive times in the 1944 All-Star Game, was the 1945 National League MVP with a league-leading .355 average, hit .423 in the 1945 World Series loss to the Tigers and was the Cubs' player/manager in 1951–53 before being fired during spring training in 1954. At 37, he batted .310 for the 1954 White Sox.

ABOUT LANE TECH: "We won the city championship all four years (1931–34) for coach Percy Moore, may he rest in peace. He was an assistant scout for the Red Sox and took me to Wrigley Field to take batting practice against Pat Malone, a grizzled old veteran. I was only 135 pounds. He thought I was the batboy, but I sprayed the ball around pretty good, and he yelled, 'Get that little guy out of there.'"

A MINOR EXPERIENCE: "I hit for the cycle in my first pro game for Class A Peoria, but Peoria was only drawing 25 people a game. So I was sent to Reading, Pa., where I met Dominic Dallessandro, another paisano. I hit .308, but I was lonesome and wanted to go home when Dom got a telegram. He read it and said, 'It's for you. You're going to Chicago.' I was 18."

ABOUT BABE RUTH: "I joined the Cubs in Boston and was getting ready at my locker when Babe Ruth came in, his big belly hanging over his shorts. A photographer took a picture of us. The Babe stared and stared at me with those sharp eyes and finally said, 'You know, kid, you should be in high school.' That photo is one of my prized possessions. Batting practice was part of Babe's promotional work for the Braves. I've never seen such a beautiful swing."

ABOUT GABBY HARTNETT: "Gabby would talk to anybody, even a wall. Al Capone had Wrigley Field seats by the visitors' dugout and wanted a picture with him. When it ran in the Tribune, commissioner Kenesaw Mountain Landis called Gabby to his office in the Wrigley Building and said, 'I ought to suspend you for posing with a criminal. Just don't do it again!' Gabby came back shaking and said, 'Well, I guess I won't be talkin' to the Big Guy anymore.'"

ABOUT DIZZY DEAN: "A great pitcher and a great guy. But if you looked at him wrong, he'd throw at you."

ABOUT HITTING: .355: "You've got to be lucky to hit that high, and I was lucky. I had a lot of flares and bleeders."

ABOUT BEING FIRED IN SPRING TRAINING: "I felt Mr. Wrigley (Cubs owner P.K. Wrigley) should know in the spring of '54 that we weren't getting any better and probably should make some trades. We needed help in center field, second base, first base and catcher. A newspaper reporter heard of it and ran it, and I got fired. (The Cubs finished seventh under Stan Hack.) Whenever I saw Mr. Wrigley after that, he said, 'I'm sorry, Phil. I never should have fired you.'"

ABOUT THE WHITE SOX: "Frank Lane, a tough old guy, signed me at a restaurant. I asked for an iron-clad contract, and he said, 'What? You're 37.' I didn't get it, but I had a great time with that team and did well for them. They gave a big bonus to Ron Jackson early in 1955, however, and I had to go. The traveling secretary, Ed Short, had to break the news. He was crying."

ABOUT TED WILLIAMS: "The first time I saw him, he was walking around the batting cage while the White Sox were hitting. I introduced myself, and he said, "I know who you are, Phil. I've heard a lot of good things about you.' I asked why he was watching us take BP, and he said, 'I learn something about hitting every day.' He signed a picture, 'To Phil, an outstanding player, a good hitter, a great guy and a credit to the game.' It's another of my treasures."

LIFE TODAY: "Lorayne and I have been married 66 years. She was a professional dancer. It was love at first sight. We live in a lovely wooded area west of Atlanta. She's my special girl."

Phil Cavarretta died in Lilburn, Georgia, in 2010, at the age of ninety-four.

For Chico Carrasquel, White Sox Are Always There

MIKE DOWNEY

Chicago Tribune July 14, 2003

A punk put a gun to a 3-year-old girl's head.

CARACAS, Venezuela—the first weekend of 2003. The girl was Chico Carrasquel's granddaughter. A sister of his was also there. So was a pregnant cousin. They had just enjoyed the holidays. They were leaving Chico's house when the two armed men jumped them.

"Give me your car keys," one said.

Or they would shoot the girl.

There was no argument. The women did as told. Given the keys, the gunmen ran off to steal the car.

Chico was in it.

A national hero. A local legend. They threatened him. They made him drive. They struck him. They took his money. They took his gold wristwatch, a keepsake from one of his four baseball All-Star Game appearances in America.

Then they dumped the old man—not three weeks from his 75th birthday—miles from home.

Another carjacking. Another robbery. Violent crime is rampant in Venezuela, and now it had come to the Carrasquel family's front door.

Chico's assailants were too young to recognize him or didn't give a damn. Paid him no honor as baseball royalty. Prince of the shortstops. Predecessor to a long line. A 10-season star in America's big leagues. The first Latin man to start in an All-Star Game.

In the resort city of Puerto la Cruz where tourists flock to the beaches, the 18,000-seat Estadio Alfonso "Chico" Carrasquel Stadium bears his name, the host to many a game.

Life has been very good for Carrasquel, but it also goes around and around, Chico's carousel.

He is now on dialysis three times a week. His sister administers the insulin shots daily for his diabetes.

"I know how sick I am," he says.

At lunch, his sister Maritza brings his plate, cuts his meat and potatoes. She is in Chicago from Venezuela on a six-month visa. Chico calls her "my chef, my nurse, my driver, my doctor, my family, my friend."

They grew up in poverty together—seven sisters, two brothers. Now they live together near 46th and Harlem, go to White Sox games together. It is just a team to some, a poor team at that. It is *the* team to Carrasquel. It always will be. It is his other family.

He says, "When I am feeling good, I go to see the White Sox. If I am feeling bad, I try to go to see the White Sox. It takes my mind from everything. I forget any troubles. I would rather be there than anywhere.

"Everything I have ever needed, the White Sox are here for me. It has been 50 years since I played for them, but still they are here for me."

In 1987, his house in Lawndale caught fire. A faulty heater. His wife got out in time. Their pet cats did not. The house burned to the ground.

He needed a helping hand. The White Sox were there.

Just as they were in 1950, when he became the man who put the "Chico" in Chicago.

In his way, he was a Jackie Robinson, breaking through a baseball barrier. A barrio barrier, you could say. Latin major-leaguers were rare. South American or Central American players in North America were all but invisible. From head to toe, the White Sox were white.

Branch Rickey and the Dodgers owned his contract. But they had shortstops galore, Pee Wee Reese among them.

It took some doing, but Rickey relented and let the Sox have him. Not every teammate was thrilled. "How can we play a guy," one asked, "who can't speak English?"

Chico remembers responding, through an interpreter, "I didn't come here to talk."

He kept to himself. He learned how to say "Comiskey Park" to the taxi drivers. He learned "ham and eggs" and had it three meals a day. He created a wild scene in a restaurant when an angry waitress misunderstood Chico's request for a fork.

Baseball he understood fine. As a rookie, he hit .282, which would be a career high. He wore uniform number 17, because "Alfonso Carrasquel" had 17 letters.

A year later, Chico handled 297 chances in the field without an error, an American League record. He beat out the league's reigning MVP, Phil Rizzuto of the Yankees, to be the 1951 All-Star starting shortstop in Detroit.

Magazines put him on the cover. He met two Presidents and movie stars. He did ads for Nokona gloves. A while back, the Detroit Tigers had tried to sign him in Venezuela by offering the poor kid a free glove. By 1951, he was giving gloves by the dozen to poor kids there, and his original one is in baseball's Hall of Fame.

Around goes the carousel. Exactly 50 years ago Monday, he was playing in the 1953 All-Star Game. He will be at Tuesday's game, at a park no longer named Comiskey, but on that same corner where the cab drivers would drop him.

An old friend from Venezuela who succeeded him as the White Sox shortstop (Luis Aparicio) will be the American League's honorary captain. A young friend from Venezuela (Magglio Ordonez) is on the team. At last count there were 38 Venezuelans in the majors. Once, there was one.

"Where I am from, the White Sox are every boy's team," Chico says. "For some maybe the Yankees are best, but in Venezuela, no."

And other things back home?

Not good. A few weeks after Chico was attacked, a boxing champion, super-flyweight Alexander Munoz, 24, was out jogging when he was jumped by three men and shot in the leg.

A workers' strike, a paralyzed economy, oil shipments cut off, travel visas denied, a political revolt . . . Venezuela has been in turmoil. Even all baseball was suspended there at one point, saddening Chico no end. No baseball? A crowd he estimates at 150,000 met him at the Caracas airport after his 1951 season. Then, the mobs cheered. Now, the mobs rob.

"I have to go back," he insists. "It is a part of me. I will always go there." There . . . and to a baseball park in Chicago.

Where he can run into his old friend and teammate Minnie Minoso and trade insults. Where he can sit with his young friend Mina Pineda, who works for the White Sox, and converse in Spanish over lunch. Where he can forget his troubles.

Robbed. Beaten. Old friends gone. In poor health. Yes, for Alfonso Carrasquel, all this is true.

But he knows what to do.

"I watch the White Sox."

How perfect—17 letters.

Chico Carrasquel died of cardiac/respiratory arrest in Caracas in
2005 at the age of seventy-seven.

Ron Santo
"I'm Way Ahead of the Game"

PAUL LADEWSKI

Daily Southtown April 6, 2002   **63**

Ron Santo had another great day at Wrigley Field on Friday.

It started when the Cubs broadcaster woke up early in his Bannock-
burn home. After a brief struggle, he made it to an upright position at the
side of his bed. He swallowed some pills and took his daily insulin shots.

Then he put on his right leg.

A few hours later, the former All-Star third baseman did one of the
most difficult things he'd ever had to do on a baseball field—balance on
his prosthesis long enough to throw the ceremonial first pitch at the home
opener.

Heck, a few months ago, Santo had thought any mention of his name
would result in bowed heads and a moment of silence.

"Absolutely, I didn't know if I'd be here," admitted Santo, who also led
the crowd in singing "Take Me Out to the Ballgame" during the seventh-
inning stretch. "I didn't know if I was gonna make it. It's almost like—and
I really mean it—a second life."

"He really is the story today," Cubs marketing chief John McDonough
said.

Just four months after he underwent the amputation of his right leg below the knee, Santo hobbled to the mound. The sellout crowd roared. Former teammate Billy Williams embraced him. Santo threw a one-bouncer
to Randy Hundley, the old Cubs catcher. Then Santo blew kisses to the
crowd on his way to the home dugout.

It was hard to tell who cried more—Santo or the 40,000 fans in the
stands.

"I'm way ahead of the game," he said. "I thank the Lord that I'm here."

Santo's eighth and most recent surgery was nearly his last. When an electrical function in his heart failed, it appeared that Santo had seen his final pitch.

"The operations were the worst times of my life," said Santo, who was diagnosed with diabetes when he was 18 years old. "Every time there had to be another one and another one, I agonized over them, and because of it, I went into cardiac arrest. But they brought me back, so I'm supposed to be here."

Santo no longer can click his heels the way he did in the heat of the 1969 pennant race. But the way he figures it, who needs to when he has so many family members and friends to lean on now?

Santo is so emotional to begin with, he can get choked up by a sacrifice fly. When he received thousands of e-mails, cards and letters from fans—"therapy," he called them—Santo knew he couldn't quit on them or himself.

Then there was Sam, who made his 62-year-old grandfather feel like 26 again.

"Grandpa, wanna ride our scooters today?" the kid would say to him.

"The competitiveness (of sports) helped me get through it," he said, "but it's not only baseball. How you've been brought up and what you're made of have a lot to do with it. If you give up, you don't have a chance.

"My family said, 'You don't have to try out for a ballclub. You can do without one leg but not your life.' They were exactly right. Because of technology, I'll always be able to do the things I always did—ride my horse, play golf, broadcast and enjoy my grandson."

While Santo isn't quite there yet, the first road trip to Cincinnati was another step forward.

Except for the fact that he couldn't take a morning shower, there was only one problem.

"My wife (Vicki) packed so much clothes, and after I took them out (of the suitcase) for five days, it took me two hours to get them back in," he said with a smile.

More good news: Friday was the fourth day in a row Santo was able to move around without the aid of a walker.

When McDonough brought up the first pitch thing several weeks ago, Santo didn't know what to expect. It was almost as if he had been asked to face Bob Gibson again. Or as he put it, "To be honest with you, I've never gone to the mound on one leg."

When was the last time McDonough had seen Santo so nervous?

"When we told him there would be a three-man booth and he would be joined by Steve Stone," McDonough kidded. "You don't know that was the day that Ron almost quit and hit me."

"To see him walk into my office today, he looks great," McDonough turned serious again.

Figures to feel and look even better in the days to come, too.

"Baseball takes my mind off it," Santo said. "I don't even think about it up there (in the broadcast booth). I don't even know that I have a prosthesis on. When the bases are loaded with two outs, I have more important things to worry about."

Because if you're Ron Santo, there are no bad days, really.

Ron Santo died of bladder cancer in 2010 in Scottsdale, Arizona, at the age of seventy. He was elected to the Baseball Hall of Fame a year later.

65

Leo Durocher
The Spit Take and the Bow
RON RAPOPORT

Chicago Sun-Times January 18, 1983

We all had had too much to drink, probably. The old guy standing a few feet away muttering how Leo Durocher was a bum certainly had, not to mention the good baseball fans who had paid $40 so they could boo Steve Garvey, who had manfully appeared at the Chicago baseball writers dinner shortly after he had spurned a free-agent bid from the Cubs and signed with the Padres.

Durocher himself may have been the soberest person in the room, which was a suite in the Palmer House that was beginning to empty as people started thinking about baby-sitters or church in the morning or having a clear head for the Dolphins and the Chargers on television.

The first time you saw him up close, you thought how frail he looked, but then you realized maybe it wasn't so bad for somebody who had by-pass surgery less than a year earlier and who was, after all, 77 years old.

They had stood for him downstairs in the banquet room earlier and though Joe Morgan and Bill Veeck and Carlton Fisk and Bill Buckner had been there, he had been the only one to get an ovation like that.

He had spoken lovingly of Ferguson Jenkins, who was also there, and of the Chicago fans, who had eaten it with a spoon, and they stood for him again when he had finished. Even if you were like the old guy and thought he was a bum, you had to admit it was a moment.

But this was an even better one. Durocher was standing in a corner and there were only a few people around him and you were glad one or two of them had been there when he managed the Cubs and knew the things to ask that he would enjoy talking about.

Soon, though, he was back beyond those years and telling two stories. They were not connected and yet, when you thought about it later, in a way they were.

One was about Sal Maglie when he was pitching for the New York Giants and how Durocher didn't like the way he was throwing the ball in a certain game and had gone out to the mound. He had no intention of taking Maglie out of the game, he said, and didn't even have anybody warming up in the bullpen, but he yelled at him and told him he was pitching like a girl and called him a dago.

Maglie had hated that, but he had started getting his back into his pitches and throwing harder and he had finished the inning without any runs scoring. He had come back to the dugout and gone to get a drink and then, on his way to his seat on the bench, he had spit a mouthful of water all over Durocher,

After the game, Maglie had come up to Durocher to apologize but Leo had told him to forget it. They had won, hadn't they?

The other story was about the time Durocher and the Giants had gone to Japan to play some exhibition games and he had been warned about taking it easy on the umpires. They were supreme authority figures, he had been told, and it was a breach of etiquette to argue with them.

Durocher was always hell on umpires, of course, and though he had tried to be on his best behavior, there was a call at third base that had started him ranting and raving.

Pretty soon, he had run the poor umpire all the way down the leftfield line and Hank Thompson, who was playing third base, was doubled up with laughter because the umpire didn't speak English and couldn't understand what Durocher was yelling.

When he got back to the dugout, Durocher was made to understand what an unpardonable sin he had committed by making the umpire lose face in front of the players and the fans. So before the next inning began, he walked out and bowed deeply in apology. The umpire bowed back and the stands exploded with delighted applause.

67

Now, somebody was asking Durocher about the Hall of Fame and didn't he feel he belonged in it. He answered with a filibuster about how when Happy Chandler, the former baseball commissioner who once suspended him for a year, had been voted into the Hall, he had taken his phone off the hook because he knew a lot of people would call expecting him to say it was a disgrace.

But finally somebody had gotten through and all he had said was that anybody elected to the Hall of Fame deserved it. He seemed very pleased with that response.

Somebody kept persisting, though. Didn't he want to be in the Hall of Fame himself? Finally he admitted that, yes, it would mean a lot to him.

He was gone soon after that and, one by one, so were the rest of us, including the old guy who kept saying to anybody who walked by that Durocher was a bum.

Whether Durocher ever makes Cooperstown or not, it cannot be too many more banquets before he is called into that other, more permanent, Hall of Fame.

What you wonder is, will the Proprietor greet him with a mouthful of water in the face or with a bow?

Leo Durocher was inducted into the Baseball Hall of Fame in 1994, three years after he died at the age of eighty-six.

ONLY IN CHICAGO

A few words say it all. The Black Sox. The Called Shot. Disco Demolition Night. The Refrigerator. And more recently, of course, only one word is needed to summon up a memory of civic infamy: Bartman.

These are events that could have taken place anywhere, I suppose, but they did not, and now they are an indelible part of Chicago sports lore, as much a part of the landscape as the el tracks and Belmont Harbor.

Here are some pieces that celebrate those special moments that will forever occupy a special place in Chicago's collective psyche.

Westbrook Pegler's presence in this section may surprise some who know him only as the "stuck whistle of journalism," a political commentator so relentlessly reactionary that even the John Birch Society stopped publishing him in its house organ. But between 1925 and 1933, he wrote a New York–based sports column for the *Chicago Tribune* that made him one of the most widely read sportswriters in the country and, according to no less an authority than Red Smith, one of the best who ever lived.

Pegler's column on Babe Ruth's called shot—was he the first to actually use those words?—in Wrigley Field in 1932 is a good example of why. It sets the scene in lively detail, contains some great quotes—though I'm guessing he made at least some of them up—and leaves no doubt where he stood on the controversy that exists to this day. Compared with John Drebinger's dry-as-dust account in the *New York Times*, it is a model of a writer capturing a moment.

Smith might have summed up Pegler's career best when he wrote, "It was during his hitch in sports that he refined his exceptional gifts as a writer, reached his peak as a light essayist, and brought more pure delight to his readers than he ever did again."

What Is Wrong with the White Sox?
Kid Gleason Asks

JAMES CRUSINBERRY

Chicago Tribune October 7, 1919

"They aren't hitting."

Those few words spoken by Kid Gleason, manager of the White Sox, offered an explanation for a large part of the cause for the fourth defeat of the south siders yesterday in the World Series against the Cincinnati Reds. They got three hits off Hod Eller and never once in the whole game had a good chance to score a run.

"I don't know what's the matter," the Sox leader continued," but I do know that something is wrong with my gang. The bunch I had fighting in August for the pennant would have trimmed this Cincinnati bunch without a struggle. We hit something over .280 for the season in the American League pennant race. That's the best hitting any ball club ever did in the history of baseball. The way those .280 hitters acted against Eller, they couldn't make a place on a high school team.

"I am convinced that I have the best ball club that ever was put together. I certainly have been disappointed in it in this series. It hasn't played baseball in a single game. There's only a bare chance they can win now. The gang that has played for me in the five games of the world's series will have to have luck to win another ball game."

While the White Sox manager was talking, it was easy to see he was terribly riled up. He was located by this writer as soon as he got into his street clothes after the game. A taxi was hailed. Three strangers climbed in. Gleason rode from the ball park to his downtown hotel without once saying a word about baseball. Once he remarked about the cleverness of the driver in getting past a couple of drays. Once he asked for a match.

After he had reached his room and closed the door, he made the remark that the gang wasn't hitting. Then he went into a tirade on all the other things they weren't doing. He clearly indicated he was mad enough to lick a lot of people and go to jail for it. He clearly indicated there was something wrong and that he intended to find out what it was.

"You know," he spoke up, "it doesn't seem possible that this gang that worked so great for me all summer could fall down like this. I tell you, I am absolutely sick at heart. They haven't played any baseball for me. I thought all of them were my boys. I felt like a school teacher might feel toward his pupils. I loved those boys for the way they fought for me this summer. Those fellows were right around me and I would have stacked my life they would have gone through for me in the world's series.

"But they aren't playing baseball. Not the kind we played all summer. If they had, the Sox would just about have the world's championship clinched by this time. Something has happened to my gang. If they would just play baseball for me the rest of the series, they might even pull it out yet. The team I had most of the time all summer would do it. I haven't had that same team on the ball field in a single game."

Regardless of what the southside manager thinks about his team, there was one fellow in the game that was in August form and that was Ray Schalk, who was put out of the battle in the sixth inning for protesting to Umpire Rigler when he pronounced Heinie Groh safe at the plate. From the press stand it looked as it Schalk might have missed tagging Heine as he slid in and that Rigler was right in his decision.

Anyway, Ray raised an awful holler, but Ray feels about this World Series just like Boss Gleason does, and his tantrum over this play might have been because of things in general instead of the play on Groh. It was apparent that Schalk was so wrought up that he was ready to tackle Jack Dempsey or anybody.

Three days later, under the headline "Kid Refuses to Believe It Was A.L. Champs Who Lost Series," Crusinberry wrote the following about the final game of one of the most notorious sporting events ever played.

"The Reds beat the greatest ball team that ever went into a World Series."

That was the first statement made by Kid Gleason when the show was over. His next statement was about like this:

"But it wasn't the real White Sox. They played baseball for me only a couple or three of the eight days."

There was logic in the statements of Gleason to one who had followed the White Sox throughout the season. The White Sox of the World Series was not the same team that won the American League pennant. The Reds of the World Series was the best Red team of the whole summer. Pat Moran had the players on their toes.

There was more discussion about the playing of the White Sox than about the peace treaty after the last game. Stories were out that the Sox had not put forth their best effort. Stories were out that the big gamblers had got to them. But all of them sounded like alibi stuff even if true and Gleason had no excuse to offer for the defeat except that the Reds played better baseball.

"I was terribly disappointed," he continued. "I tell you those Reds haven't any reason beating a team like the White Sox. We played the worst baseball in all but a couple of games that we have played all year. I don't know yet what was the matter. Something was wrong. I didn't like the betting odds. I wish no one had ever bet a dollar on the team."

73

The Called Shot Heard Round the World

WESTBROOK PEGLER

Chicago Tribune October 2, 1932

There, in the third ball game of the World Series, at the Cubs' ball yard on the north side yesterday, the people who had the luck to be present saw the supreme performance of the greatest artist the profession of sport has ever produced. Babe Ruth hit two home runs.

Now, Lou Gehrig also hit two home runs, and Jimmy Foxx of the Athletics or any other master mechanic of the business might have hit three or four home runs and you would have gone away with the same impression that a factory tourist receives from an hour of watching a big machine lick labels and stick them on bottles of mouthwash or pop. The machine might awe you, but would you love it?

The people who saw Babe Ruth play that ball game and hit those two home runs against the Cubs came away from the baseball plant with a spiritual memento of the most gorgeous display of humor, athletic art and championship class any performer in any of the games has ever presented.

The Babe is 38 years old, and if you don't know that he is unable to hike as far for fly balls or stoop as nimbly as he used to for rollers coming to him through the grass, that must be just your own fault, because he would not deceive you. As an outfielder he is pretty close to his past tense, which may mean that one more year from now he will be only a pinch-hitter. He has been breaking this news all year to himself and the customers.

Why, when Bill Jurges, the human clay pigeon, hit a short fly to him there in left field and he mauled it about, trying for a shoestring catch, he came up off the turf admitting all as Jurges pulled up at second.

The old Babe stood up, straightened his cap and gesticulated vigorously toward Earl Combs in center. "Hey!" the old Babe waved, "my dogs ain't what they used to be. Don't hit them out to me. Hit to the young guy out there."

The customers behind him in the bleachers were booing him when the ball game began, but they would have voted him president when it was over, and he might not be a half-bad compromise, at that.

Somebody in the crowd tossed out a lemon which hit him on the leg. Now there are sensitive ball players who might have been petulant at that and some stiff-necked ones who could only ignore it, boiling inwardly. But the Babe topped the jest. With graphic gestures, old Mr. Ruth called on them for fair play. If they must hit him with missiles, would they please not hit him on the legs? The legs weren't too good anyway. Would they just as lief hit him on the head? The head was solid and could stand it.

I am telling you that before the ball game began the Babe knew he was going to hit one or more home runs. He had smacked half a dozen balls into the right-field bleachers during his hitting practice and he knew he had the feel of the trick for the day. When his hitting practice was over he waddled over toward the Cubs' dugout, his large abdomen jiggling in spite of his rubber corsets, and yelled at the Cubs sulking down there in the den, "Hey, muggs! You muggs are not going to see the Yankee Stadium any more this year. This World Series is going to be over Sunday afternoon. Four straight."

He turned, rippling with the fun of it and, addressing the Chicago customers behind third base, yelled, "Did you hear what I told them over there? I told them they ain't going back to New York. We lick 'em here, today and tomorrow."

The Babe had been humiliating the Cubs publicly throughout the series. They were a lot of Lord Jims to him. They had had a chance to be big fellows when they did the voting on the division of the World Series pool. But for a few dollars' gain they had completely ignored Rogers Hornsby, their manager for most of the year, who is through with baseball now apparently without much to show for his long career, and had held Mark Koenig, their part-time shortstop, to a half share. The Yankees, on the contrary, had been generous, even to ex-Yankees who were traded away months ago, to their deformed bat boy who was run over and hurt by a car early in the season, and to his substitute.

There never was such contempt shown by one antagonist for another as the Babe displayed for the Cubs, and ridicule was his medium.

In the first inning, with Earle Combs and Joe Sewell on base, he sailed his first home run into the bleachers. He hit Charlie Root's earnest pitching with the same easy, playful swing that he had been using a few minutes before against the soft, casual service of a guinea-pig pitcher. The ball would have fallen into the street beyond the bleachers under ordinary conditions, but dropped among the patrons in the temporary seats.

The old Babe came around third base and past the Cubs' dugout yelling comments which were unintelligible to the patrons but plainly discourteous and, pursing his lips, blew them a salute known as the Bronx cheer.

He missed a second home run in the third inning when the ball came down a few feet short of the wire screen, but the masterpiece was only deferred. He hit it in the fifth, a ball that sailed incredibly to the extreme depth of center field and dropped like a perfect mashie shot behind the barrier, long enough to clear it, but with no waste of distance.

Guy Bush, the Cubs' pitcher, was up on the top step of the dugout, jawing back at him as he took his turn at bat this time. Bush pushed back his big ears, funneled his hands to his mouth, and yelled raspingly at the great man to upset him. The Babe laughed derisively and gestured at him. "Wait, mugg, I'm going to hit one out of the yard." Root threw a strike past him and he held up a finger to Bush, whose ears flapped excitedly as he renewed his insults. Another strike passed him and Bush crawled almost out of the hole to extend his remarks.

The Babe held up two fingers this time. Root wasted two balls and the Babe put up two fingers on his other hand. Then, with a warning gesture of his hand to Bush, he sent him the signal for the customers to see.

"Now," it said, "this is the one. Look!" And that one went riding in the longest home run ever hit in the park.

He licked the Chicago ball club, but he left the people laughing when he said good-bye, and it was a privilege to be present because it is not likely that the scene will ever be repeated in all its elements. Many a hitter may make two home runs, or possibly three in World Series play in years to come, but not the way Babe Ruth made these two. Nor will you ever see an artist call his shot before hitting one of the longest drives ever made on the grounds, in a World Series game, laughing and mocking the enemy with two strikes gone.

Babe Ruth proved to be as good a prophet as he was a hitter. The Yankees won the final game of the Series the following day to sweep the Cubs in four straight.

Ten Years after Woodstock, There Was Veeckstock

DAVID ISRAEL

Chicago Tribune July 13, 1979

The man who brought baseball midgets, much laughter, and myriad promotions, Thursday night brought it the game's first rock riot.

And when it was over, after one game was cancelled, one field destroyed, and the idyllic greensward of Comiskey Park overrun by several thousand crazed teen-agers, even Bill Veeck, the man who has seen just about everything, was a bit amazed by it all.

He sounded every bit as astonished but hardly as euphoric as John Sebastian did when he gazed out from the stage at the half-million folks camped on Max Yasgur's farm in New York in 1969, and announced, "People, we're a whole city."

"I was amazed," Bill Veeck said. "We had anticipated 32 to 35,000, We had more security than we ever had before. But we had as many people in here as we ever had."

While Veeck, the president of the Chicago White Sox, was amazed, many members of both the Sox and the Detroit Tigers, who somehow managed to play the first game of a scheduled double-header, were angry, scared, and bemused.

They were forced, you see, to play that first game under a constant bombardment of records and firecrackers.

This was the impromptu portion of an anti-disco promotion co-sponsored by the Sox and a rock radio station. The promotion was very clever. Anyone carrying a disco record was admitted for 98 cents. When the promoters were planning the promotion, they apparently forgot that records make wonderful frisbees, and fly twice as fast and hit twice as hard.

"How'd you like to get hit in the eye with one of those?" said Wayne Nordhagen of the Sox. "These people don't realize it only takes one to ruin a guy's career."

The planned portion of the promotion was a ceremony in center field hosted by Steve Dahl, the maniac disc jockey from WLUP-FM. At the conclusion of his ceremony, Dahl blew up a crate full of disco records. At the conclusion of the explosion, fans poured out onto what had been a neatly manicured field.

As far as riots go, this one was lovely. I mean, this isn't going to make anyone forget Grant Park or the Days of Rage. It was a lot of sliding into second base and "Look-at-me-ma" jumping around for the benefit of the television cameras.

When it started, Sox pitcher Ken Kravec was on the mound warming up for the second game. He retreated to the safety of the dugout, as did the rest of the players from both clubs.

Some of the Sox took up hats to protect themselves, but it never went that far. Eventually, the riot started to lose energy, and then police, who waited patiently outside the ballpark, came in to disperse the crowd and clear the field.

"It was crazy," said the Tigers' Mark Fidrych, who knows about such things. "I stayed in the dugout and watched the whole thing."

"Beer and baseball go together, they have for years," said Sparky Anderson, the Detroit manager. "But I think those kids were doing things other than beer." Rusty Torres, the Sox right fielder and player representative, was on the Cleveland Indians in 1974, when their 10-cent beer night turned out much the same as 98-cent ticket night did here.

"This wasn't as bad," Torres said. "In Cleveland, they were throwing lighters and bottles."

Basically, this figured. It would have happened any place 58,000 teenagers got together on a sultry summer night with beer and reefer. It wasn't

mean-spirited—it couldn't have been, the only serious injury was a fractured ankle—but it certainly was a nuisance. And it really had no place
at a ballpark.

One thing it did prove, though, was that while the Sixties might be
over, you still can get a lot of people excited through rock 'n roll.

"This wouldn't have happened," said Sox pitcher Richard Wortham,
who's a Texan with a natural preference for Willie Nelson and Waylon
Jennings, "if they had country and western night."

Lee Elia Swings for the Seats, Hits Fans

ROBERT MARKUS

Chicago Tribune April 30, 1983
"I guess I lost it." Cub manager Lee Elia very nearly lost it all Friday afternoon. He lost a ballgame, his temper and almost his job.

"When I heard that tape, it (Elia's job) was in jeopardy, I'll guarantee
that," said general manager Dallas Green.

He was referring to the most sizzling footage recorded since the Nixon
tapes, a scathing, raging indictment of Cubs' fans by the frustrated Elia,
who had just seen his team drop a heart-rending 4–3 game to the Los
Angeles Dodgers.

"All these so-called Cubs' fans, ripping everything we do," Elia began.
"I hope we get hot—just to stuff it up those 3,000 people who show up
every day. If those are the real Chicago fans they can kiss my ass right
downtown—and print it."

Liberally sprinkling his tirade with expletives that a roomful of Rose-
mary Woodses could not delete, Elia stormed: "They're really behind you
around here. What am I supposed to do, go out there and let my players get destroyed every day and be quiet? For the nickel-and-dime people
who show up every day? They don't even work. That's why they're out at
the ballgame. It's a playground for the suckers . . . Rip those country suckers like they rip the players.

"About 85 percent of the world is working. The other 15 percent come
out here."

About two hours later, after he had been called into Green's office and forced to listen to the damning tape, Elia explained that he had just singed his players with the same kind of withering language. "If it hadn't been for a good 15-minute tirade with our club, maybe I wouldn't have gotten cooking so bad," he said.

Elia said he was not aware that right-fielder Keith Moreland had to be restrained from climbing onto the dugout roof to get at three fans who were taunting the Cubs as they walked off the field.

"I saw it," said Green. "They were drunk. There were three guys with their hands full of beer, and Keith tried to get over the dugout."

Elia was venting his frustration over a game the Cubs lost when Lee Smith wild-pitched home the winning run in the eighth inning. It was a game in which the Dodgers got only four hits—two doubles, a two-run homer by Ken Landreaux and a solo blast by Mike Marshall. It was a game in which the Cubs once more left runners stranded in scoring position at critical times. It was a game that dropped them to a 5–14 record, "and tonight," screamed Elia, "some jerk on TV will say that the Cubs are 5–14 with the worst record in baseball. That's lovely.

"I get frustrated," Elia said after he had calmed down, "because a lot of positive things have transpired around here in the last year and a half and that doesn't show on the record."

"I'm aware the fans have to be frustrated also because we haven't executed when we should and we haven't hit like we could and like we can. My frustrations just peaked. It's obvious the fans have the same frustrations and I was out of line." Green took it one step further. "We're not performing," he said. "We're not doing the job on the field. And the players and Lee Elia and Dallas Green are responsible for that. The fans are not. The fans have a right to expect more from us because we popped off and said more was going to come from this team."

"The only place we can look to the poor performance of the Cubs to date is the organization itself," concurred board chairman Andy McKenna. "This kind of action we cannot condone. We have the greatest fans in the world and we know it."

If Elia's blast was triggered by postgame questioning, it was not apparent. He had kept the clubhouse closed a bit longer than usual, but no more than 10 minutes. He had just calmly told a roomful of reporters, several of whom had tape recorders, that he had not been able to get starter

79

Paul Moskau out of the game before Landreaux's game-tying homer in the sixth because, "I just couldn't get to Bill Campbell in time."

He did not seem to object to a question about why he had let Campbell bunt instead of pinch-hitting for him in the seventh (Campbell bunted into a double play), but began to get agitated as he went along. "What do you want me to do, use five guys (from the bullpen) every day? There comes a time when you've got to execute. That's one of the things that have hurt us."

And then he was off and screaming. At first he said he was not upset at the media, but later he raged about "all those editorials about Ron Cey and Phillie-itis. The thing that fries my ass is the nickel-and-dime editorials. How anyone that ignorant could spend a quarter and read it is beyond me.

"It'll take more than a 5–14 record to destroy the makeup of this club," he vowed. "There are some pros out there who want to play this game. If you want to rip somebody rip me, but don't rip those guys. They're trying to do more than God gave them and that's why we're making mistakes."

Green said that when he first talked to Elia, the manager was not even aware of what he had said. "He called me before taking a shower and at that time didn't know what he had said," said Green. "We played the tape back so he understood at that time how bad it really was. It was not handled professionally and Lee has told you his feelings about that."

Lee Elia remained manager of the Cubs another four months before being fired. The team finished fifth with a record of 73–89.

William Perry
Fat Is Where It's At
MIKE IMREM

Arlington Heights Daily Herald October 22, 1985

As of Monday night, William Perry is the biggest thing ever to hit network television. Bigger than Jackie Gleason, Cannon and My Mother The Tank rolled into one lump sum.

The Refrigerator's show is a short-running comedy series, to be sure, but never to be confused with a miniseries. Nobody 308 pounds is a mini-anything, especially when he's thundering at you with mayhem in his eyes.

Perry, the Bears' part-time defensive tackle and full-bodied fullback, made his second appearance as a ball carrier in as many weeks. As a result, he did more for ABC's ratings without a toupee than Howard Cosell ever did with one.

After carrying twice against the 49ers last week, the Refrigerator was on the offensive for three first-half plays Monday night against the Packers and helped turn them all into touchdowns. Twice he blocked the socks off on Walter Payton touchdown runs, and once he rambled a yard for a TD of his own. Monday Night Football will never be the same, and Green Bay might not be either. With the Fridge putting the Packers in the deepfreeze, the Bears rolled to a 23–7 victory and a 7–0 record.

"I just want to help the team," said Perry, who played more on offense than defense. "I'm blocking for Walter, I scored a touchdown. I'm just happy. That touchdown was great. My first in NFL. I can't describe it, it was just great.

"My running style? There's no style," he said with a big smile. "I haven't gotten the ball in the open field yet. It's just been on the goal line, and I just go straight ahead."

Thanks to highlights like Perry, this might have been the most entertaining bad football game in history. There were assorted interceptions, fumbles and penalties, but enough fights, trick plays and funny incidents to keep any audience awake.

But most of all, there was William Perry.

The Fridge was used only in short-yardage, goal-line situations, but he lit up Soldier Field every time the occasion arose. In homes nationwide, football fans must have rushed back from the refrigerator to watch The Refrigerator rush the Green Bay defense.

He didn't disappoint his fans, at least not in the first half.

Perry was licking his chops and the Packers wound up licking their wounds. On his first and third plays, the Fridge blocked linebacker George Cumby 5 yards off the ball while leading the way for Payton.

"No," the Fridge said, "Cumby didn't say anything to me. I think I rung his bell." On one of his blocks, Perry took out two men. "I'm obligated to

81

block the linebacker," he explained. "If there's anybody else in my way. I take him out, too."

In between playing bell ringer with the Packers, Perry carried the ball and the defense into the end zone from 2 yards out. Payton enjoyed that. But he enjoyed The Refrigerator's chilling blocks even more.

"Believe me, the guy (Perry) is unbelievable," said Payton, who was upstaged despite rushing for 112 yards in 25 carries. "He does whatever is asked of him. That last touchdown, I felt like I was stealing. He cleared out that side and I walked in. He's great to have out there because I just hide behind him.

"He's so wide, when he's in there nobody expects him to move with such speed and agility. I just hope they don't move more defensive linemen there. They'll move all the running backs out."

To celebrate his first touchdown since entering puberty, Perry slammed the football so hard it bounced up and pierced the sky. "No," he said innocently, "that's no penalty. I was just having fun."

So was everybody but the Packers. The audience went wild. This Perry guy has charisma, he has pizzazz, he has show biz written all over his ample girth.

"I'm not going to renegotiate my contract," Perry chuckled. "I gotta play the last three years."

If the last couple weeks is any indication, he'll continue doing it as an all-purpose running back, a sturdy defensive tackle and a menace covering kickoffs. Bears coach Mike Ditka loves hitters, and Perry loves to hit.

"I had those goal-line plays in with William last week, too," Ditka said. "I just wanted to use 'em tonight. Until they put somebody bigger in to plug up the hole against him, you might see those plays the rest of the year."

And we're all liable to see more and more of William Perry on national television. The 49ers game was on CBS, the Packers game on ABC, and now NBC wants a piece of the Fridge.

David Letterman phoned Monday to book Perry on his "Late Night" show for tonight. Practice might force the Fridge to take a rain check, but he'll likely make it soon.

Hey, the guy is the biggest thing to hit network TV since . . . well, you know.

The Bottom Line
Acupuncture Puts Jim McMahon's Troubles behind Him

BOB VERDI

Chicago Tribune January 23, 1986

NEW ORLEANS—Jim McMahon dressed up like a billboard, ambles gingerly down a restricted corridor of the Bears' hotel headquarters, then bangs on the door of his room. Kurt Becker appears. "Don't you have a key?" asks the injured lineman. "What's going on?"

McMahon leads a contingent of five into the darkened suite, then raises his arms to the ceiling, triumphantly.

"It's acupuncture time!!" chirps this quarterback, this piece of work, this free spirit whose tale of a wounded tail has become the cause celebre of Super Bowl XX. And with that exclamation, McMahon sheds his adidas, his blue running tights, his purple bikini underwear, his multicolored sweatshirt, his baseball hat, his sunglasses. All he wears now, stretching out on the bed with chest down, is a sheepish grin.

"Aha," says Hiroshi Shiriashi, reaching for his bag of needles. "Now we start." This is Wednesday, shortly before noon, about an hour after the now-famous acupuncturist from Tokyo had flown in from Chicago. McMahon's gluteus maximus, battered during the Bears' NFC Championship victory over the Los Angeles Rams two Sundays ago, is still a sore subject to the victim, not to mention the team's management. Clearly, this is a medical emergency.

"Please, quiet," says Shiriashi, a pleasant man of few words. He motions toward the television set, which is broadcasting a soap opera for the edification of Becker, who is occupying the other bed, looking rather perplexed by it all.

"You gonna stick more pins into my roommate?" says Becker, shutting off the TV. "Tell you what, doctor. There's a $36,000 winners' share for beating New England Sunday. You stick all the pins in him you want, long as he's ready."

McMahon, on horizontal hold with feet resting atop the pillows, laughs. His head protrudes from the other end of the mattress, so he can spit his

Skoal drippings into a glass. He does not look like an athlete concerned about missing the biggest game of his life.

"I told them in the press conference this morning there's no way I won't play Sunday," McMahon says. "I don't know if they believe me. They also asked me what my behind looks like. I said I didn't know. It's behind me. What does it look like, Hiroshi?"

Shiriashi is busy preparing an alcohol rub for McMahon's affected area, the left buttocks, which is a mosaic of bruises and ominous hues. Anybody who doubts that McMahon is in severe pain, anybody who surmises that he had concocted this story just to capture attention, or miss practice, needs only to take one glance at this bereaved soul, lying there in his birthday suit, staring at the wallpaper ahead.

"You guys didn't go out last night?" asks Steve Zucker, McMahon's representative from Chicago.

"Nope," Becker says. "We barricaded the door at 6 o'clock. That's 6 p.m., not 6 a.m. Lots of sleep."

"Needed it," McMahon says. "Had a good time Monday night. Went to tape that Bob Hope show. He's a legend. We talked about his golf game and my golf game. Like to play in his tournament some day. Then I left with Tony Eason (Patriots' quarterback) and got something to eat. Then ran into Jay Hilgenberg. I really like Bob Hope. Like him so much, we went back and knocked on his door about 2 a.m. Hilgy wanted to get at the leftover sandwiches. Woke Bob up. I don't know if he appreciated that."

Shiriashi is probing McMahon's posterior now with his acupuncture needle, a filament-thin apparatus designed not to maim but to relieve pressure at specific points in the body. The doctor makes two or three dozen different light pierces, all the while closing his eyes, as if to meditate.

"He's a master at what he does," whispers Bill Anderson of the Illinois State Acupuncture Association. That organization was aroused when Bears' president Michael McCaskey, upon learning that Shiriashi visited McMahon Monday without official sanction, vetoed any further treatments. Or so it was interpreted.

"McCaskey's saying now that it's okay, that he'll pay the bills for Hiroshi?" McMahon says. "You know why McCaskey did that? I told him, 'Do you want me to play or not?' That's why he changed his mind all of a sudden. It's his team, yeah, but it's my rear end. I don't know why everybody's got their noses out of joint. This isn't a knock at (trainer) Freddie Caito, or anybody else. Hiroshi here. He's a specialist."

After about 20 minutes with his pins, Shiriashi briefly massages the problem, then instructs McMahon to run a hot shower on it.

"Another treatment tonight," Shiriashi says. "Then two tomorrow. Maybe tomorrow he can run at practice, see how it feels."

Suddenly, from the bathroom, a booming voice.

"Hey, doc, how long do I have to stay under this thing?" McMahon yells. "I'm melting in here." McMahon emerges shortly, red as a beet. Now he starts prancing about the room, making like he's dropping back, pivoting, throwing a pass, bending over the center for the snap.

"All the beautiful women in the world," Becker grouses, "and I got to watch this."

"Feels better," McMahon says. "I tried to run a little yesterday, but I only lasted about 10 yards. If I try to go again today, it'll probably tighten up. But it's improved over what it was. It improves every day. See, I can bend my left leg a lot higher up than I could before."

McMahon returns to the bed for another short session. Someone mentions that Gary Fencik suggested he wear a headband Sunday for United Way. How, Fencik wondered, could the NFL fine him for advertising its official charity?

"No, I think I might wear a headband saying 'ACUPUNCTURE,'" suggests McMahon. "I'll have to write small, though. That's a pretty big word, isn't it? Maybe I'll wear a label on my butt, too. 'Made in Japan.'"

Shiriashi, ever the craftsman, oblivious to all this tomfoolery, resumes his project on McMahon's contusion. There's a knock on the door.

"Is it working?" asks Walter Payton, upon entering.

"Of course," McMahon says. "Needles don't even hurt, either."

"They asked me today at that press thing, am I strange? No, I said, I'm normal. I just don't worry about what other people think. Too many people are hung up on other peoples' opinions. I'd like to just win the Super Bowl, then vanish for a while. Play golf. That's another reason why I gotta get this butt fixed."

"Mac," says Becker. "We better catch that last bus."

85

Shiriashi completes his task, and McMahon rises, takes a fresh dab of Skoal, puts on his purple bikini underwear, his blue running tights, his multi-colored sweatshirt, his hat, his sunglasses, his adidas.

"Thanks, doc," McMahon says. "Can you come to practice to take a look at me there? I'm sure management will be happy to see you."

Not so fast. Predictions, please.

"Go Bears," says Shiriashi.

McMahon heads down the hall, singing "Needles and Pins," feinting here and there, as though he's getting ready for Sunday. His roommate follows.

"Man's got the most famous rear end in the world right now, and I've got to live with him," Becker says, shaking his head. "Crazy. Only the Bears. This could only happen on the Bears."

Steve Bartman
In the Middle of the Maelstrom

JOHN KASS

Chicago Tribune October 16, 2003

With 40,000 Wrigley Field fans screaming their rage at him, tossing beer on him, hurling hatred his way, I stood next to the Human Goat and asked him a question the night the Cubs began to choke.

What were you thinking?

"I don't know," said Steve Bartman, more numb than terrified, although he had plenty to be terrified about. "I don't . . . know."

His was the hand that inspired the worst Cubs collapse in baseball history. He reached for a foul ball in Game 6—a game in which the Cubs had the lead and should have won and taken the Series.

But he knocked it away from Moises Alou. The Florida Marlins got an extra out, and that unnerved the Cubs. They folded and broke, tossing Game 6 away, while digging a hole for Game 7.

We're using his name because he released a written statement Wednesday afternoon, apologizing for breaking the hearts of his fellow Cubs fans.

Sadly, Bartman no longer owns his name. He has given his name up to a larger purpose because now it's a verb. He has Bartmaned himself, firmly fixing him and all other Cubs fans in the mythology of pain.

On Tuesday night, with the fans screaming at him, I didn't want a written statement. I wanted to hear what he had to say.

"I-I don't know," he said, as the beer sprayed toward him, in perfect arcs against the night sky. "I don't know."

I was there by chance, sitting a few sections down with my boss, who thought it would be a good idea if a White Sox fan showed up at Wrigley for what would be a historic event.

But it was historic. The Cubs choked historically.

And after the fans started screaming at Bartman, I ran over to where he was sitting and saw something strange and terrible. It was a man in the center of a maelstrom, trying to shrink himself, trying to become small and disappear, reaching for some refuge inside himself, to hide in front of 40,000 fans who wanted him hurt, or worse.

The fans around us screamed that they wanted to beat him to a pulp, they wanted him dead, and I jotted the notes down on the back of a grocery receipt—it was the only paper I had on me—and asked again.

What was on your mind?

"I do not have a statement at this time," he said, as I stood next to him, jotting notes.

"I have no comment. No comment. No comment. No comment. No comment."

Hey, you might have just cost the Cubs a chance at getting into the World Series.

And as soon as I said it, I regretted it. But he knew the truth of what he'd done.

Bartman stared at me as if he'd heard a strange language, then half turned, sat back in his seat and began rocking back and forth. He had radio earphones on, and as the fans shrieked epithets, he clamped his palms over those earphones, and put his head down, and kept rocking, quietly, staring into left field.

"He touched the ball," said Kim Ward, a Cubs season ticket holder whose seat was an arm's length away from Bartman.

"He touched the ball. He started everything. He started the downward spiral. He touched the ball." Then she started to cry.

A fan sitting next to Bartman came up with the bouncing foul ball that Alou should have caught. "He said that he wants to crawl under his seat and die," said Jim, who grew up in Oak Lawn, a Cubs fan in Soxtown. "He just wants to die and, if they lose, everything is going to be blamed on him."

If he's as great a baseball fan as his friends say, then he should have been paying attention and he should have let Alou catch the ball.

Yet there were five or six other Cubs fans reaching for that ball, too, kids with gloves and older men, all of them reaching, all of them in the front row of a key game, all of them selfish. And they're lucky, because they're not wearing the horns.

"That fan saved our season," said Luis Castillo of the Marlins. "That fan gave us a chance we shouldn't have had. And you can't give extra chances."

What ruins the story is that Bartman didn't tense up on the mound and hang curve balls for smacking. Mark Prior did. Bartman didn't forget to walk out of the dugout and settle Prior down. Manager Dusty Baker forgot. Alex Gonzalez made the key error at shortstop, not Bartman. And with bases loaded in a tied game, Bartman didn't catch a fly ball for the second out and stupidly throw home, missing the cutoff man and putting runs in scoring position. Sammy Sosa did that. If Sammy hits the cutoff man, the Cubs are out of the inning down only 4–3. But Sammy gets praise.

The Cubs lost their chance at a World Series on Tuesday. They choked again on Wednesday. But Steve Bartman is taking all the blame.

To say the Cubs were Bartmaned and that he alone cost them the pennant probably isn't fair. But this is Chicago and they are the Cubs, and fairness has nothing to do with it.

MAGIC MOMENTS

"Chicago is a town of masochists," says Marvin, a character in *Bleacher Bums*, the wonderfully evocative play about Cubs fans that was first performed in 1977. "They like to see themselves get beat. A bunch of losers."

That may be a little harsh, but it cannot be denied that over the years Chicago fans have become the dictionary definition of the term "long suffering."

Which may explain why the city experiences such an outpouring of jubilation when things go right.

Hugh Fullerton describes the excitement that greeted the realization the Cubs would face the White Sox in the 1906 World Series. I. E. Sanborn celebrates the wonders of the prelapsarian Cubs. Warren Brown offers a detailed account of the 1940 Bears historic championship-game victory. John P. Carmichael throws his hat in the air for the Bears' 1963 championship.

Fans of a more recent vintage well remember the excitement that greeted the Bears' win over the Patriots in Super Bowl XX that Don Pierson describes. It had just taken so long, and so many bad seasons, to get there. The fact that the Bears had such a great team that year, and such a goofy one, only added to the enjoyment.

Then there were the estimated 1.75 million fans who celebrated the 2005 White Sox' World Series victory parade that wound from U.S. Cellular Field to the Loop. And the crowd that turned out for the Blackhawks after they won the Stanley Cup in 2010, which was said to be even larger, perhaps because it was June and school was out.

And did those repeated championship celebrations in honor of the Bulls ever get old? Not in my book.

But for all the excitement and gratification Chicago's great sporting moments have brought the city over the years, surely none ever resonated throughout America—throughout black America, at least—quite the way Joe Louis winning the world heavyweight championship in Comiskey Park did in 1937. While accounts in the white press centered on the defeat of the popular Irishman Jim Braddock—"Death came to the champion," was Carmichael's lead in the *Daily News*—Dan Burley's coverage in the *Defender* began with a high-decibel celebration of the emotion Louis's fans felt and never once turned down the volume.

Burley, who wrote for the *Defender* and other black papers for thirty-five years, has a résumé no other sportswriter can match. He was a jazz piano player and composer who wrote such songs as "Pig Foot Sonata" and "Chicken Shack Shuffle." He was also the author of *The Original Handbook of Harlem Jive*, which was a source of the beatnik vocabulary, and he is said to have coined the word "bebop." When Burley died in 1962, the writer of his obituary in the *Defender* couldn't resist quoting a few lines from his jive parody of John Greenleaf Whittier's "The Barefoot Boy." (Blessings on thee, little man, / Barefoot boy, with cheek of tan!) Neither can I.

> Blessings on Thee, Little Square
> Barefoot Cat with the unconked hair;
> With thy righteous pegtop pants,
> And thy solid hepcat's stance,
> With thy chops so red and mellow,
> Kissed by chicks so fine and yellow.

Sox Join Cubs, Pennant Is Won

Thousands of Baseball Fans Frantic with Joy over Victories Which Bring Both Flags to Chicago

HUGH S. FULLERTON

Chicago Tribune October 4, 1906

Chicago is the baseball center of the earth.

Since last night a combination pennant pole, marking the site of Chicago, has served as the earth's axis, and around it something less than 2,000,000 maddened baseball fans are dancing a carmagnole of victory, while in every other city in the American and National League there is woe.

Next week in Chicago the two teams who have made the most marvelous races in the history of baseball and given to Chicago the honor of being the first city that ever won two major league pennants in a season, will meet and fight it out for the world's championship.

Today Chicago does not care. The fact that the Sox have joined the Cubs in the pennant-winning class is honor enough for the present and whoever wins the world's championship will recognize the antagonist as a great ball club.

The news of the downfall of Clark Griffith's New York Highlanders' hopes ended the anxiety of the fans, the fear that the White Sox, worn by their long and desperate struggle, might break at the last jump and lose the race.

Last night Chicago was baseball mad. The entire town talked baseball. Crowds stood cheering on corners at the mention of the game, everywhere there was rejoicing. Men stood and cheered in elevated trains when the news was passed along that the Sox were safe and that Chicago had two pennants—and the world's championship.

The climax of the tense race in the American League came with a suddenness that was startling—and when New York fell before Philadelphia the Chicago fans realized that the coveted prize finally belonged to the White Sox and that the desperate struggle for the American League flag, which has lasted since the Sox reached the top on Aug. 12 after one of the most sensational upward fights in history, was over.

The winning of the pennants by two Chicago teams was accomplished by two wonderful races. Frank Chance's Cubs—by far the best ball club in America today—playing brilliant ball, jumped into the lead of the National League race before the season was a month old, and, playing steady ball, held that lead to the end with only a few days out of it. Then New York flashed to the front, and fell back, and from that time to the finish Chance's men won out alone, beating all comers decisively, winning every series, and outclassing all rivals in all departments of the game.

It went out after the world's record for number of games won, and cinched that, setting the mark of number of games won so high, 116 with only 36 losses, that it will be difficult to equal.

Chance had the best team, and it was in the best condition throughout the year. His pitchers wobbled a bit early in the season, then rounded into form, and, with the assistance of the recruits President Charles Murphy hurriedly summoned whenever things went wrong and the buying up of players, who were not needed but who helped make it unanimous, he put his team out so far ahead that interest in the race as a contest died out.

But if the Cubs won because it was the best team, the White Sox won because it is the gamest, best handled, and most scientific team.

They won the championship of the American League after a fight which has no parallels in the history of baseball. They conquered odds that ordinarily would beat any ball club. They beat out stronger teams after overcoming heavy handicaps and fought it out practically alone against the united opposition of six of the clubs of the League.

To start with, there are four clubs in the American League which, on paper, are stronger than Chicago has been at any stage of this season. When a team which figures fifth in the league wins a pennant honestly and squarely against terrific odds, there is a reason for it. In this case the reason is found in the owner of the club and its manager. Charles Comiskey, the owner, always has been admitted the smartest baseball general the game ever has known. In Fielder Jones he has found a field manager who can carry out his ideas—and add to them.

Jones has by winning this pennant marked himself the smartest manager of the year. When a manager has the best team and has nine best players to go out and win games for him the task is simple. When he has a weak team and, by sheer generalship, wins he is a wonder. When, in the face of overwhelming odds, tough luck, discrimination, umpiring, sickness, and repeated injuries, he pulls off a pennant by brains and nerve, simply by making the best use of mediocre material, he is more than that.

The victory of the White Sox is a triumph of mind over matter. It was won by brains, not brawn, by thinking and generalship, and not by mechanical playing on the ball field.

The story of the fight of the White Sox for the American League championship this season is one of the most thrilling and stirring bits of baseball history, and that Chicago won the pennant is a triumph of honesty and hard work. It is small wonder that the fans who have followed the fortunes and misfortunes of the team went half mad with enthusiasm when it won.

93

The White Sox upset the heavily favored Cubs, winning the World Series four games to two. Fullerton was the only writer who correctly predicted the outcome.

Cubs Supreme in Baseball World
Final Victory over Detroit Gives Chicago Club Greatest Record in History of the Game

I. E. SANBORN

Chicago Tribune October 15, 1908
DETROIT, Mich.—When Orval Overall shut out Detroit's Tigers 2 to 0 in the fifth and final game of 1908 World Series he drove the final nail into the greatest honors that ever fell to one baseball club—two straight world's championship pennants, floating on top of three straight league championship emblems.

There have been other clubs which wore the title of three times champions, but Chicago has worn it twice, once when Cap Anson's old White Stockings were at their best in the middle of the '80s and once again when Cap Chance developed and led an even greater team in the young years of the twentieth century. Boston, Baltimore, and Pittsburgh share with Chicago the honor of having won three consecutive National League pennants. Never has any club been able to add to those laurels the winning of two world's pennants. Nor is that the end of Chicago's laurels for Chance's men today gave the great metropolis of baseball its third consecutive world's championship, including that won by the White Sox in 1906.

Not in the memory of this generation of fans has any team ever won its honors with greater credit than that which belongs to Frank Chance's warriors. Not in a thousand years has a team been compelled to fight as hard for its titles as the Chicago team which won the National League pennant twice inside of five days under the most trying circumstances. But, once assured of the National League's banner, the rest proved comparatively easy. For the same reason undoubtedly today's final crowd of the year was the smallest that has watched a World Series battle under modern conditions, the official count showing only a little over 6,000 fans present, despite ideal conditions.

Overall was the final selection for the game that was to end the series, and Overall was extremely right. That was shown in the first inning, when he struck out four men, thereby establishing a new strikeout record. Before he was through whiffing for the day he had the scalps of ten batsmen dangling at his belt and seven of these strikeouts were put over when there were men on bases. Three hits were all the Tigers could get off Overall, yet two of these coming together a single round made the outcome of the game doubtful for the actual space of five minutes. In that time the tall Californian disposed of the two batsmen who stood between him and victory.

Against Overall was pitted "Wild Bill" Donovan, who came back for a second pitched battle with Overall in an effort to win one more game in the series. The spectators settled back to watch a contest such as electrified the west side crowd for seven innings last Sunday, but it was only a minute or two before it was shown that "Wild Bill" was not nearly as fit as in his previous battle, for the Cubs batted him hard in the first inning and actually settled the game right there.

One Cub run was made with three hits in the opener, and with that Overall could have won his spurs, for with his grand pitching the Tigers had no real chance to score, although on two occasions they threatened rather seriously. After the fifth inning, when the Cubs scored their second run off Donovan and the Tigers failed in their bitterest rally because

Overall struck out the slugger Sam Crawford in the pinch, it was an easy task for Overall. He finished the string out as strongly as he began and registered his second victory over Donovan.

As Johnny Kling camped under a high foul from Schmidt's bat in the ninth inning and caught it for the twenty-seventh out the band of Cub rooters gathered in the grandstand let out a wild and prolonged yell, while the Tiger adherents folded their banners and hid their megaphones under their coats in the double distress of having watched their idols humiliated for the second year in succession.

Gamely Jennings' men trotted over to the Cub bench and congratulated Chance and his men on their triumph and the two-time world champions hurried away to their camp to dodge the wildly enthusiastic fans who tried to head them off and make them a feature of a parade downtown.

What those gray clad modest young warriors have accomplished will be remembered longer than any of them lives. For in this series, as never before, they have demonstrated the perfection of their machinery. Flawless, save for Kling's failure to make an almost impossible play when Claude Rossman struck out in the first inning on a ball so low that it hit the ground, was the work of that machine today, and even the dismally disappointed Detroit fans were compelled by sheer force of its excellence to acknowledge they never have seen anything like the airtight baseball of which the Cub have given them two demonstrations in as many days.

That stonewall infield has never been better, and Chance, Evers, Tinker and Steinfeldt have written their names above those of Anson, Pfeffer, Williamson, and Burns, Chicago's original and long famous stonewall defenders. That lightning fast outfield, Frank Schulte, Artie Hofman, and Jimmy Sheckard, has nothing to ask or learn from the fastest that ever won three pennants before. And in the batteries there is nothing in stonewall history in Chicago or elsewhere to equal the gameness and cunning that have been exhibited by those Cub twirlers who have borne the severest burdens of the battle, Mordecai Brown, Overall, and Ed Reulbach, with the help of catchers John Kling and Patsy Moran.

Today brought out the defensive excellence of Chance's magnificent machine in greater prominence than ever before, for the Tigers were battling desperately to stave off the final defeat for yet another day if possible. They were at Overall's delivery with all their might and strength and when they did not strike out breaking their backs after his phenomenally fast drop curve, they hit the ball on the nose occasionally, giving the Cubs' fielders some difficult chances.

In their attack the Cubs did not shine as brilliantly as they have, but that was through no fault or slip of theirs. It was due to the perfect work behind Donovan and the determined efforts of his feline supporters to give him the best they had in stock. The Cubs played their usual dashing, tearing game on bases, but were checked up repeatedly in brilliant fashion by their beaten but game opponents. The Tigers were battling brilliantly all the way, but found themselves up against a tribe of warriors equally game and determined and far better equipped both offensively and defensively.

It was a furious assault the Cubs made right at the start, and it drove the Tigers into their dens for a moment in swift retreat, but they emerged again later on. Evers led the assault that won with a swift poke into center field out of all reach. A minute later the Tigers' Matty McIntyre was tearing in after Schulte's single to left, and one more trip of the second hand around its tiny circle brought a ripping single from Chance's bat into center field. That scored Evers with the only run Chicago needed to earn the lion's share of the diamond laurels of the twentieth century.

With the fifth came Chicago's second run, and it was due as much to Wild Bill's wildness as to the Cubs' own efforts. Kling was given a pass and Overall dumped a sacrifice bunt, which advanced Johnny to second. Sheckard also was passed and Evers stung a liner so far through left center that drove Kling across the plate with the second and final run of the game.

With two runs to overcome, the Tigers rallied strongly to the task in the fifth. Bill Coughlin gave them the chance with a little scratch, which eluded Steinfeldt on a crazy bounder to his right. Donovan perished in a futile effort to bunt Coughlin down to second base. McIntyre responded with a terrific smash close to the first base line, for which Manager Chance made a desperate lunge. It went into the crowd for two bases and Coughlin was stopped on third by the ground rules.

There were men on third and second and only one out, and the yellow and black streamers and rooters made themselves heard once more. Charley O'Leary could only raise a little fly back of second base, and Coughlin dared not try to score on it after the exhibition of Hofman's throwing prowess he already seen. Crawford was next and a hit would tie the score, but that deadly poison of Overall's was put into operation again and Crawford struck out with a terrible lunge at his sharp drop curve.

The whiff of their pride and joy broke Detroit's back. Never again did the Tigers become at all dangerous, and no more was the yelling of hopeful rooters heard. Only the steadily swelling joy of the comparatively small array of Chicago noisemakers broke the stillness of the closing moments of the obsequies.

Sanborn's mention of the Cubs winning the pennant twice in five days is a reference to the notorious base-running mistake by Fred Merkle that prevented the New York Giants from winning the National League title and led to the game being replayed, which resulted in a Cubs victory that allowed them to advance to the World Series. . . . As of this writing, Orval Overall remains the last Cubs' pitcher to win a World Series–clinching game. . . . Elsewhere in that day's Tribune *sports section, the following note appeared: "Those who hold reservations for tomorrow's game in Chicago can retain them for the 1909 Series. They will need them."*

White Sox Beat Giants: Crepe Dims
Happy Lights of Broadway
Chorus Girls Weep, Waiters Sulk, and Joy Is Gone

JAMES CRUSINBERRY

Chicago Tribune October 16, 1917

NEW YORK—Even the electric signs along the gay white way seem dim tonight! New York has had a blow that made it sick. A bombardment from German flyers couldn't have done much more damage. New York was so sick it didn't even fight.

The idea of some fellow from Cascade, Iowa, coming in here and beating John McGraw's all-star National League champions out of the world's title has so affected Gotham that it will take weeks for it to recover. Of course, it was Chicago's fiery White Sox who got the credit, but the chances are that they are celebrating the 4–2 victory out in Cascade, the home of winning Sox pitcher Red Faber, with greater éclat than they are on Clark Street.

It's calm tonight from Harlem to Bowling Green and if one stands at Forty-second and Broadway, one might think he was in Evanston, for all New York is sick. The only live persons in town are the few from Chicago, who are marching on the sidewalk and pushing all the citizens into the new subway excavation.

New York died harder than it did in 1908, when the Cubs beat the Giants out of the pennant. At that time there was fighting on the Polo Grounds when the deciding battle was settled. There wasn't a blow struck today, so far as could be learned. New York took its defeat quietly, and didn't care to discuss it. John McGraw himself waited when it was all over to shake hands with Clarence Rowland and Eddie Collins, Faber, and some more of the new world's champions. The New York rooters who saw what took place walked sorrowfully away. There wasn't anything to say.

They had seen Heinie Zimmerman run a foot race with Collins from third base to the home plate. Eddie had four feet of a start and he finished just four feet ahead of the Bronx boy. That was the first run for Chicago, and Heinie Zim had actually chased it right over the plate. The last report was that Heinie was not present at his Bronx "café" tonight.

The New York theaters opened their doors tonight just the same as if nothing had happened, but all the show girls were weeping, the stage hands were in the way and only a few live fellows from the middle west were down in front. The Friars' club and the Lambs' were in mourning. Times Square was dull. The waiters in every restaurant were surly and got one's order mixed. New York was dead.

The only life was found at the Ansonia Hotel, where the White Sox are housed. All the gayety of Gotham tonight is right in the Ansonia, where Rowland and his new champions of the earth were celebrating.

Down in a quiet room at the Biltmore was Charles Comiskey, owner of the White Sox. He was hiding away and reveling over the victory which he has wanted since 1906 when his boys last won the big title. His only desire was to get back to the loop in Chicago as soon as possible and gather together his friends, the hundreds of Woodland bards and the thousands of common citizens, and buy one for everybody. He hates New York, and he has righted all the wrongs he has felt for a quarter of a century or more.

Comiskey waited 11 years for this event, and he fears he may have to wait another 11 for another. Consequently, he proposes to celebrate the event as it should be, and he even went so far as to say it mattered little what happened in the future in baseball. He said he had finally landed another championship for Chicago, and he felt now as if his life's work in the old national game was completed.

In many ways the final game was the best game of the series. The biggest crowd of the series was present, just under 34,000. A balmy breeze from the other side of the Hudson blew over Coogan's bluff and across the historic Polo Grounds. The sun shone and the grounds were in fine shape.

Soon after noon, the big place was filled with fans. They had their back to the wall, for defeat meant ruin. They had confidence in McGraw and his men because the Giants had shown them two games here in which it seemed that only an accident would permit the White Sox to beat them. But when the sun was sinking behind the bluff and the shadows were gathering the gloom was doubled because of the feeling in the minds of that throng.

It wasn't a mad throng at all and for the first three innings the crowd was live and alert and confident. It felt that McGraw would surely beat the Sox today and then the rest would be easy.

But in the fourth inning came the footrace between Zimmerman and Collins and Eddie was fast enough to keep his lead for the first run of the combat. From that moment on the crowd was discouraged. When the eighth inning arrived many a staunch supporter of McGraw walked out of the park, more interested in getting home in time for supper than in anything the Giants might do on the ball field.

After Chick Gandil had slashed a hit in the fourth that drove in two more runs the game seemed as good as over. However, there was a revival of hope in the bottom of the inning when Buck Herzog stung a triple that drove in two New Yorkers. Now it was a close game, and during the balance of the fight Faber hurled as he never hurled before and held the enemy at bay until the end. It was a great victory and Faber is one of the big heroes of the champions tonight, for he was credited for three victories in a world's series.

As a matter of fact, it seems that no one is a bigger hero than Faber, now that it is all over. Even though he was defeated in one game and even though he pulled the biggest boner of World Series history in stealing third when it was occupied, there is no one on the team deserving of more credit for the victory.

At a late hour tonight it wasn't known what the White Sox would do to complete their celebration. A barnstorming party was booked to take place after scheduled game at the soldiers' camp here tomorrow, but the national commission was opposed to such antics. However, there were no plans made for the return to Chicago, and the new champions are likely to divide the pelf here tomorrow morning and not appear in a body in Chicago again until opening day next year, so the fans out home might just as well cut loose and celebrate without the presence of the players.

The eight players who would later become the Black Sox all appeared in this Series. The only hint of scandal came when Heinie Zimmerman was accused of having purposely allowed Eddie Collins to score in the fourth inning of the final game. Zimmerman denied it, but two years later he was banned for life after John McGraw accused him of attempting to bribe Giants' players. . . . When, after a forty-year absence, the White Sox appeared in the 1959 World Series, Red Faber, age seventy-one, threw out the first ball.

Tan Tornado Tears Loose with a Right
Joe Louis Writes His Name in Book of Champions at Sox Park
DAN BURLEY

Chicago Defender June 26, 1937
An amber glove, encasing bruising, battered knuckles wrote JOE LOUIS in the Book of World's Champions Tuesday night at Comiskey Park. A battered Jim Braddock, his face a duplicate of a freshly beaten steak, sprawled on the canvas while 66,000 went mad. Jim Braddock isn't champion any more. Joe Louis is. Jim Braddock tried hard, but didn't. Joe Louis tried and did.

Prayers in the valley of the southland; supplications, some silent, some audible from denizens of a thousand city streets in America, backed the Alabama boy who made good in the big show. God didn't fail him—and neither did that right cross, delivered to Braddock's jaw in the first minute of the eighth round.

History and legend have recorded famous bouts. Children and grown-ups too, remember the story of Robin Hood—but Robin Hood never drew a bead with his trusty eye brow on the sheriff of Nottingham more accurately than the right Louis drew on Jim. It was delivered with a finality that WAS final. It rang down the curtain on an uninterrupted reign of white heavyweight champions from the time John Arthur Johnson shielded his eyes from the sun and cat-napped on that canvas in Havana as a surprised referee tolled off the count, through Max Schmeling and Max Baer.

Ladies and Gentlemen: Meet Joe Louis, heavyweight champion of the world!

A Tan Tornado . . . a shuffling devil-man with hell in either glove and a killer's instinct that glows like the volcanic furnaces under Mt. Vesuvius . . . that's Joe Louis, the modem fighting man.

"His mental attitude" . . . wrote the experts . . . shows clearly that Louis isn't the Louis of Carnera and Baer days . . . He's sluggish . . . he's lazy . . . he's dumb . . . He has too much money . . . he has no imagination . . . he hasn't been trained right . . . Braddock will win because he is a smart fighter . . . he has never been knocked out . . . He is a ring craftsman . . . his generalship has guided him through 87 encounters, some of which he lost, but not because of inability to box or to exhibit at all times the fighting instinct he brought to America from his Gaelic sires.

But a Brown Boy from 'Bam, who dropped his cotton sack a few moons ago to twist bolts into autos in Detroit, turned back the white man's clock to 1910 when John Arthur Johnson whipped Jim Jeffries at Reno. Tonight the same situation—a hue and cry for a white hope—resounds in the swank men's club. They're already discussing the chances of Max Schmeling in his return bout with the new champion this fail.

The Louis I saw tonight was Joe Louis. He was the Joe Louis of legend and fact . . . perfect! Referee Tommy Thomas told the two men to "shake hands and come out fighting and may the best man win."

Braddock threw a right to Joe's face, missed and clinched. Louis drove in, leading with his left as Braddock danced away. Louis swung with his right, stopped it and crossed over a left to the head. The Tan Tornado lanced the champion with a left to the jaw as Braddock forced him on the ropes. Louis reversed the situation and lashed at Braddock's head with both hands as they danced into a corner.

Braddock seated Louis with a right to the head as the crowd rippled up out of its seats as Joe immediately jumped up. They sparred at the bell. Louis ran out for the second round and Braddock led with a right to the head which was short. Louis smacked him with both hands to the head and then drove in as Braddock's right glanced off his ear. Braddock pushed the challenger onto the ropes and landed a long right to the head. Braddock scored with rights to the head and body as Louis missed a vicious left jab.

Braddock hit Louis with a right and then missed a left as they started a flurry which left Braddock a bit groggy at the bell. Whiskey was flowing in the stands like water as Louis' rally made him look like a million dollars. Louis again ran out for the third heat and they sparred as Braddock missed a long right. Louis went in with a left-handed attack to the head as ox sweat rolled down his glistening hide. Braddock scored twice with rights to the head. Louis banged him with a right to the head, followed by another.

Louis made the champion miss twice as they clinched. Braddock followed Louis, pitching his right hand to the head. Louis cracked over a terrific right to the head at the bell. The round was slow as Louis sought an opening and Braddock seemed content to score with random rights to the head and body. Braddock hooked Louis' head with a right at the start of the fourth and they exchanged in the southwest corner off the ropes.

Louis jabbed his chin with a left that worked like a piston rod. Braddock missed a right to the jaw and they clinched. Louis made Braddock look bad as the champion missed a twin barrage to the head and then the Bomber darted in and rained lefts to his mouth which rocked him like a skiff on a stormy sea. He pecked at Braddock's face with both hands. The crowd howled as Braddock missed. Louis was getting the range and gunning for that chin. Braddock was game to the core . . . he seldom retreated.

They exchanged right crosses as the bell for the fifth sounded and Braddock touched Louis' jaw with a right. Joe worked in close and pounded at his head with both hands and then drove him around the ring with a left hand fusillade as damaging as a tommy gun spraying a nest of Boches. Braddock's face reddened and his eyes grew swollen under that terrific onslaught. Joe was scoring at will and Braddock looked decidedly bad in the exchange.

They clinched and Braddock missed a vicious uppercut as the challenger shuffled off to the side. Louis kept jabbing away, his amber hide gleaming like an oiled python's as he weaved and bobbed with murderous intent. Louis' aim for Braddock's left eye improved and the Bomber slammed away at it like Babe Ruth swinging on one down the middle. Jim's touted right hand wasn't bothering the Bomber at all.

Louis suddenly retreated in the sixth and Braddock missed with both hands as he drove in. Louis' left caught his chin and the Bomber forced him off with lefts to the jaw which no human could stand much longer. They bombarded each other on the ropes and Louis kept that left in his face and marched him about the ring as he scored to the head. The crowd rose like the rippling ocean-tide as Braddock grew noticeably weaker. The Bomber cannonaded Braddock's face with a left that would have broken in a steel safe. The Irishman took it like the man he is. The crowd rose and sat down and applauded as the tough Gael took his punishment.

Braddock opened the seventh fighting, but fell away as Louis started drumming that left jab into his face with the monotonous regularity of a Haitian tom-tom. Louis was methodical as he went about his work. He was sizing Braddock up much like an executioner figures out the best way to guillotine a culprit by noting the vulnerable points around his neck. Braddock was missing and Louis started cracking him again. The champion was swinging wildly as though he were loading a wagon with hay. Louis slipped under his offerings and came up into a spirited exchange in which Braddock scored several rights to the head.

At this stage Braddock's face was ready, if it were a steak, for the grill. But the Irishman could take it. No doubt he was thinking of his wife and little ones and the days he spent on the WPA. At the same time Louis was thinking of the millions who would gain new hope and courage through his efforts here at Comiskey Park in this battle for pugilism's highest award, the heavyweight championship of the world. So Joe fattened him for the kill. He left the champion a shell-shocked shell at the end of the seventh.

They clinched in the eighth and then exchanged two-handed blows to the head in the middle of the ring. Braddock stepped back a second and in that second the world fell. It came tumbling down all around him. A million noises sounded and the Falls at Niagara could make no greater sound than the jolting, jarring right cross Louis sailed to his chin.

Braddock went down. He went down, I say, and stayed down. Who could get up after being hit by a baseball bat.

The Homer in the Gloamin'
"Lord God Almighty"
JOHN P. CARMICHAEL

Chicago Daily News September 29, 1938

We surrender to inadequacy. This Cub-Pirate pennant fight has gone far beyond our poor power to picture in words. When you squirm to fashion the proper pinnacle for a "Dizzy" Dean only to find that you need at least its twin, that a Gabby Hartnett may also brush the stars, word-painting becomes a magic art not given to the mine run of mortals to diffuse.

So let this be, today, a confession of helplessness to treat an afternoon which beggars description; an afternoon in the life of a stout-hearted Irishman who, as darkness almost wrapped him from the sight of 35,000 quaking fans, changed the map of a baseball world with one devastating blow. And that he is alive and in one piece at the moment, ready to carry on from that smash, is no fault of a Cub team and a Cub populace gone mad.

For a second successive night we stood in a clubhouse of crazy men in play suits. Only this time they weren't even articulate. We can still see 'em fighting for words, staring at one another with glazed eyes. We can still see 'em pushing Hartnett from wall to wall with the irresistible force of robots gone wild. We can still see Gabby trying vainly to free himself from idolatrous teammates.

We can still see Billy Herman, standing in the middle of the floor, arms akimbo. When he could talk it was first just a whisper of awe: "Lord God Almighty." Dawning consciousness of the moment brought it out again, louder, hoarser: "Lord God Almighty." Then the full realization of the terrific sight he had just watched in the twilight smote him. "Lord God Almighty," he suddenly screamed and hurled his glove he knew not where.

He wasn't even swearing. It was as though he was asking the heavens above to witness that this thing he'd just seen with his own eyes could really happen to him and those caught up in the maelstrom around him.

Dean's day was great. This one was greater. This was everybody's day until Hartnett wrested it from them all with that miraculous, breathtaking blow in the ninth with two down, two strikes against him and a tie game about to be put over for a double-header today because it was no longer possible to see in the gloom. Far out in the stands a mailman caught the ball and even while Gabby struggled in the arms of his men, it appeared in the clubhouse with a plea for the Hartnett name.

"Give him a new one and I'll sign it," ordered Gabby. "I want to keep this one forever. I've had the greatest thrill of this old life now."

Over in a corner "Rip" Collins, himself one of the day's heroes at that plate, tried to break the hysteria with his inevitable gag. "I get some credit," he yelled. "Gabby used the Collins stance at the plate." Elbowing his way to Gabby's side strode Trainer Andy Lotshaw, a comic figure with his cap awry and wiping away at streaming eyes with a huge towel.

"You big lug," he wept, "you hit it just like I used to do." He was shoved aside, sniffling, and "Dizzy" Dean leaped upon the managerial desk behind which Gabby had sought refuge. "Diz" teetered there back and forth on the balls of his feet, matted gray hair hanging over his forehead like an old crone's disheveled locks.

"Oh," he moaned. "You . . . you Gabby." He tried to talk with his hands, but lost his balance and fell back into unsympathetic arms. Sheer exhaustion at relief from the tension of what they'd gone through finally drove some to their chairs, where they slumped like marionettes whose guiding strings had let them down. Through the half-open door came the frenzied roar of the crowd from which, only minutes before, Andy Frain's ushers had barely saved Hartnett in his entity.

Now up, now down, now up again, the Cubs and Pirates went all the heart-straining day. The tide of battle surged bitterly through breaks, good and bad. It was almost too much for human flesh and blood to watch. And that hat we do not own is off once more to HIM and THEM.

Dizzy Dean, his arm hurting and near the end of his career, had beaten the Pirates 2–1 a day earlier in what he called the greatest game he ever pitched. . . . Associated Press writer Earl Hilligan is believed to have coined the phrase, "The Homer in the Gloamin.'" . . . The Yankees swept the Cubs in four games in the World Series that followed.

Bears Shock Redskins, and Everybody Else, 73–0

WARREN BROWN

Chicago Herald-American December 9, 1940

WASHINGTON—In the years to come, when any future devotees of professional football get together, sooner or later, we fear, the subject of the Chicago Bears' 73 to 0 victory over the Washington Redskins in Griffith Stadium yesterday will come up for discussion.

We have been gazing upon football for more years than we care to reckon, yet never in any previous enterprise, professional, collegiate, prep school or sandlot have we seen the like of the ruthless havoc wrought by the Bears.

After all, folks, this WAS the championship playoff of the National League. The Redskins had won the eastern divisional title, the Bears the western. Undoubtedly the Bears were properly installed as favorites going into the game, and probably they did believe they would win handily enough. But neither Bears nor the 36,034 who watched them ever dreamed that the score would mount to an unbelievable 73 to 0 before the day was done.

It was at once the record score of the eight years of playoffs as the Bears gained for Chicago a championship that has been absent since 1933 and it was a record score for any and all sorts of professional football since some Philadelphia team in a bygone era ran up 64 points.

Appreciating the fact that you'll be asked or be asking questions about this game in the days to come, we intend to list the scoring first, and in their order of making the four Bear touchdowns in the first half to account for 26 points and the seven touchdowns in the second half—perhaps the Bears' way of replying to Washington owner George Preston Marshall for having characterized the representatives of Halas U. as a "first half" team.

No. 1 was Bill Osmanski's, made on the second play from scrimmage in the game when he raced 68 yards down the side of the field. On it, George Wilson threw a mighty block at a critical moment that took out everybody in a Redskins uniform save the leader of the Marshall musicians.

No. 2 was Sid Luckman's on a quarterback sneak of one last foot after the Bears had come eighty yards in seventeen plays.

No. 3 was Joe Maniaci's, a forty-two-yard jaunt patterned after Osmanski's eye-opener, but without the sensational blocking, since none was needed.

No. 4 was Ken Kavanaugh's as he made a spectacular grab of Luckman's 30-yard pass into the end zone. This was the seventh of a series of plays in which the Bears had come fifty-six yards.

No. 5 was Hampton Pool's when he intercepted a pass by Sammy Baugh and went fifteen yards for the score, right after the second half began.

No. 6 was Ray Nolting's, in two plays, one of eleven yards and one of twenty-three yards.

No. 7 was George McAfee's when he intercepted a pass by Roy Zimmerman and raced thirty-five yards to score.

No. 8 was Clyde Turner's twenty-one-yard dash after he intercepted another of Zimmerman's passes.

No. 9 was Harry Clark's, when he broke away for a forty-four-yard touchdown on the first play of the fourth quarter.

No. 10 was Gary Famiglietti's after Redskins quarterback Frank Filchock fumbled on the 2-yard line.

No. 11 was Clark's again, when he scored from the 1-yard line 11 plays after Maniaci intercepted a pass by Filchock.

To complete the record, this is the second successive year in which the National League title has settled in the West without the eastern representatives being able to score a point.

A year ago it was Green Bay, 37; New York Giants, 0. So that a simple mathematical process will indicate that the West has scored exactly 110 points in these playoff games while the East has scored exactly nothing.

Nearest the Redskins came to a tally yesterday happened in the last few seconds of the first half when they saw their hopes ended as Osmanski intercepted a pass on his own 8-yard line.

In all probability the Redskins realize by now that they couldn't have been much worse off if they had tried to vary their game by rushing. However, their judgment wasn't quite as bad as that of the man at the public address system, who, while the score was Bears, 54, Redskins, 0, attempted to air a plug for next year's season-ticket sale. Honestly, we can still hear the Bronx bellow he got for that.

The Bears' margin of victory remains the largest in the history of the National Football League. The winning share for each player was $873.99.

A Tale of Three Bears—and the NFL Title

108

JOHN P. CARMICHAEL

Chicago Daily News December 29, 1963

The Bears were leading 14–10 at the end of the third quarter and, during an official timeout, George Halas strayed down to the bench, which is tucked in the northwest corner of Wrigley Field. His eyes shone with a feverish excitement in a cold, wind-whipped face.

"We need one more, we could use one more," said a neighbor and Halas embraced the thought as a drowning man reaches for succor. "Oh yes, yes," he agreed in prayerful tones, "That would be wonderful . . ." They didn't get it, but they didn't need it and today the world is the Bears' oyster, with the pro football championship of the world on the half-shell. After 18 fruitless years, during which they only once got into the title bracket, the Bears brought tears of joy to their coach's eyes.

The ducts simply couldn't contain all the happiness of the occasion. "What a day to remember," said George before he was shaken out of his dream world to face the aftermath realities of radio and television.

In fairyland's fantasy, there were just three Bears. This time, even as all season, there were anywhere from 22 to 30. And yet, as if the old story was being re-enacted in its triumvirate form on Sunday, there still were three big Bears: Larry Morris, Ed O'Bradovich and Mike Ditka.

They set up both Bears touchdowns, which Billy Wade scored, Morris with his 61-yard return of a Giant aerial, O'Bradovich with his pickoff of a screen pass and Ditka with his third-down catch on the one-yard line.

"Morris played the greatest game of linebacking I ever saw," said Rudy Bukich, the reserve quarterback. "He's never got the full credit he deserves." And from the next locker came the amen from Richie Petitbon, who intercepted the last Y. A. Tittle thrust in the end zone: "You can say that again."

This was the end for which the beginning was made last September and, for a few early minutes it looked like the Bears might crack the big game wide open. With the score tied 7–7, the Bears kicked off and Charlie Bivins recovered the Giant fumble on their five.

Folklore was in the making, a day to be remembered as maybe that of the sitting ducks, a day of shooting fish in a barrel. From here, the Bears could roll as they didn't all year.

But the kickoff was called back. A Bear lineman was offside, involving one of the rarest and worst penalties in football. Upstairs they said Steve Barnett was the offender, but Bob Jencks asked for all, or part, of the blame.

"I thought I gave Roger Leclerc (the kicker) a couple of steps," said Jencks, "but maybe I moved up too fast or he might have slowed a little."

This was understandable, since Jencks had been kicking off most of the year and was used to the quick runups. So from that point on, the game settled down into a dogfight, giving increasing evidence of the low score by which it was settled.

In spite of the intense play, the penalties totaled only 60 yards, a tribute to what O'Bradovich called "good composure on both sides."

It was O'Bradovich who, a year ago, cost the Bears a penalty by getting into a fight that let these same Giants win a seasonal game. But this time he not only promised to curb himself, but told newspapermen afterwards that "to lose your temper and get into fights is just being selfish, because you penalize your team."

So in the spirit of comparative sweetness and light, the championship was awarded without undue incident, although both sides hewed hard to the line. Between halves, Cecil Isbell, the erstwhile Packer quarterback, was putting on a mock shiver and he said it wasn't entirely from the cold. "The way they're hitting down there makes me shake even in retirement," he laughed.

When Petitbon intercepted that last Tittle "bomber," there were just two seconds left. Then came the glory rush to the Bear clubhouse, with Ditka sinking onto a chair and ribbing: "Look at everybody, you'd think we won a title or something." One player in the exuberance of victory, lighted a cigar and said: "I think I'll start celebrating now."

But Halas saw him and said: "Put it out . . . no smoking in the clubhouse."

The guy did. Papa Bear didn't want smoke getting in his eyes when they were already misty with triumph!

No Contest

Bears the Best, Win Super Bowl XX

DON PIERSON

Chicago Tribune January 27, 1986

NEW ORLEANS—This is as good as it gets. The Bears won the Super Bowl 46–10 in an awesome display of football encompassing all the joy and fury of an awesome season.

Their destruction of the New England Patriots was so complete it went beyond Super Bowl proportions and recalled only the record 73–0 victory by the Bears over the Washington Redskins in the 1940 National Football League championship game.

The Bears have a tradition that transcends Super Bowls, and Sunday they ended years of frustration for their city and themselves and showed a nation they play even better than they talk or sing.

They simply blew your minds like they said they would.

After an early Patriots' field goal ruined their bid for an unprecedented third straight shutout, the Bears scored and scored until they reached the appropriate final number, stamping the "46" defense forever on NFL history.

They scored until the Cubs and White Sox had won the World Series, until the Black Hawks and Bulls had won world titles. They scored until all the doubts and fears of all those awful years were replaced by the deafening cheers of a Superdome crowd chanting "Let's Go Bears."

Quarterback Jim McMahon, changing headbands more quickly than he changes plays, scored twice. Fullback Matt Suhey scored once. William "The Refrigerator" Perry scored after coach Mike Ditka called on him for a rollout pass he never got off.

Cornerback Reggie Phillips, subbing for injured Leslie Frazier, scored on an interception and defensive lineman Henry Waechter scored a safety.

McMahon answered the pressure of Super Bowl week with a near-perfect performance helped by a different kind of needle than his bally-hooed acupuncture treatments. He received a pain-killing shot in his sore rear end from team physician Dr. Clarence Fossier and was able to move away from the Patriot rush with ease. He was sacked only once.

"The Doc's needle worked," said trainer Fred Caito. "We went back to basic NFL treatment."

McMahon chose to wear several headbands out of the hundreds he said were sent to him.

"I decided to stick with the charities," said McMahon, who started with "JDF Cure" in honor of the Juvenile Diabetes Foundation; POW-MIA; and finished with "PLUTO" for former Brigham Young teammate Dan Plater, a cancer patient who is now in medical school at USC.

Only the cries of "Payton, Payton" went unanswered. Walter Payton failed to score, providing a harsh reminder that like their 18–1 record, not everything is perfect. He blocked, as usual, and ran hard, as usual, and said, as usual, that it wouldn't really sink in until next year.

"Right after we win it again," he said.

"I wanted to get Walter into the end zone," said Ditka. "But our plays are designed to score and I didn't know who had the ball."

"I feel very sad for No. 34," said McMahon. "I also would have liked to have seen a goose-egg up there. We could have got to 60 points, but we ran out of time."

This was the completion of a mission that Ditka said meant more to him than the Bears' and Chicago's last title in 1963 under George Halas.

"What you do in life by yourself doesn't mean as much as what you accomplish with a group of people," said Ditka. "It's because of Mr. Halas that I'm here. I'm just trying to pay some dues."

They were paid in full in a little more than one devastating opening quarter, a microcosm of the season.

The Patriots scored first after Payton fumbled and the Bears scored twice after two Patriot fumbles. Quarterback Tony Eason could do no more than take five steps back and duck. When he got passes off, they looked like ducks. After three sacks and no completions in six attempts, the Patriots brought in veteran Steve Grogan, who finally got them a first down with 4:06 left in the half.

"We have to communicate," yelled middle linebacker Mike Singletary after the play. "They got a first down. It was ridiculous."

The Patriots had minus yardage until the third quarter. Grogan was sacked four more times and was intercepted twice.

Bears defensive coordinator Buddy Ryan broke down and admitted his defense was the best he had ever seen, a sentiment that provoked no argument.

"This was a 10," said Singletary. "Or at least a 9.999."

Ryan also broke down in a team meeting Saturday night.

"He told us, 'Win or lose, next week you guys are my heroes,'" said safety Dave Duerson. "By the time he was able to finish, his eyes filled with tears and they were running down his chin. His entire face was quivering. We stood up and gave him a standing ovation. Then Steve McMichael proceeded to destroy the chalkboard."

"We love each other. That's why we're so good," said McMichael.

Defensive end Richard Dent was the game's most valuable player because he was in on the Patriots' two early fumbles. After that, it was hard to see who was getting to the Patriot quarterback first.

Appropriately, defensive players scored the final three times. Phillips ran back an interception 28 yards for a touchdown and Perry's one-yard touchdown plunge preceded Waechter's safety.

The Bears got going shortly after McMahon found receiver Willie Gault behind cornerback Ronnie Lippett for a 43-yard pass. The Bears isolated Gault on Lippett by flopping their formation to get Gault away from Patriots' cornerback Raymond Clayborn.

The Patriots came out passing because they figured they couldn't run. But the Patriots simply couldn't block anything.

"His eyes were moving around," Duerson said of Eason. "John Hannah's eyes were moving. Brian Holloway's eyes were moving. The reason was we were creating havoc. They couldn't block, man."

Eason fumbled when sandwiched by Dent and McMichael, leading to a Bears' field goal.

Then Craig James fumbled when he was picked up and tossed aside by Dent, leading to a touchdown.

McMahon faked to Perry and followed a huge path for the touchdown that made it 20–3.

McMahon's perfect 60-yard pass to Gault early in the third quarter set up McMahon's second touchdown that made it 30–3 and ended any thoughts of respectability by the Patriots. Payton ended up with 61 yards in 22 tough attempts, but the Bears established the run early with Matt Suhey, who had 52 yards in 11.

Singletary said the only subtle difference in Ryan's "46" plans for this game was a "59" blitz that sent Singletary, Marshall, and Wilson all after the quarterback. But the rush of the front four was more than the Patriots could handle.

"I've got to be honest," said Singletary. "I thought New England was a lot better than what I saw today. They were trying to talk their way through us."

"We've never been a team to talk," said Duerson, who didn't mention barking. "When Les Frazier and Mike Singletary got hurt, the Patriots were cheering and patting each other on the back. When their tight end (Lin Dawson) went out on a stretcher, our whole defense all clapped and cheered for him. They were a cheap organization that showed no class."

As usual, the Bears were mild-mannered and subdued afterwards, refusing to let that chip fall off their shoulders.

"You don't see any of us hyperventilating," said Duerson. "We knew we were the better team."

Now everybody should know it.

"People kept saying we weren't that great of a team," said Gault.

An article by a Boston columnist headlined "Chicago will choke again," was posted inside the Bears' locker room.

Chicago did the choking all right. And the Patriots did the gagging.

"No, it wasn't easy," said Singletary. "Maybe we made it look easy. But it wasn't easy."

White Sox Seize the Day, Own the City

JAY MARIOTTI

Chicago Sun-Times October 29, 2005

Where there was concrete, they stood. Where there were roofs, they climbed. Where there were poles, they hung. Where there was space between bodies, they squeezed in and tried to breathe.

I'm not certain where they came from or where they've been, but on an October afternoon in a city supposedly dominated by another baseball team, White Soxdom encompassed more than a few scattered zip codes.

It was an army at long last, numbering in the tens of thousands at the paralyzed corner of Wacker and La Salle, where the river loosely separates the South Side from the North. Chicago remains a Cubs town in sheer fan density, as all-time-low World Series TV ratings might have a hand in indicating. But know this: Having beaten the embarrassed crosstown rivals to the holy grail, the Sox obviously have become the more accomplished and relevant club . . . and seem to be gaining ground in popularity.

A world championship has that sociological effect, we now realize. Especially when 32,153 days have passed since the last one.

"Chicago! Second team, no more!" Paul Konerko told the throngs. "We knew this would be a big deal, but we didn't know it would be like this."

"Make no mistake, this is all about you guys. And quite frankly, I didn't know there were so many of you out there," said Ken Williams, the deal-maker, stunned by the enormity of the crowd and a blinding flurry of confetti as the double-decker buses passed the Board of Trade.

New York has its canyon of champions. For a day, the Second City had its boulevard of impossible dreams. "This here is the greatest feeling of my life," Mark Buehrle said. "From the minute we left U.S. Cellular Field, I had goose bumps the whole way."

He spoke for many. As title celebrations go, this one was more memorable and regal than some of those cheesy Bulls hoedowns in Grant Park, where the Luv-a-Bulls and cigar smoke made us cringe and the team's perpetual internal strife turned the mood awkward. Chicago was a Michael Jordan town then, but never has it been a basketball town. It's not in the blood like baseball, which is handed down generationally around here like a family name. Whichever team won the Series first, we knew the celebration would be a landmark day for all of us, mostly the owner.

Jerry Reinsdorf wasn't viewed favorably by the masses in the Bulls' glory days, when he always wondered if he and Jerry Krause would be booed at post-title parties. Once, when we were on speaking terms, he called to thank me about a piece urging fans not to boo him and said he would send it to his mother in Brooklyn. Those tense times, as Friday proved, are long gone.

Baseball is his true passion, and to finally break through and win—after 25 years of swinging and missing—has refreshingly brought out the emotional side of a clout-wielding man who often has faded from sight when his clubs haven't performed. He'll never admit it, but it was important for Reinsdorf to win a title without being overwhelmed by the Jordan ghost. He has done that, making him the rare owner to win championships in two major sports.

"Everyone kept asking me the last couple of days what I did with the last ball, that last out," said Konerko, whom some theorized might keep the symbolic baseball much like the undeserving Doug Mientkiewicz last autumn in Boston. "Well, it's going to the man right here. Because he earned it."

That would be Reinsdorf. His eyes were damp in Anaheim. His voice started to crack in Houston. On a gorgeous day in Chicago, the day even he thought he might never see, he broke down and let the tears flow. Imagine what Donald Fehr, Scott Boras and all his enemies thought when tough, gruff Jerry raised the ball for everyone to see, then rushed to make a quick comment at the podium before he cried like a baby.

"Getting this ball from Paul Konerko," he said through sobs, "is the most emotional moment of my life."

"I've got to tell you, all year, we had to listen to people out there who told us we didn't have the team to do this," Konerko said. "We were in first place at the (All-Star) break, and people didn't want to believe. We win the division, and people say we're gonna get beat by the Red Sox—didn't happen. We go to Anaheim, and we've got to hear about umpires' calls. We go to the World Series, and now we've got to hear about domes and all kind of stuff.

"I was trying to think in my mind what would make people think we're a good team. The only thing I could come up with is maybe we'll have to come back and do this again next year."

There was one painful moment, which tends to happen during these affairs. That came when Buehrle demanded that the three players who came up with this corny "Don't Stop Believin'" thing be held accountable. With former Journey singer Steve Perry dusted off for the occasion, Buehrle asked the culprits—Aaron Rowand, A.J. Pierzynski and Joe Crede, the self-described "Three Stooges"—to join Perry in a singalong. The only words Pierzynski seemed to know were, "A singer in a smoky room, smelled of wine and cheap perfume."

It was so awful, it was beautiful.

From Glad to Verse
For Sox Fans, There's No Rhyme or Reason behind 2005 Season

MIKE DOWNEY

Chicago Tribune October 30, 2005

In October of two thousand and five,
A very strange thing occurred.
In fact, you might even think it
As strange as you've ever heard.

After eighty-eight years of failure,
A team that the whole world mocks
Finally won the big one;
We mean the Chicago White Sox.

You probably don't believe it,
Or can't believe what you're seein'.
But it's true, the White Sox have won it;
So bless you, Ozzie Guillen.

They did it for Shoeless Joe Jackson,
For Looie and Nellie Fox.
For Fisk and Zisk and Baines and Raines
And hundreds of other Sox.

Since nineteen hundred and seventeen,
We haven't known how this feels.
Our field of broken dreams has been
At 35th and Shields.

We suffered with Veeck (as in wreck),
And with Thomas, the Big Hurt;
We felt for some of the "Black Sox"
Stained by their teammates' dirt.

We watched as the Sox changed colors,
Wore pajamas and even shorts.
And saw them disappear each year
From the wide world of sports.

They never once took the pennant
From 'nineteen to 'fifty-nine,
And then the Sox famine continued
Right up to the present time.

They fought off Cleveland Indians
Throughout the month of September.
And then proceeded to give us
A Soxtober to remember.

First came a series with Boston,
A team to weaken one's knees.
For how would you like to be pitching
At Fenway to David Ortiz?

But the right Sox did come to prevail
When all was said and told,
By grounding to Graffanino
Through whose legs it rolled.

Next came a stronger opponent,
From Anaheim (via Los Angeles).
And what a play we saw one day!
Rarely been one so scandalous.

On strike three to A. J. Pierzynski,
And only by God's good grace,
A catcher, Josh Paul, rolled the ball and
Pierzynski stole first base.

You'd think God would side with Angels
And give them a helping hand.
Instead, it was up to the umpire
Who let the "safe" call stand.

And finally came the World Series,
A wondrous sight to behold.
To remember Chicago's last one
You'd need to be pretty old.

After decades of Sox frustration,
Of losers and laggers and lemons.
They went right out and won Game 1
And even rocked Roger Clemens.

The opponents, the Houston Astros,
Came in buzzing with Killer B's.
Bagwell and Biggio, Berkman and Burke
Making Astronomical fees.

But Contreras was up to the challenge,
Then the Jenks kid showed his power.
He buzzed a strike three by Bagwell
At a hundred miles an hour.

Game 2 was quite a bit different.
The Sox found themselves in a jam.
But that was before Konerko
Konnected on his grand slam.

Into the game's last inning, though,
The score remained tied at six.
Who thought the bat to win it would be
Uh . . . Scott Podsednik's?

Well, as any Sox fan can tell you,
This is as weird as it gets.
But then comes Game 3 down in Texas
And you ain't seen nothin' yet.

It dragged on for fourteen innings
Till roundabout one a.m.
Both sides were clearly exhausted;
Us as well as them.

The longest World Series game ever
Left Houston's fans even more glum.
Down to their subs, as dead as the Cubs,
The Sox sent to bat Geoff Blum.

He homered right into a corner
Of Minute Maid Park ("the Juice Box").
And very much alive were our boys of '05
The never-say-die White Sox.

One more win, just one more win
And the whole team could come home early.
Crede, Uribe, Iguchi and Rowand
Garcia and Garland and Buehrle.

One more win, just one more win
Till fireworks light up the sky.
Till Nancy Faust, our key player,
Plays "Na Na, Hey Hey, Goodbye."

One more win, just one more win
Is all that a Sox fan asks.
And then we can go out to trick-or-treat
Disguised in our Ozzie masks.

Oh, nothing you've seen on Halloween
Could ever be quite so spooky
As kids of Chicago dressed up for a party
As Guillen or Jenks or El Duque.

No candy you eat could be half as sweet
As a White Sox parade going by.
Millions in the street giving cheers to Politte!
Hey, look . . . there's Jermaine Dye!

And Hermanson, Harris, Vizcaino, Perez,
Ozuna and Widger rate props.
Don't worry, we haven't forgotten to mention
A very fine pitcher, Neal Cotts.

One more win, just one more win
How would the White Sox get it?
We didn't know how, we didn't know when,
Just knew we would never forget it.

They easily won the World Series;
Smashed the Astros four in a row.
But did a sweep by the Sox come as a shock?
The answer, quite frankly, is "No."

Wildcats Pinch Themselves — All the Way to Pasadena

GENE WOJCIECHOWSKI

Chicago Tribune December 29, 1995

PASADENA, Ca.—There are stranger things than seeing this dateline and Northwestern share the same paragraph. Like how about Gary, Ind., and the Bears?

But here the Wildcats are, 47 years removed from the legacy of Aschenbrenner, Murakowski and Tunnicliff, the proud owners of the first, second, third and, so far, only Rose Bowl touchdowns ever scored by Northwestern players. Who knew it would take five more decades, eight more head coaches, 327 more defeats and 992 more lettermen before the Wildcats returned to college football's oldest bowl game?

That's what makes this latest visit so special. This is football through the looking glass. If you hadn't seen it with your own eyes, you'd think somebody got their W's and L's mixed up. Isn't Northwestern supposed to beat Miami of Ohio and lose to everyone else? Shouldn't Darnell Autry be running for the USC Trojans, not against them? And since when does a team lose its star linebacker to a broken leg, its star kicker to a bizarre knee injury and still go from 3–7–1 in 1994 to 10–1 in 1995?

"On the plane, it hit me big time," cornerback Chris Martin said after arriving in California last week. "Now we're here, and it's overwhelming."

Of all the improbable, nearly unimaginable sports stories of this decade or any other, none has more charm than Northwestern's. The Wildcats were college football's equivalent of Neil Armstrong dipping his toe into the Sea of Tranquility.

In a season when almost everything went by the book, Northwestern was the one reason to keep turning pages. The Wildcats led the nation in "did-you-see-that?" upsets. They won the Big Ten. Better yet, there were no agent sightings, no Pell Grant scandals and no law firms on retainer. NCAA investigators wouldn't know their way to Evanston without a road map. The closest thing to a paper trail was homework. In short, this is mom-and-pop football at its squeaky-clean best.

The last time Northwestern was here, the team arrived by train. Raccoon coats were in. Rust wasn't the predominant air color of Southern California.

Now you wonder if the Wildcats have any actual idea how to be in a bowl, especially the self-proclaimed granddaddy of bowls. After all, 47 years is 47 years. Maybe an instruction booklet for the players would have been useful.

For example:

Tip No. 1: No, you don't get to ride on one of the parade floats.

Tip No. 2: You know, that's not a real queen and her court.

Tip No. 3: When exploring Los Angeles, trust no one who offers to sell you "a genuine Rolex" for $50.

Tip No. 4: During the pregame coin toss, please refrain from asking

USC team captains for their autographs. And sorry, flash photography is not permitted at midfield.

Like it or not, this is the image Northwestern still must overcome. For all of their accomplishments, the Wildcats haven't completely convinced America they're for real. USC a four-point favorite? Apparently, warm and fuzzy doesn't transcend the spread.

"They're the Cinderella and we're the Wicked Witch of the West," said USC assistant coach Mike Sanford, "and we plan on fulfilling that role."

That's where Gary Barnett comes in. Barnett, whose stay as an assistant coach at Colorado included six bowl appearances, two national-championship games and one national title, is doing what he can to serve as the Wildcats' postseason tour guide.

Club Gary, it isn't.

Before boarding the charter flight last week, he told his assistants to expect long hours—and he didn't mean by the hotel pool. He told his players to enjoy themselves, but then he issued a challenge: "Do you want to go out and just play in the Rose Bowl?" he said. "Or do you want to win the Rose Bowl?"

Some Rose Bowl coaches have sequestered their teams as if they were the O.J. Simpson jury. Others have considered curfew a suggestion, not a requirement. Barnett has insisted on a happy medium. Have fun, but within reason.

Barnett remembers the 1989 season, when Colorado went to the Orange Bowl undefeated but left with a loss. The Buffaloes were too busy looking at palm trees, too concerned about sampling the South Beach nightlife, too distracted by their newfound status to focus on their national-championship game against Notre Dame. Final score: 21–6, Irish.

The next year, again at the Orange Bowl, again against Notre Dame and again with a national title at stake, hardly a Colorado player ventured outside the team hotel. The Buffs won the game and a championship. A lesson learned.

"We're just counting on the leadership and the character of this football team to realize what's at stake, what the opportunity is," said Ron Vanderlinden, Northwestern's defensive coordinator.

The truth is, not everyone is buying this purple glass slipper stuff. The way USC star receiver Keyshawn Johnson figures it, nobody beats Notre Dame, Michigan and Penn State in the same season and wins the Big Ten because of magic dust. Granted, Johnson can't name more than two players on the Northwestern roster, but he knows determination when he sees it.

"All that Cinderella crap . . . get it out," he said. "Everyone's going off the history with Northwestern. Let's trash the history."

Johnson's major at USC? History.

Nobody is quite sure whether Northwestern will be back here anytime soon. Roseanne hosted Frank Sinatra's recent TV special, so anything is possible. But just in case, maybe it's time to appreciate Northwestern's season for what it really is: as perfect as a rose petal, as amazing as the Gary Bears.

Northwestern's bubble burst three days later when it lost to USC, 41–32.

Say Cheesesteak
Blackhawks Win Stanley Cup

DAVID HAUGH

Chicago Tribune June 10, 2010

PHILADELPHIA— On the day Patrick Kane first picked up a hockey stick as a boy growing up in Buffalo, he imagined this moment. And Kane probably has envisioned it every day since the Blackhawks drafted him No. 1 overall in 2007.

Yet not even all that mental visualization prepared Kane for the emotion that overwhelmed him Wednesday night when he made every hockey kid's fantasy his reality.

"It's pretty crazy and it hasn't sunk in yet that I scored the goal to win the Stanley Cup," Kane said, still shaking, after the Blackhawks' 4–3 victory in overtime beat the Flyers in Game 6.

It took a while for it to sink in for the 20,327 at the Wachovia Center and the millions watching back in Chicago.

At the 4:06 mark of overtime, Kane picked up the puck along the wall and shot it toward the net past Flyers goalie Michael Leighton. It landed on the far side of the goal and required an officials review to verify a goal Kane already had begun celebrating.

"I saw it going right through his legs," Kane said. "I tried to sell the celebration a bit."

He may not stop for a while.

This was the artful, perfect ending for Chicago, Kane frolicking down the ice with a finger raised into the air and smiling like the kid he is. This was hockey symmetry, one of the Blackhawks' franchise players ending 49 years of Stanley Cup futility for the franchise with a legendary goal.

Lord Stanley, welcome back to Chicago. It has changed a lot since 1961. But the satisfaction is still the same.

"It was storybook with Patrick scoring the game-winner," Blackhawks Chairman Rocky Wirtz said. "I dedicate this to my father, my grandfather, my uncle and everybody in our family who worked their asses off for so long."

In the city in which a fictional boxer inspired generations of underdogs in a movie telling his story of redemption, another Rocky celebrated a rags-to-riches triumph that only felt too good to be true. Six years after seeing his family's team ranked the worst organization in professional sports, Wirtz now can boast being an owner of the best hockey team in the land.

From Wirtz to first indeed.

"Everyone has a piece of this, it was much more than just me," Wirtz said as players and coaches congratulated him on the ice.

With both hands, Blackhawks captain and playoff MVP Jonathan Toews, the other franchise player, hoisted the silver chalice on the ice as cameras clicked photos of Toews and his giddy teammates for posterity.

Say Cheesesteak.

"Oh, my God, it's like that commercial," Toews said. "I'm speechless."

The young Blackhawks struggled to grasp the fact they really had done it, with skill and speed and strength that never failed them when they needed it most. They did it with a combination of force and finesse, grit and grace, that was no accident.

This was the vision of President John McDonough, who spent 24 years in the Cubs front office but made his North Side friends envious by presiding over a Stanley Cup champion in his only third season running the Blackhawks. This was the design plotted by GM Stan Bowman, more than just the son of Scotty, since he assumed his new job last summer after eight years in the Hawks front office.

This was the plan executed by Joel Quenneville, the coach with the legendary mustache, who now has a resume even more impressive.

"You live for this," Quenneville said as fans chanted, "Thank you Q!" "It's a proud moment for our whole team."

Yes, Kane and Toews fulfilled the promise surrounding them since their rookie season of 2007 when the magic returned. Duncan Keith and Brent Seabrook gave the '85 Bears a run for their money as the toughest defensive line in Chicago sports history. Goalie Antti Niemi disproved doubters from here to Helsinki, coming up bigger than ever after the Flyers' late third-period goal tied it 3–3 and sent it into overtime.

Dustin Byfuglien, whose first goal came on a power play with nemesis Chris Pronger in the penalty box, became the name first mentioned in any Chicago discussion about clutch playoff performances. Marian Hossa dispelled any thoughts of a Stanley Cup curse by winning in his third straight finals with his third different team. John Madden and Patrick Sharp and, well, find a roster because it just became a collector's item.

"Winning with this group of guys makes it even more special," Toews said.

Give the Flyers credit. They were harder to get rid of than hiccups. After Andrew Ladd's goal off a redirect from Niklas Hjalmarsson gave the Hawks a 3–2 lead at the 17:43 mark of the second period, they wouldn't go away. There were 3 minutes, 59 seconds left to the champagne celebration when Scott Hartnell banged in a goal that came off Ville Leino's stick and bounced off Hossa's skate and past Niemi.

It was the type of play that made many back home in Chicago start to worry about Game 7. But worry no more.

Kane's goal won it for you and your neighbor hanging the Hawks flag and everybody who watched the game five-deep at a bar back home. This was for you guys.

This was for Keith Magnuson and Doug Wilson, Eddie O. and Cheli, and all the other proud former Blackhawks who never won the Cup. This was for Bobby Hull and Stan Mikita, whose return to the organization

125

helped bridge tradition with potential. This was for Dale Tallon and Denis Savard, the former GM and coach, respectively, whose work identifying and developing the young talent on the Hawks made all this possible.

This also was for all the fans who stuck behind the team when you couldn't find them on TV and you couldn't talk about them on sports-radio shows because hosts were ordered to discuss anything but the Blackhawks.

This was one for the ages.

"This is a night," McDonough said, "that we'll remember the rest of our lives."

So that's why his eyes were moist.

ANY TEAM CAN HAVE A BAD CENTURY

n a short story titled, "The Last Pennant before Armageddon," W. P. Kinsella, the author of *Field of Dreams*, conjures up a season in which the Cubs are about to win the World Series when their manager is troubled by a recurring nightmare that the world will end if they do. To which any true Cub fan would ask, "What's the catch?"

Cubs' managers and players sometimes try to wave aside the fact the team hasn't won a world championship since 1908 by saying they weren't around while this dismal streak was taking place, not all of it at least, and people should stop dwelling in the past.

Cub fans know better, of course. *They* were here as losing season followed losing season, as were their parents and grandparents. Not for them the luxury of just passing through, nor can they trade their allegiance or declare themselves free agents. Instead, they must wallow in their misery, pondering over and over the litany of the curse of the Billy Goat and the seventh-game humiliation in the 1945 World Series, the Black Cat in 1969, the ground ball going between Leon Durham's legs in 1984, the overmatched 1989 team being crushed by the Giants and . . . well, the less said about the 2003 National League Championship Series the better.

Charles Dryden, whose piece on the first game of the 1918 World Series leads off this section, deserves special mention and not only because Ring Lardner's admiration was so great that when someone praised his humorous baseball writings he replied, "Me, a humorist? Have you guys read any of Charley Dryden's stuff lately? He makes me look like a novice."

Dryden certainly had a knack for phrasemaking. He is credited with the first use of "pinch hit," "ballyard" and "horsehide." He called the 1906 world champion White Sox "the Hitless Wonders," named Charles Comiskey "the Old Roman," Frank Chance "the Peerless Leader" and Fred Merkle "Bonehead." And it was Dryden who, in 1909, wrote of the downtrodden Washington Senators, "First in war, first in peace and last in the American League."

Dryden's coverage of Babe Ruth's 1–0 victory over the Cubs' Hippo Vaughn is representative of his work. He interrupts his account of what sounds like a sensational game to ponder the weather, the crowd, a fleet of blimps appearing over Comiskey Park—a World War I version of to-day's military flyovers—and to offer a comical description of the umpires and other assorted trivia. Like other baseball writers of his era, Dryden occasionally neglected to identify the players he wrote about by their first names—I have taken the liberty of filling in the blanks—and as was also the custom he never visited the locker rooms after games where he might have asked Ruth or Vaughn for comment on their magnificent perfor-mances. And as to Dryden's mention of "deans" in the fourth paragraph, I checked with several baseball experts and lexicographers and none of them had any idea what he was talking about.

Brent Musburger's column, which is the only ray of sunshine in this otherwise grim recounting, shows just how excitable Cub fans can be when things are going their way. Rick Talley, on the other hand, gives a painful dissection all the all-too-familiar flip side, one that is made even more excruciating by the fact that it depicts the worst Cub flop of all.

Then there is Mike Royko, who didn't write about sports regularly, but when he did, full-time sports columnists could only react the way Oscar Peterson says he did when he first heard Art Tatum play the piano: with despair. One of Royko's greatest attributes, and one of the hardest to emu-late, was the common touch. If you had a PhD in nuclear physics—or English literature for that matter—you got no more enjoyment out of his columns than if you never made it out of high school.

As for the piece reprinted here, it is, in my estimation, the funniest sports column ever written. Try to read it without laughing out loud. I dare you.

1918

The Curse of the Bambino, Chicago Style; Ruth Triumphs over Vaughn, 1–0, in First Game of World Series

CHARLES DRYDEN

Chicago Herald-Examiner September 6, 1918

Without doubt this was the softest World Series combat on record for all concerned with the possible exception of the Cubs. A pass to Dave Shean in the fourth and the singles of George Whiteman and Stuffy McInnis off Hippo Vaughn scored the only run of the opening game which Boston naturally copped 1–0 before 19,274 people who spent $30,348 to see it.

Aside from that round there was nothing doing in the way of visible assets. The Cubs were so keenly organized to prevent Babe Ruth from knocking any homers they forgot to score any runs for themselves. Not an error was made on either side, the umpires stood around like statues in a park and the hitting was modest to a degree. The Red Sox whacked Hippo five times and the Cubs collected six hits from Ruth.

Where the Cubs should have won but didn't was in the first round. They loaded the bases with two out and Charlie Pick skied to left. In the sixth with two on and two out, Charlie Deal slammed a foul so far that the pill returned in a badly damaged condition. These were the only large openings. The home champions had a runner on second with one gone in the third and he was left on third base to look at airships and other scenery.

Altogether it was a cozy and homelike affair. The attendance was not up to expectations. Neither was the climate, but that alone should not account for the gaps in stand, bleachers and pavilions. Nor were the deans crowded as heretofore, though the press coop contained several female deans, which are said to be more deadly than the male.

Incidental to the main doing a fleet of airships loomed up in the smoke and clouds. When the pilots sighted the World Series they sheered off and went throwing fits in the sky. Being keyed up for any type of entertainment the bugs watched the evolutions, keeping one eye on the national pastime.

By all rules of organized superstition Babe Ruth should have lost the battle. He struck out the first batsman, but the rule doesn't always hold

129

good. On the other hand, Manager Fred Mitchell inherited a mammoth floral horseshoe from the Cubs' Claws Club and had a moving picture of his smile of acceptance. There is no luck in the floral horseshoe except when the Greeks wish them on Heine Zim and he was far away. The Cubs were favorites and they certainly looked mighty nice in clean white uniforms. Somebody forgot to send the official mascot to the laundry and this soiled kid no doubt queered the proceedings.

It didn't take as long as usual to get the show started. With the bouquets out of the way the four umpires emerged and did a little pointing at nothing in particular while Ruth and Bullet Joe Bush warmed up on the sidelines. Finding nothing worth pointing at, the cameramen having withdrawn, the umpires took their stations. Hank O'Day in shining armor went behind the plate. Mr. George Hildebrand camped within a few feet of first base. Bill Klem folded his shapely thumbs across his stomach at second and Brick Owens went into retirement at third base. Brick had nothing to do but pose as part of the scenery.

Ruth was a disappointment in one respect. He didn't glean any homers. Every time the southpaw came up the bugs howled for his specialty but Vaughn was there to fool him. Hippo twice whiffed the slugger and had Babe swinging his neck loose. On the slab, however, Babe was the big works. His job was to steer the Cubs away from the plate and he succeeded. Another prominent victim of Hippo's wiles was Fred Thomas. That gallant young able seaman struck out twice, but Fred has a good alibi. Fred just naturally shied at the bean ball having spent several months in the Navy.

Shean, the hero of the cracked digit, cracked the first hit, a single in the opening round. After that, Dave walked a couple of times and the first pass won the ball game. Perhaps Hippo realized that if Dave clicked a triple or something the jar would sting his sore finger. After two defunct in the Cubs share of the first round Les Mann and Dode Paskert smote singles. Fred Merkle was favored with a pass which stocked the bases. Charlie Pick landed a fly in George Whiteman's mitts and that noble chance blew up.

In the fourth Shean copped the first of his sore finger passes. Amos Strunk thought a sacrifice would help some. He bunted a fly to Vaughn and that was the last of Amos for a while. Whiteman poked a single to center and McInnis followed that knock with a safe blow to left. Shean scored and rested his sore finger on the water cooler until they got the side out. Scott bunted a fly which Charlie Deal captured in neat style and Thomas fanned.

The Cubs started something in the sixth and were unable to finish it. After one out, Paskert and Merkle astonished Ruth with a couple of singles. Pick sacrificed them along one notch. Here was where Deal tore off a foul fly that routed Phil Douglas and Tom Clarke out of the distant bullpen. On the next try, Deal skied to Whiteman.

In the ninth, Mitchell ordered out the militia, but it was then a hopeless case. Merkle skied and so did O'Farrell, batting for Pick. Deal came through with a single and Bill McCabe went forth to gallop for him. Bill got set on his mark and Bill Killefer hoisted a fly to right which ended the combat.

131

Shean's "cracked digit" was his middle finger, which was tightly wrapped after some of the nail and skin were ripped off during practice before the Series began. The Red Sox won the Series four games to two.

1945
The Great, the Good, and the Awful
WARREN BROWN

Chicago Sun October 11, 1945
The world's baseball championship, such as it is, belongs to the Detroit Tigers.

It became theirs in the presence of 41,590 witnesses at Wrigley Field yesterday when the Chicago Cubs, who have been trying off and on since 1908 to win one of these post season skirmishes, up and blew game and series in a most dismal fashion.

The final score was 9 to 3.

The ball game, however, was decided as early as the first inning when the Tigers drove out Hank Borowy after only three men had faced him, and carried on against the wildly inept Paul Derringer, until five runs were scored.

Those, as it turned out, were more than the Tigers needed to take the championship, four games to three. Yet they picked up another off Derringer in the second inning, one off Paul Erickson in the seventh, and a final pair off Claude Passeau in the eighth. If it matters, they didn't score off Hy Vandenberg, who fitted in between Derringer and Erickson, and added 3 1/3 scoreless innings to the few of the same he had pitched earlier in the season.

Borowy, trying to operate for the third time in four days, found the task too trying. Derringer, unable to get the ball over the plate most of the time and rocked in the first by Paul Richards' bases-clearing double, may have need rest, too, for all we know.

At all events, when he passed three Tigers in a row in the second, forcing a run across, Manager Charlie Grimm gave him the winter off to relax.

The Tiger hurler, Hal Newhouser, appearing on the scene for the third time, had no trouble of great moment with any of the Cubs save Phil Cavarretta and Harry Lowrey, who annoyed him constantly. Were it not for those two, and an occasional nudge from Don Johnson and Bill Nicholson, the Tiger hurler might have closed out his first World Series string with a shutout.

Along the way, Newhouser, in winning his second game of the series, fanned 10. One of the three runs scored against him was the result of some of the quaint outfielding methods of Roger Cramer, who lost sight of a fly ball, as Tigers had been doing now and then, ever since the series began.

The set of seven games, played before an aggregate of 333,457 fans, will stand as a record for wild and wooly baseball, since the coming season should see the return of enough major league ballplayers from the service to elevate the game once more to a measure commensurate with the $7.20 ticket price than the one which ended yesterday.

Borowy's stay in the ballgame was of less than five minutes duration. Skeeter Webb ran the count to three and two and singled to right. Eddie Mayo pushed the first ball in the same direction for a single, and when Doc Cramer looped a single into left field, scoring Webb, Derringer was summoned from the bullpen.

He was greeted by Hank Greenberg's sacrifice, and was then ordered to pass Roy Cullenbine, which filled the bases. Rudy York eased some of the pressure by popping out, but Derringer was unable to get a single pitch over to Jim Outlaw, who walked, forcing in Mayo. This left the bases filled, and Richards quickly cleared them with a double into the left-field corner.

The ninth Tiger, Newhouser, grounded out to end the inning, at last.

The following day, Brown analyzed the major reason for the Cubs' defeat in the World Series, which, as of this writing, is the last in which they ever played.

It would, perhaps, be more charitable to forget the whole thing, but people do insist on pawing over the wrecking of the Chicago Cubs 1945 World Series model, in an attempt to find out just what happened. Or, knowing what happened, their needs must keep on wondering how it did.

If you consult your nearest composite box score, you will find the answer part way down the summary.

It goes like this: BASES ON BALLS—Off Passeau, 8; off Derringer, 7; Off Borowy, 6; Off Wyse, 4. Off Vandenberg, 3; Off Erickson, 3; Off Prim, 1; Off Chipman, 1—Total, 33.

Off Trucks, 5; Off Newhouser, 4; Off Trout, 3; Off Bridges, 3; Off Overmire, 2; Off Tobin, 1; Off Mueller, 1—Total, 19.

You will not need to look any further for the main reason why the Cubs are still seeking a world's championship to put beside the last one they won, some 37 years ago.

Detroit's pitchers, the great, the good and the ordinary, were able to get the ball over the plate.

The Cubs' pitchers, the great, the good and the awful, were not.

The Detroit pitchers, despite some of the weirdest fielding displays, especially in the outfield, that any World Series has ever know, continued to place their trust in the baseball truism that there is always some kind of chance to make a play on any ball which is hit—unless it goes outside the park—but that there is no chance at all to make a play on a man who is drawing a base on balls.

The Cub pitchers, though witnessing in almost every game several instances of truly spectacular defensive work in both outfield and infield, failed utterly in this business of getting the ball over the plate.

133

It seemed to me that the Detroit pitchers stood in awe of none of the Cub hitters, not even Phil Cavarretta, who was the best seven-game ball-player the Cubs had on the field.

The Cub hurlers, however, were gravely concerned over Hank Greenberg. Yet the extreme caution excusable in pitching to Greenberg was also exercised, with dubious results, in working on several of the lesser members of the Nine Old Men, whose record in season or in series didn't indicate that they could hurt anyone much if they did get a good ball to hit, instead of a base on balls.

Brock for Broglio
Joined at the Hip

JEROME HOLTZMAN

Chicago Tribune January 22, 1995

I was talking to Ernie Broglio when Lou Brock walked in and sat down at the table.

"Do you know why I'm here?" Broglio asked Brock. Then, without waiting for a reply, Broglio said, "I'm here because of you."

"History put us together," Brock acknowledged. "We're joined at the hip."

This little dialogue occurred Friday at the Hilton Hotel when the Cubs were opening their annual weekend winter fan convention. As an added attraction, John McDonough, the Cubs' marketing director, had the inspired idea of bringing Brock and Broglio together.

It was perhaps the most disastrous deal in Cubs history: Brock to the Cardinals for Broglio on June 15, 1964. Brock had a Hall of Fame career with the Cardinals. Broglio won a total of seven games for the Cubs.

In the years since, they have been together on five or six occasions, usually at old-timers games. Broglio recalled his last Wrigley Field appearance:

"It was an old-timers game. I got a standing ovation; 40,000 people booed me. Leo Durocher brought me back. But he was so mad he didn't pitch me."

When the deal was made, the unanimous reaction, here and in St. Louis, was that the Cubs had pulled a major coup.

The report in the Chicago Daily News began, "Thank you, thank you, oh, you lovely St. Louis Cardinals. Nice doing business with you. Please call again any time."

Bill White, the recent National League president who was then the Cardinals' first baseman, remembers that none of the St. Louis players liked the deal. Some fans carried a banner that read: "Broglio for Brock. Who could make such a deal?"

While visiting with Broglio here Friday, Brock admitted that he was also surprised.

"Here's a young guy with two left feet who doesn't know where he's going and I was traded for a 21-game winner," Brock said. "I knew the kind of quality pitcher he (Broglio) was. Until the trade, I had no idea of my value in baseball, what my stock was worth.

"It gave me some indication how good I might be. It solidified my confidence. The day before the trade I hit a two-run homer to win a ballgame 3–2. So I was feeling pretty good. But most of the time I was worrying, thinking I might get sent back to the minors."

That changed the day he reported to the Cardinals. As soon as he suited up, manager Johnny Keane put his arm around Brock's shoulder and told him, "We traded for you because we think you can play. You're in right field."

Keane was right, of course.

Brock, a bit player during his 2 ½ years with the Cubs, was hitting .251 when he was traded. He finished the season with the Cardinals batting .348 and had 33 stolen bases to lead the team to the pennant. Broglio, in the meantime, had nothing but woe in his maiden season here, winning only four of 18 starts.

What the Cubs' brass apparently didn't know was that Broglio had suffered a minor arm injury a month before the trade. "At the time, it wasn't very serious," Broglio said Friday. "It kept getting worse."

Broglio won one game for the Cubs in 1965 and two the next year. He was then traded to the Cincinnati Reds and never appeared in another major-league game. Lifetime he was 77–74. In 2 1/2 seasons with the Cubs, he was 7–21.

135

Brock had a blockbuster career. He finished with 3,023 hits, a .293 lifetime average and a major-league-record 938 stolen bases, since broken by Rickey Henderson.

"I don't agree with the people who say it was the worst deal in history," Broglio said Friday. "Brock made himself. He would have done the same thing here in Chicago if they had let him play. I'm happy that he got into the Hall of Fame. And I'm happy that I got to play in the big leagues as long as I did."

Madness in Wrigley Field; Enjoy It While It Lasts

BRENT MUSBURGER

Chicago American July 3, 1967

Fantasyland is raging out of control.

Fun is fun but who ever heard of an entire city wanting to sleep inside a baseball stadium after the game was over? The farmers don't even do that for King Lombardi up in Green Bay.

For most of the last two decades, P.K. Wrigley couldn't give away space inside his friendly ball park. Yesterday, he couldn't get anybody to leave.

That sellout crowd of 40,464 stood and roared and stomped and shouted and hollered and cheered and whistled and the game had been over for nearly 20 minutes. It was like an overwhelmed theater audience demanding encore after encore. Nobody could remember the last time that ever happened at a baseball game.

Not even Don Larsen, the man who occupied center stage during baseball's most dramatic performance: his perfect game for the New York Yankees against the Brooklyn Dodgers in the 1956 World Series.

"I was in a stupor when I pitched that game," admitted Larsen, salvaged by Cub manager Leo Durocher from the minor leagues last week. "Today, I could sit in the bullpen and watch what was happening. I couldn't believe it. If this team wins the pennant, those fans will tear the park apart."

For an hour after Ferguson Jenkins wrapped up his three-hit performance in a 4–1 victory over the Reds, his Cub teammates all but forgot about the reason behind this spontaneous hysteria—the fact that the Chicago Cubs, a 100-to-1 shot last April, are in first place in July. That's like watching hell freeze over right before your eyes.

The players, though, guzzled beer, ate Ron Santo's pizza, dealt cards, and raved endlessly about the fans, many of whom were still milling about outside the dressing room, chanting: "We're No. 1 . . . We're No. 1," or "We want Leo."

A ruddy-faced Irishman with a green and white banner—no doubt left over from his Saturday afternoons in the shadow of the Golden Dome— led a parade down Waveland Avenue, into a German pub. Another chap with a dazed look in his eyes walked about with a sign that read: "I love the Cubs." He acted as if he meant it.

Mitch Miller (yes, the fellow with the beard) walked away from Wrigley Field with a young lovely under one arm, shaking his head in disbelief. He probably was thinking what a great opportunity he'd just missed to stage a singalong.

Dick Radatz, a relief pitcher with a sense of humor matching his physical stature, put a Nazi helmet with a "Hell's Angels" lettered across the top, stepped outside the dressing room door, held up both hands in the politician's familiar "V" for victory salute. The crown threw Radatz kisses in return.

An Andy Frain usher, tired of throwing cross-body blocks at the fans who stormed the field after the game said to a buddy, "From now on, I'm going to demand combat pay before I work in Wrigley Field."

"I don't believe eet, I don't believe eet," chirped Adolfo Phillips. "Eet ees like the bull fights. The people are crazy. And Ernie is upstairs on the radio, screaming. "We did eet. We did eet."

Mr. Cub, Ernie Banks, sidelined Saturday when Pete Rose spiked him, spent yesterday sitting between Vince Lloyd and Lou Boudreau in the WGN radio booth.

"No, we haven't got a microphone in the Cubs' dugout," explained Boudreau at one point. "That's just Ernie Banks sitting here cheering his teammates."

Ernie resembled Leonard Bernstein leading the New York Philharmonic orchestra when he led the people beneath the radio booth in an organized ovation for the Cubs during the seventh-inning stretch.

Even the Cincinnati Reds were impressed.

When Art Shamsky batted in the fourth inning, he looked down at Cub catcher Randy Hundley and commented:

"Baby, they've got the fever in this city. We could be in first place by five games but we'd draw about 5,000 in Cincinnati."

When the scoreboard posted the fact that the Mets had tied the Cardinals in the eighth inning of the first game, Tommy Helms, who was then batting, turned to Hundley and shouted:

"Man, I can't even think out here today."

Santo was the batter when the Mets' dramatic ninth-inning victory was posted. When the crowd exploded over that, Ron tightened up so much he couldn't swing at a perfect strike.

"There's only one word to describe this—be-you-tee-ful," exclaimed Durocher, curled up on a chair in a corner of his office.

"Ebbets Field was never like this. This is mad hysteria. The closest thing I can recall is after Bobby Thomson's home run and we won the 1951 pennant. There were 30,000 people standing outside our centerfield dressing room and they kept cheering us until all the players stepped outside and took a bow.

"But did you see those rooftops across the street? I can't remember seeing people over there since the early 1960s when the Cubs had those real good teams.

"I think those people are staying upstairs until they find out what the Mets did to the Cardinals in the second game."

Durocher was the perfect host. He broke out a couple of bottles, a tray of ice cubes, glasses, and told reporters to help themselves. There isn't anything in this world quite like seeing Leo Durocher in first place.

Frank Sinatra has assured Leo that he'll sing the National Anthem in Wrigley Field Oct. 3.

The Cubs lost nine of their next eleven games and finished the season in third place, fourteen games behind the National League and World Series champion Cardinals.

1969
Trial by Torture, One Day at a Time

RICK TALLEY

Chicago Today September 11, 1969

PHILADELPHIA—What's it like to live and eat and travel with a seven-game losing streak in September?

It's torture. Especially if you're a Chicago Cub and you've been in first place all season. Until today.

Now you're second and it's gnawing on you. The prize is there in plain sight. The playoffs. The World Series. Money, fame, pride of accomplishment. Everybody says you're the best and that you will win.

But you're losing and you can't stop and you're crying inside.

On the outside, you try to stay calm. Professional.

But you think and you read and you go to the ball park early so you won't have to kill time at the hotel. You read telegrams. You play cards, and you talk, and get yourself "up" for the game. But you lose again and cripes, here they come. The reporters. The vultures from Philadelphia and New York and Newsweek magazine and the guys you know from Chicago, and you don't want to talk but you've got to show your class, so you do.

You explain how the breaks are going against you . . . how the poor hitter in the ninth hit one off the end of the bat into right field off your best relief pitcher, Phil Regan, and who wudda figured that? And you tell about how the hits aren't falling . . . how you can't seem to get the big hit . . . the game breaker, and how your pitcher did a good job . . . but threw that bad pitch in the fourth, a changeup when it should have been the fast ball, and how the team is in a slump . . . just like a hitter gets into a slump. You can't change. You won with this and you've got to stay with it. It'll work out. Tomorrow. A win. That's all we need.

Ballplayers like humor, even in times of stress. Their humor in recent days, however, has been grim.

"Have you heard about how well the Cub Power record album has been selling," said one Cub yesterday in Doc Schueneman's training room. "It's breaking all sales records. People are using the album covers for dartboards." (Pictures of Cub players border the album covers.)

139

It was still raining in the afternoon and Hank Aguirre, a man who fought for a pennant in 1967 with the Detroit Tigers, only to see it slip away on the final day, said grimly:

"If it rains us out today, we're gonna celebrate the victory."

But attitudes change just like pennant races change.

The Cubs didn't get rained out yesterday. They lost to the fifth-place Phillies, 6–2, and the common statement heard was "I can't believe it." Followed by, "It's not over yet. Don't count us out."

Yesterday, while waiting for the rain to stop, WGN radio announcer Lou Boudreau visited the clubhouse and made an attempt to "loosen up" the players. He did an excellent job. He told stories about handling pitchers Satchel Paige and Jim Bagby during the 1948 pennant race with the Cleveland Indians and he had the Cubs rolling on the floor with laughter.

"Anything to help them relax," admits Boudreau, who gets so keyed up himself that he gets up and walks out of the radio booth when things are going bad.

"We have no excuses," says manager Leo Durocher, in assessing the Cubs' decline. "We played horrible baseball."

"We can still win it," says Regan, who has been hit hard recently and when somebody told him he did a good job yesterday, he said, "It's about time."

"We can win," repeated Regan. "We just can't get down on ourselves."

Ron Santo is there. The Captain. He shouldn't have played against the Phils, but he did. He couldn't run because his knee was swelling again, and filling with fluid, but he played because you don't step out of the lineup in September.

In St. Louis, he'll have that knee drained again. Until then, he'll sleep with an icepack, and he'll play. His ankle is heavily taped from a sprain, his knee is discolored and swollen, his right wrist is still puffed from a Jerry Koosman fast ball. But he's not making any excuses. He's playing.

A healthy Ron Santo would have thrown Phillies' third baseman Tony Taylor out by eight steps last night in the first inning. But he couldn't move quickly enough to get the ball. Taylor was safe. Infield hit. He scored the run, and once again, as so many times in this losing streak, the Cubs fell behind.

"No comment," said Leo Durocher. It's his decision. He isn't talking to sports writers, particularly those from other cities. He's polite. He smiles. But "no comment," and perhaps that's why Cub players are patient and understanding and feel a responsibility to talk to writers.

It doesn't matter, really. I'm sure Durocher agrees. His feud with the press is not important when you consider the importance of the Cubs winning or losing a pennant.

Maybe it's his ploy. A way to sidetrack pressure from the players. It doesn't matter. To Chicago, the Cubs matter. No Leo versus sports writers. That's second-page stuff.

Let's face it. The Cubs are snakebit. When a reserve catcher hitting .173 (Dave Watkins) played outfield and stabs you with a home run, you're snakebit.

Better now than later. That's the only rallying thought about the Cubs' plight. They still have time to recover.

One down, 19 to go. And the Cubs have an ambition. They'd like to see the New York Mets come to Chicago on Oct. 1–2 trailing by three games. Then the Cubs' regulars could show up in street clothes and watch the game from the front row.

That's something to work toward. A chance to see Tom Seaver try for a perfect game against the farmhands. The same Seaver who watched a TV replay the other night and said: "Thatta way, Santo. Way to move after that pizza."

The Cubs know all of this. They read, too, about Mets pitcher Jerry Koosman admitting he deliberately threw to hit Santo. They don't say much about that but they're thinking.

Tonight, the lowly, nothing-to-lose Phils again. Another day to kill and another attempt to break that losing streak.

The Cubs, who had led National League East by eight and a half games on August 19, lost fourteen of their last twenty games while the Mets won thirty-nine of their last fifty to win the division by eight games and went on to win the World Series.

45 Runs Later, Cubs Come Up One Short

DAVE NIGHTINGALE

Chicago Tribune May 18, 1979

Larry Bowa, the littlest Phillie, put 243 minutes of playing time, 10 innings, 45 runs, 50 hits, and 11 homers into a nutshell.

"That," said Bowa, "had to be one of the greatest games ever played."

A weary band of Cubs might reluctantly tend to agree, even though they were on the short end of a 23–22 score as the gloamin' rolled over Wrigley Field Thursday.

Mike Schmidt's second homer of the game was the decisive blow off Cub reliever Bruce Sutter in the 10th inning, but it seemed anticlimactic.

In fact Schmidt wasn't even the batting star of the day.

Bob Boone had three hits and five RBI for the winners. Garry Maddox had four hits and four RBI. Pete Rose and Schmidt batted home four apiece.

And the biggest hitting numbers were on the losers' side of the scorebook: seven RBI for Bill Buckner, including a grand slam homer, and six RBI for Dave Kingman, who three times drove the ball over the left-field wall.

"I've never seen anything like this one, not even in high school or grammar school," said Phils' Manager Danny Ozark. "After this one, I guess we proved the National League can get by without using a designated hitter."

"What a game!" said Cub Manager Herman Franks. "But it's gone, and my guys won't be holding onto it when they go on the field Friday, not the way they played today. We got nothin' to be ashamed of, the way we kept fighting back. And they didn't give us a thing in those comebacks. We earned them."

The Cubs Thursday were reminiscent of the old joke about the father who stops by the sandlot to watch his kid play and inquires about the score. And the kid says: "We're behind 15–0." And the dad says: "Gee, that's terrible."

And the kid says: "Don't worry, pop, we ain't been to bat yet."

The North Siders were behind 7–0 from the start, thanks to homers by

142

Schmidt, Boone and Phillie starting pitcher Randy Lerch off Dennis Lamp and Donnie Moore, before any Cub first swung a bat.

And before you knew it, the deficit had been chopped to only one run, with Lerch chased in the bottom of the first by a six-run rally that featured Kingman's three-run homer.

The Phillies hammered back with eight in the third, ousting the beleaguered Moore and continuing the assault against a wild Willie Hernandez. Still, the visitors refused to get overconfident.

"We all knew it was going to be one of those kind of days," said Bowa. "I mean, what the heck, the Cubs had a field-goal kicker warming up on the sidelines for three innings. That ought to tell you something."

The Cubs got three more runs in the fourth off Doug Bird on homers by Kingman and Steve Ontiveros. But, still, their deficit continued to increase—to 12 runs, 21–9.

"When we got up by 12, I figured we could win it if we could hold them under two touchdowns and could block a couple of extra points," said Bowa.

If Larry really felt that, it was tongue-in-cheek. A few innings later, Bowa nearly swallowed that tongue.

So, too, did Tug McGraw, the top lefty reliever in the Phillies' bullpen.

"It's funny," said McGraw. "I mean, when you're sitting out there in the pen and you see the way things are going, you don't exactly beg to come in the game. And yet, all the time you're saying to yourself: "Well, I know I could stop all of this foolishness.' So, what happens? I get my chance to stop it, and blowie!"

"Blowie" took the form of a seven-run Cub fifth, comprised of a single, a Schmidt error, two walks, a Buckner grand slam, another walk, Jerry Martin's two-run homer, and an ensuing academic double by Barry Foote, cutting the Phillie lead to a mere 21–16.

Even though it was only the fifth inning, the assault on McGraw forced Ozark to reach for his ultimate relief weapon, right hander Ron Reed and his 4–1 record and 0.43 ERA.

Except that Reed nearly proved the ultimate disaster. A single by Steve Dillard, Ivan DeJesus' double, and still another Kingman homer cut the margin to 21–19.

By now, the pages of the record book were flying, and fingers were pointing to the Cubs' 26–23 victory over the Phils on Aug. 25, 1922, a 61-hit extravaganza (in which the Cubs nearly blew a 25–6 lead after four innings) rated the top offensive outburst ever.

And the fingers kept pointing as a triple by Greg Gross and Boone's double gave the Phils a 22nd run, a 22nd run that they sorely needed because the Cubs pounded Reed for three in the eighth to tie the score on RBI singles by Buckner, Martin and Foote, the last two coming with two out.

"After a game like this, the first thing you do is check to see if you have any broken bones," said Reed, somewhat crestfallen at his failure to check the losers.

Now, although no team in National League history had ever come back from a 12-run deficit to win, it seemed as if the pendulum had swung toward the Cubs. Why? Because the ninth-inning pitchers were Sutter (one win, six saves) and the Phillies' Rawly Eastwick, a onetime World Series star with Cincinnati who has of late fallen on evil times (8.00 ERA).

But in the 10th, with two out, Sutter's 3-and-2 split-finger fastball to Schmidt didn't sink. Instead, it rose off Schmidt's bat and into the left-field bleachers and the game, mercifully for both teams, was over.

1984
"This Will Hurt for a Long, Long Time"
BOB VERDI

Chicago Tribune October 8, 1984

SAN DIEGO—Rick Sutcliffe spoke in a whisper and still could be heard. It was that quiet, that shocking, that final.

"They're going to the World Series and we're going home," he said. "This will hurt me for a long, long time. It will stay with all of us for a long time. It's hard to deal with. Very hard."

Keith Moreland's eyes were redder than his hair. Dallas Green stared through the hole in the top of a beer can. And Jim Frey's voice cracked for the first time all season. The Cubs had gotten beaten up for 39 years, and now they had picked a most untimely occasion to beat themselves.

It wasn't supposed to turn out like this, this American dream for America's Team. Not after the Cubs won the first two games in Chicago. Not after Thursday night's defeat. Not even after Saturday night's thrill theater, as delicious a game as was ever played.

Because Sunday, for the National League pennant, the Cubs had the big guy on the mound. Rick Sutcliffe. You could feel the great expectations in the bus going to Jack Murphy Stadium and during batting practice. You could sense it through five innings when the lead was 3–0 and the destination Detroit.

"Instead, now we go home and pack our bags and pick up the pieces," said Sutcliffe (17–2). He had lost his first game in three months, but three months from Sunday, when the San Diego Padres beat him 6–3, that's what the big guy will be thinking about. Whether he has a fishing pole in his hand, a book or a child.

A lesser man might have hidden from the crush of interrogators wondering what happened. A free agent who should win the Cy Young Award and double his $900,000 salary could have pinned the donkey's tail on Leon Durham, who waited for the ball to come up, or Ryne Sandberg, who thought the ball would stay down.

But Rick Sutcliffe, elegant in depression, blamed himself. For not holding a lead, for yielding a leadoff walk to Carmelo Martinez during the Padres' four-run seventh inning, for letting Steve Garvey get around on a fastball.

"I take the responsibility for this," he said. "It's my fault. These guys have been great behind me all year. The key wasn't Durham's error. The key was the four pitches to Martinez. It was my loss. My loss. And I don't know quite how to describe the hurt."

A big crash landing this was, with the big guy taking the blame. He said what he did during the regular schedule didn't matter now, and before he wills his body to the highest bidder in the off-season flesh market, he's got to rectify Sunday in his head. Where it went wrong, and why.

Sutcliffe maneuvered comfortably through five innings, surrendering but two hits. His breaking ball wasn't the best, and his location was less than pinpoint. But he's gotten by before, and Sunday, he was getting by again. Until the summer turned to winter.

Now, many people will try to unravel the cosmic significance of Sunday's comeuppance. People who have lived, but mostly died, with the Cubs. And people who just discovered baseball within the last two weeks. And people who maintain that tagging up on a deep fly has deep sociological impact.

Forget it, whether you're a season-ticket holder or one of the millions of dilettantes who joined the parade. Failure is letting a kid go hungry, not letting a pennant slip away. The Cubs won 98 games during a year when most experts figured they'd be fortunate to win 78. They were entertaining, energizing and, above all, promising.

In the end, as Rick Sutcliffe was saying, the hurt comes because the Cubs got a taste and never swallowed. This was a better team than anybody expected from April to Wednesday but too good a team to allow what happened from Thursday to Sunday.

If anything, it wasn't the four pitches to Carmelo Martinez that killed the Cubs; it was the euphoria surrounding them. They came here with one game to win but with thousands of friends, relatives and fans assuring that it was only a formality. Nobody can look into an athlete's head; let it just be said that the possibility for distraction was everpresent.

"I know what you're driving at," said Green. "The celebrating before the job is finished. I don't know if that happened here. But I do know that at a time like this, you need all 25 guys to sacrifice like they've never sacrificed before."

And so, Sunday evening, there was nothing left to celebrate and even less to say. Frey shook every hand of every player but made no speeches. He had a suspicion that he could talk until he was blue and still not be heard.

"It was my loss," said Sutcliffe, repeating the lie. It was everybody's, not to rationalize or to dwell on, but to rectify and build on. Sunday's gloom has nothing to do with 1969, but 98 wins from April to Sunday doesn't guarantee that next year will be better. Chemistry is a fragile item.

"39 More Years" the banner proclaimed as the Padres danced about Jack Murphy Stadium Sunday afternoon. Not likely. But not this year, either.

Ticket scalpers in Chicago will be sad; Las Vegas bookies will be relieved there's a big election next month; and the in-laws still want to come over for Thanksgiving dinner.

A Very Solid Book

MIKE ROYKO

Chicago Tribune March 12, 1987

A New York publishing house has sent me a copy of a new paperback book it has just brought out.

With it came a note that said: "We take pleasure in presenting you with this review copy and ask that you please send two copies of your notices to our offices."

I seldom review books in my column. The Chicago paper for which I write has a section that takes care of that. But in this case, I'm going to make an exception.

The book is called "If At First . . ." with a subtitle that says "With the exclusive inside story of the 1986 Championship Season."

The author is Keith Hernandez, who is the first baseman on the New York Mets baseball team. Actually, he didn't write it—some professional ghostwriter did.

But the words and story originated with Hernandez. I will begin my review by saying that this is a very solid book. The moment I opened the package and saw what it was about, I threw it against my office wall as hard as I could.

Then I slammed it to the floor and jumped up and down on it. I beat on it with a chair for several minutes until I slumped onto my couch, emotionally and physically spent. Although slightly scuffed, the book was still intact.

It is also a book that can cause excitement. I dropped it on the desk of a friend who has had weekend season tickets at Wrigley Field for the past 10 years. It immediately stirred him to emotional heights. He shouted:

"Why are you showing me that piece of (deleted)? I say (deleted) Hernandez and (deleted) the Mets and (deleted) the whole (deleted) city of New York. And (deleted) you, too."

Then he flung it against a wall and gave it a kick. It still remained intact. I told you it was a solid book.

It's a book that can move a sensitive reader to tears, as I discovered when I showed it to a man who has been going to Cub games since 1946, a year that is known as The Beginning of Darkness.

When he looked at the cover, he choked back a sob, a tear trickled down his cheek, and he said: "Why them? Why not us? What was our sin? How can we atone for it? You know, I asked my clergyman that, and he said he wishes he knew, because he lost $50 betting against them."

And it's a powerful book. As reviewers like to say: It can hit you right in the guts. This was proven to me when I showed it to a confirmed bleacherite who said: "Excuse me. I'm going to throw up."

But enough of generalities. Let us consider the contents of this book.

On the very first page, Hernandez and his ghostwriter say: "ad made the second out on a long the Mets were through for 1986: o out, nobody on, two runs down, ox already leading the World Series en our scoreboard operator at"

And on page 81, Hernandez says: "round during infield practice, I draw a line man and myself and call our manager over avy? I ask. He laughs."

Moving to page 125, we find: "Oh, sweet bird of youth, however, were a different story. It's diff- quietly as I work my way out of a bad me to listen to his judgments. I wrong with my swing. I know hot to th hard-headed. Dand and I have had"

I know, it sounds kind of garbled, incomprehensible. But that's the way a story reads when you rip the pages of a book in half, one by one, as I've been doing.

Don't misunderstand me. I'm not doing that out of spite. I'm a good sport, a cheerful loser. Why, in the last two years, I don't think I've watched my video of the movie "Fail Safe," in which New York gets nuked, more than 30 or 40 times.

The fact is, I have found this to be a useful book.

I have been tearing out the pages and crumpling them into little wads.

When I have about 30 or 40 of these wads, I will put them in my fireplace under the kindling and light them. They're excellent for getting a fire started.

Then I pour myself a drink, lower the lights, sit back, and stare at the crackling flames.

And I pretend that I'm looking at Shea Stadium.

1989
The Boys of Zimmer Leave Their Hearts in San Francisco

PHILIP HERSH

Chicago Tribune October 10, 1989

SAN FRANCISCO—The Giants' celebration brushed past Cubs second baseman Ryne Sandberg. He was standing a few feet beyond first base, where he had stopped running a minute earlier. Sandberg was thrown out at first, the third out of the ninth inning, the last out of the game, the final out of the Cubs' 1989 season.

The shortest way for Sandberg to reach the Cubs' clubhouse was to continue up the right-field line. He went the other way, through the mini-cams and still cameras and the players whose joy over winning the National League pennant was being recorded forever. In the distance the Candlestick Park scoreboard furnished the numbers: Giants 3, Cubs 2.

He walked past the mound and into the Cubs' third-base dugout, picked up his glove and took off his batting helmet, sipped from a paper cup and stood there. The sun was still bright and warm on the field where a Cub game and a season of unexpected passion and tension had just ended Monday afternoon. Sandberg was drinking it all in.

"I just wanted to go to the dugout and gather my thoughts," Sandberg said. "I just stood there and watched. I couldn't believe it was over."

If he stayed in the dugout long enough, maybe this would become a field of dreams and the players would come back out of the fog and there would be another game for the Cubs. This one, the fifth and final game of the National League Championship Series, was too good to be over.

The Cubs season was that way, too, and Sandberg knew it, even as he tried to regroup after the loss that made the Giants 4-games-to-1 winners in the best-of-seven series. Another minute went by, and then he walked the length of a diamond for the last time this season, past first base, down the right-field line and into the tunnel to the clubhouse.

Now, was our glorious summer made a winter of discontent by the Giants?

The temptation is to answer yes, to say that the playoff defeat was just another scene from "Bleacher Bums," to carp about Don Zimmer's persis-

149

tently unorthodox managing strategies and Les Lancaster's not knowing the count before giving up the winning home run in Game 3. Isn't such second-guessing the essence of Cubness, which nearly rhymes with neurosis? You wouldn't feel that way if you had watched the Cubs stumble out of spring training with all the finesse of the Bad News Bears. You wouldn't feel that way had you been here, watching three oddly wonderful baseball games in perfect weather.

"Thank You, Cubs—the fans in the cheap seats," said a banner towed over Candlestick Park in the fifth inning. Somebody up there understood what had happened between April and the late September day when the East Division title had been clinched.

"It was a crummy ending to a wonderful season," said Cubs first baseman Mark Grace.

"I had a blast. This is the most fun I've ever had. I'm going to cherish this."

Who could have failed to enjoy the amazing Grace and the thrill of Will Clark, the Giants' first baseman, in the last five games. Grace hit .647, not bad. Clark batted .650, his last of 13 hits in 20 at-bats driving in the two runs that broke a 1–1 tie in the eighth inning.

"My heart was racing a little bit," Clark admitted.

The Cubs showed they had plenty to leave in San Francisco. After two routine outs in the top of the ninth, they mounted, remarkably enough, another of their patented comebacks. The rally scored one run and put runners on first and second before Sandberg grounded to second for the final out.

"It was disappointing and discouraging, but a lot of good things came out of this season," Sandberg said.

"How do the Cubs spell tradition?" asked one sign in Candlestick Park. "L.O.S.E."

"It's not the same old story," said pitcher Scott Sanderson. "We had a great year. People told us we weren't any good and we couldn't win anything. I think we answered those questions."

What was lost, in the end, were only a few baseball games. No Chicagoan need feel like a tortured soul over a baseball team's defeat. Baseball may sometimes look like life and feel like life, but it is just a diversion.

One may feel for Andre Dawson, who suffered one ignominy after another in these playoffs only two seasons after he could do no wrong. He left hundreds, thousands, millions of runners on base, and pitchers actually walked Grace to pitch to Dawson, and he was on the bench for the final inning, replaced by Mitch Webster as Zimmer juggled positions in the batting order.

And Dawson will make nearly $2 million next year to play baseball.

"I don't think Andre would want anyone to feel sorry for him," Grace said.

Nor should anyone feel that way for or about the Cubs or Chicago. This wasn't like 1984, when all they needed to make the World Series was one win in three games in San Diego. This time, they were a good team beaten by a better team, and it was, as Grace said, "a blast."

So it was that Zimmer, a baseball lifer, a man for whom this game may seem bigger than life itself, could still joke when he was asked about the best thing he would take out of this season.

"Well," he said, "I'm having cartilage taken out of my knee next week."

In Chicago, where the series would have returned had the Cubs won one game in San Francisco, the temperature Monday evening was heading for the 30s. At Wrigley Field it was no longer the time for baseball. But for as long as it lasted, we had the time of our lives.

2003
One More Desolate Night at Wrigley Field
RICK MORRISSEY

Chicago Tribune October 16, 2003
This was the fading sound of the last subway train rumbling away from the station at 3 a.m. It was the loneliest silence Cubs fans ever have had to endure, and that's saying something.

Fans were walking out of Wrigley Field on Wednesday night, and the full weight of the desolation was hitting them hard. You could see it in their heavy steps and their drawn faces. A defeated people. They walked silently, as if waiting their turn to view the deceased.

But they already had seen this body, year after year after year. After picking the Cubs off the floor all Wednesday night, after slapping their faces and pacing with them to keep the blood circulating, the crowd finally realized there wasn't anything more to be done. In truth, maybe there never was anything to be done, not after that almighty collapse in Game 6 of the National League Championship Series on Tuesday night. My, how that game had drained the city of its thimble-full of confidence.

Game 7 went to the Marlins 9–6 and with it a trip to the World Series. The Cubs got a lovely parting gift of nothing. They immediately put it in the closet with all the other nothingness.

The poor soul who was vilified for deflecting a foul ball in Game 6 deserved better than this. He deserved a victory. After 58 years without a World Series appearance for the Cubs, that would have been the best part of a trip to the Fall Classic. Why? Because the vast majority of us have hearts. Chicagoans understand suffering better than most, thanks to sports, and this guy suffered enough for the Cubs' sins Tuesday night.

But, no. He gets lumped with a stupid goat. Alex Gonzalez and his eighth-inning error don't. The guy with the headphones does.

The Cubs fought hard Wednesday night, but by the seventh inning they could hardly raise their arms. Noble, yes, in the vacuum of the game, but hugely disappointing from a team that returned to Chicago with a 3–1 series lead. Two games to go, Mark Prior and Kerry Wood locked and loaded in the chamber, and what more did the Cubs want in the way of golden opportunities?

Was a Marlins' forfeit asking for too much?

Manager Dusty Baker spent the better part of a season trying to shield his team from all this rotten history, but he didn't understand the heaviness of the past, how it pressed down on chests and restricted breathing. He probably didn't understand it through seven innings Tuesday, when the Cubs were leading the Marlins 3–0. But surely he understands now what this city, the Cubs-loving part of the city, feels on a yearly basis.

After that eighth inning, he has to understand why Cubs fans sometimes approach the future by hardly bearing to look. And surely he saw how his team felt the negative vibes in the eighth Tuesday all the way to the end of Wednesday night. Or maybe he didn't.

"We didn't lose the pennant," he said. "The Marlins won it."

Baker said he wanted to change the culture of losing in this town, and now he knows the only real way to do it is to get to the World Series. Never mind that for the first half of the season, the Cubs had no business thinking about the playoffs. But a magical September changed everything, to the point where the entire season forever will be defined by that Game 6 collapse.

The franchise forever will be defined by that collapse.

"Maybe when we win next year, (fans) will forget about it," Cubs left fielder Moises Alou said.

Fans came looking for a reason to believe in Game 7. A bone. A glimmer of hope. Anything. And then Juan Pierre tripled to start the game, Wood walked Ivan Rodriguez, and 20-year-old rookie Miguel Cabrera golfed a low fastball into the left-center seats.

Hope arrived in the second inning when the Cubs scored three runs, two on Wood's dramatic shot to left-center. And hope seemed to establish residence when Alou hit a two-run homer in the third. Wrigley sounded like a flock of military jets. It was 5–3, and why not the Cubs?

If there is one thing we have learned about these Marlins, it's that they don't ever stop hitting. And so the fifth inning rolled around, Wood started struggling with his control and the Marlins kept hitting. They scored three runs and then brought in Josh Beckett on two days' rest to pitch in the fifth. The Josh Beckett who threw the two-hitter in Game 5.

What's the cliché? World Serious, that's it. The Marlins were World Serious.

And the Cubs, worn to the nub emotionally, couldn't respond in kind. Wood was knocked out in the sixth inning after throwing 112 pitches. He was spent, worn-down, of no use.

Such a slim, flimsy thing, a 7–5 lead, and yet with Beckett on the mound in the sixth, it looked to have the tensile strength of a steel girder. Florida kept hitting, and the Cubs kept hitting long fly balls that found homes in Marlins gloves.

Left fielder Jeff Conine caught Paul Bako's fly ball to end the game, and the Marlins danced like kids on the field. Cubs fans looked on, like anthropologists studying a foreign people.

"Fate wasn't on our side," Cubs center fielder Kenny Lofton said. "The plan was set beforehand."

It wouldn't be such a big deal if the ending varied once in a while.

153

MICHAEL

rnie Banks was Mr. Cub. Walter Payton was Sweetness. Bobby Hull was the Golden Jet.

Michael Jordan was Michael. No nickname ever seemed necessary. ("Air Jordan" was the invention of an Oregon sporting goods company. No one in Chicago ever called him that.)

It can be argued whether Jordan was the greatest athlete ever to play in Chicago. But there is no dispute that his talent, competitiveness, and force of will made the Bulls of his era the most successful sports team in the city's history.

Beyond that, Jordan's impact radiated out from Chicago in a way that made him the symbol of the city throughout the world in a way no one else, with the possible exception of Al Capone, had ever been. His effect was equally profound in the realm of sports marketing and advertising, which can be divided into two eras—Before Jordan and After Jordan.

I covered Jordan in his first years with the Bulls and distinctly remember the moment I had my first glimpse of the future. It was in the first week or two of his rookie season and the Bulls were playing Milwaukee in the Stadium. Jordan received an in-bounds pass at the baseline and proceeded to dribble the ball around and through every Bucks player on the floor until the only player left between him and the basket was Sidney Moncrief, who had been named the NBA's defensive player of the year the previous two seasons. Jordan leaped over Moncrief as if he weren't there and threw down a thunderous dunk.

"Holy smoke," I thought, or words to that effect.

Here are six pieces that show some of Jordan's greatest moments, and two of his lowest—by Melissa Isaacson and Bob Greene—that show how a writer can sometimes be rewarded by just sitting and listening.

Bernie Lincicome's column, it should be noted, was written when Jordan retired the first time to try his hand at baseball, but it resonates with the sense of loss Bulls fans feel to this day.

"The Shot" Is Too Good Not to Be True

TERRY BOERS

Chicago Sun-Times May 8, 1989

RICHFIELD, Ohio—The instant Michael Jordan put up The Shot Sunday you just knew this time it was going to be true.

You knew it not because of the softness of his touch or the beauty of his follow-through or the trajectory of the ball as it floated toward the hoop. No, you knew it because there was not a chance that Michael Jordan was going to miss another game-winning shot.

While Jordan has long been playing basketball at such an incredibly advanced level that he can seemingly will things to happen, he did clang a jumper off the back iron that would have won Game 4 for the Bulls Friday night at the Stadium.

And Jordan, as is his wont, was tough on himself for that misfire. He was far tougher on himself, though, for the two free throws he missed in the final 48 seconds of that contest, which Cleveland won in overtime.

He was the guy, after all, who boldly had predicted it would take the Bulls just four games to dispose of the favored Cavaliers in this best-of-five playoff series, and the chance to do just that had slipped through his very own fingers.

That would seem enough to dissuade even Jordan from playing the role of soothsayer again, but with three seconds left on the Richfield Coliseum clock Sunday, he had one Tarot card left to play.

Tilting toward Craig Hodges on the bench during the final Chicago timeout, Jordan promised his downcast running mate he was going to make the winning basket.

The reason that Hodges was feeling rather poorly had everything to do with the previous play. Assigned the task of guarding Cleveland's Craig Ehlo with six seconds remaining and the Bulls ahead 99–98, Hodges made one of the worst defensive mistakes you'll ever see.

After tossing the ball in, Ehlo, on a simple give-and-go play from Larry Nance, ran right past Hodges and scored the uncontested layup that gave the Cavs back the lead they'd held for most of the afternoon.

"I was jumping up and down trying to distract him (Ehlo)," Hodges said about his short nap. "He threw the ball in and blew by me like a streak at the same time.

"I was mad at myself, but Michael told me on the bench not to worry about it, that he was going to go ahead and make the winning basket.

"Michael just did what he always does—he really stroked it."

That stroke happened only after Brad Sellers made two snap—and correct—judgments. Sellers, the trigger man on the sideline inbound play, first took a brief look at Hodges, who'd squirted free. Then he looked at Scottie Pippen, who also appeared to be in the clear.

But this was no time to play a hunch. Sellers knows no game is over until Michael Jordan says it's over, so he did the right thing—he gave the ball to him.

Although Ehlo stuck with Jordan so closely he actually made the Divine Mr. M. do a double-pump from the free-throw line, The Shot rose unmolested.

The ball rattled on the rim for a brief moment, finally dropping in as the clock hit triple zero.

Cleveland, a 57-game winner during the regular season, and winners of all six games they played against the Bulls, was out of the playoffs, 101–100.

Jordan, as part of his celebration, turned to the sellout crowd of 20,273, which had been exceedingly rowdy, and screamed, "Go home," a move that he would later call "uncharacteristic."

"It's just that people were starting to talk to me about my tee times and how I'd choked," Jordan said. "I was also pumped up by the crowd here because they were trying to take me out of my game."

Of course, no one who ever has played the game can do that.

Those final two points gave Jordan 44 for the day, a decent enough follow-up to the 50 he scored Friday.

"You just saw one of the great clutch performances of all time," said Bulls coach Doug Collins. "It was only justice that Michael Jordan should make that shot."

He'll get no argument here.

*The Bulls went on to lose the Eastern Conference finals to the
Detroit Pistons before winning their first championship two years*

*later. But in the years to come, "The Shot" would symbolize the
beginning of the Jordan dynasty.*

When Jordan Cried behind Closed Doors

BOB GREENE

Chicago Tribune May 15, 1991

"I went to my room and I closed the door and I cried," Michael Jordan
said. "For a while I couldn't stop. Even though there was no one else home
at the time, I kept the door shut. It was important to me that no one hear
me or see me."

Now the National Basketball Association playoffs are entering their
most exciting and dramatic phase. Jordan's likeness and electronic image
are everywhere; sometimes it seems he is as much logo as he is human.

In a sense, Jordan owns the world. To me, though, perhaps the most
remarkable part of the Jordan story is the fact that, as a sophomore in
high school, he was cut from his school's basketball team. I kept wondering about how it affected him at the time it happened. Back then, he didn't
know that someday he was going to be Michael Jordan. Back then, he
wanted to play with the others, and was told that he wasn't good enough.

One evening, as we sat and talked in the hours before a Bulls game, he
spoke about it. I wasn't surprised that Jordan remembered every detail.
How could he not? Back then he had no idea what was going to happen to
him in the years ahead.

"For about two weeks, every boy who had tried out for the basketball
team knew what day the cut list was going to go up," Jordan said. "We
knew that it was going to be posted in the gym. In the morning.

"So that morning we all went in there, and the list was up. I had a
friend, and we went in to look at the list together.

"We stood there and looked for our names. If your name was on the
list, you were still on the team. If your name wasn't on the list, you were
cut. His name was on the list. He made it. Mine wasn't on the list."

As we talked, other members of the Bulls walked past—Scottie Pippen, Horace Grant, John Paxson, Bill Cartwright. Jordan's voice was soft,
and he nodded hello to each of them and continued with his memories.

"I looked and looked for my name," he said. "It was almost as if I thought that if I didn't stop looking, it would be there."

Was the list in descending order of talent? Were the best players at the top of the list, with the marginal players at the bottom?

"No," Jordan said, as if envisioning the list anew. "It was alphabetical. I looked at the H's, and the I's, and the J's, and the K's, and I wasn't there, and I went back up and started over again. But I wasn't there.

"I went through the day numb. I sat through my classes. I had to wait until after school to go home. That's when I hurried to my house and I closed the door of my room and I cried so hard. It was all I wanted—to play on that team.

"My mother was at work, so I waited until she got home, and then I told her. She knew before I said anything that something was wrong, and I told her that I had been cut from the team. When you tell your mom something like that the tears start again, and the two of you have an aftercry together."

At the end of that basketball season, Jordan said, he asked the coach if he could ride the bus with the team to the district tournament. Just to watch the other boys play.

"The coach told me no," Jordan said. "But I asked again, and he said I could come. But when we got to the tournament gym, he said he didn't know if I could go in. He told me that the only way I could go in was to carry the players' uniforms.

"So that's what I did. I walked into the building carrying the uniforms for the players who had made the team. What made me feel the worst about that was that my parents had come to watch the tournament, and when they saw me walking in carrying the uniforms, they thought I was being given a chance to play.

"That's what hurt me. They thought I was being given a chance. But I was just carrying the clothes for the others."

He is the best basketball player in the world; he is very likely the best basketball player who ever lived. If you ever wondered why he continues to work so hard, the answer may lie in this story. It is doubtful that any other professional athlete was ever cut from a high school team. The men who make it to the pros have always been the best on every playground, the best in every class, the best in every school.

"It's OK, though," Jordan said. "It's probably good that it happened."

Good?

"I think so," he said. It was almost time for him to go upstairs onto the Stadium floor and hear the amazing, shuddering roar that comes from the crowd every time they catch sight of him.

"It was good because it made me know what disappointment felt like," he said. "And I knew that I didn't want to have that feeling ever again."

Champions
Bulls Stampede to First Title
SAM SMITH

Chicago Tribune June 13, 1991

INGLEWOOD, Calif.—Champions!

"I never lost hope," said a tear-stained Michael Jordan, whose 30 points and 10 assists helped the Bulls wrap up their first NBA title Wednesday with a thrilling 108–101 victory over the Los Angeles Lakers. "I'm so happy for my family and this team and this franchise. It's something I've worked seven years for, and I thank God for the talent and the opportunity that I've had."

Champions!

"I'm just happy for everyone, all of us—the organization, the city, the people of Chicago," said John Paxson, whose 20 points included 10 in a crucial three-minute stretch late in the fourth quarter after the Lakers had tied the score at 93. "It's an unbelievable feeling because we did it as a team. I can't wait to get home and share this with the city."

Champions!

"Pax was the key," said Bulls coach Phil Jackson. "M.J. was finding him and he stepped up and hit the shot."

"That's why I've always wanted him on my team and why I want him to stay on my team," said Jordan, holding the Larry O'Brien championship trophy while flanked by his wife, Juanita, and father, James, in the gleeful Bulls locker room.

"I've never seen a celebration like this," said Jackson, drenched in champagne and the warmth of success. "I was with the '70 Knicks and the '73 Knicks, and there was never anything like this. This has been a poised team and they just lost it."

Champions!

They almost lost the game. The Lakers—led by Magic Johnson's 16 points, 20 assists and 11 rebounds and Elden Campbell's 21 points—made it difficult all the way on the Bulls.

But this was not a Bulls team to be denied, as they won the last four games—including all three at the Forum—to win the series 4–1.

Champions!

"We were fortunate and we were destined," said Jackson.

The Bulls plowed through the playoffs with a 15–2 record (an amazing 7–1 on the road), second best in NBA playoff history. They became the second team in the modern NBA era to win the title with the league's leading scorer on the team. They set five-game Finals records for best shooting, 52.7 percent; best defense, allowing only 91.6 points per game; most assists and steals; fewest turnovers and holding the opposition to the fewest rebounds.

They became the team of the '90s.

Champions!

"It's going to taste sweet for them," said Johnson, who came into the joyous Bulls locker room to congratulate Jordan.

Rock breaks scissors and Air grounds Magic.

But it didn't look like it was going to work that way.

The Lakers, without the injured James Worthy and Byron Scott, fought like aging champions, throwing blow after blow at the Bulls.

The Lakers stormed the backboards early in taking a 49–48 halftime lead. Campbell came off the bench to score on pass after pass from Johnson. Tony Smith added 12 points and Terry Teagle nine. But it would not be enough.

"We just couldn't overcome the loss of Worthy," said Johnson, who played the full 48 minutes. So did Jordan and Scottie Pippen, who led the Bulls in scoring with 32 points, the first time a player other than Jordan has been the Bulls' leading scorer in the playoffs.

Champions!

"It was a hard-fought game," said Jackson. "We had to dig down. I didn't think our energy was great, but we worked hard and then Pax was the key."

Often unappreciated, always overlooked, especially this week by the Lakers, Paxson was brilliant. He gave the Bulls a lead they would never surrender with a 19-foot jumper. Then, after a Sam Perkins jumper fell short, Jordan found Paxson for an 18-footer.

"It was a tribute to Michael finding the open man like that," said Jackson.

"When I'm in rhythm, I feel like I'm going to make them," said Paxson. "I got good looks at the basket. You don't feel anything. You just catch the ball and shoot it."

And the opposition goes down.

The Lakers would make one last run, closing within 103–101 when Perkins converted a three-point play with 1:13 left.

But back came Paxson, hitting nothing but bottom from 18 feet for a 105–101 lead with :56 left. The Lakers wouldn't score again.

Champions!

And they exulted.

Pippen, who also had a playoff-high 13 rebounds, popped the first champagne bottle as the team came sprinting into the locker room, dumping the bubbly over a bubbling Horace Grant as the locker room resembled a fraternity party.

"We're going to celebrate for at least two days," said Pippen.

The players immediately gathered in a circle for a prayer and then grabbed champagne bottles, dousing one another, Bill Cartwright quietly saying "Finally," and Paxson running up for the trophy presentation from Commissioner David Stern.

"I've got to be a part of this," he yelled.

Bulls owner Jerry Reinsdorf smiled and laughed and wore champagne like a comfortable suit.

"I thought maybe we'd get two here, but three . . . ," he said. "This is unbelievable."

Champions!

General Manager Jerry Krause hugged Craig Hodges. Hodges lived.

"It doesn't get any better than this," said Hodges.

Championship hats and T-shirts were distributed. June Jackson looked

163

for husband, Phil; Donna Grant for husband, Horace. Everyone screamed and hugged.

Champions!

Will Perdue dumped champagne on Cartwright, and Hodges stood alone, shouting, "Yeah, yeah, yeah!"

For a long time, Jordan sat along one of the long benches in the visitors' locker room. In many ways, it was his party.

He hid his head in the arms of his wife for a long time after receiving the MVP trophy and cried.

Finally, he picked up his head as reporters and photographers gathered in a tightening circle.

His eyes were red and tears glistened on his cheeks, reflecting in the lights. It could have been champagne, but it wasn't.

"I never showed this kind of emotion before in public," he apologized.

He didn't have to. He really is human. For years, he's threatened and cajoled, been praised as the best example of team basketball and vilified as the worst example. He basked in the spotlight put on him, but was also cursed by it. Could he be a winner?

"We started from scratch, on the bottom, not making the playoffs when I got here," said Jordan. "It took seven years, but we won. This should get rid of the stigma of the one-man team. We have players that make us an effective basketball team."

All champions!

Baseball, Birmingham, and Dreams of His Father

MELISSA ISAACSON

Chicago Tribune July 24, 1994

BIRMINGHAM, Ala.—The best way Michael Jordan can describe it now is that he has good days and bad days. Days when the ball looks big and the pitcher looks scared. Days when he has to figure out how he let himself get picked off third so it won't happen again.

And then there are the days, he said, like one recently when "I cried all day long."

It was in another faceless hotel, on another minor-league road trip, on another rainy day good for nothing but watching cable movies, and that was exactly what Jordan was doing.

"It was a Wesley Snipes movie," he said. "And at the end, his father died. The room was dark and I was lying on the bed and I guess it hit the right buttons because all of a sudden, I couldn't stop crying. I talked to my wife. I called everyone I knew. And I still couldn't stop crying. I never had a day in my life that I felt that sad."

James Jordan would have been 58 July 31. This week marks a year since he was taken from his family suddenly and brutally in a murder expected to be replayed in the as-yet-unscheduled trial of two young suspects in North Carolina. Defense attorneys have said it could be as late as next March or April before the case is tried.

Whenever it occurs, many of Jordan's family will be there. Michael will not.

"The damage has been done," he said in Birmingham last week. "Whatever they do to those guys is not enough. So I've blocked it off. My father died because of something stupid, and I won't let that hurt me again by going through it again. Justice may prevail, but there's no justice when there's no life."

His family seeks closure. His wife Juanita, he says, "has to see everything to the end. But to me, the end was when he was taken."

A perpetually positive person, Jordan is his father's son. And so he weathers the good days and bad, pursuing one of their mutual dreams and feeling James' presence as he makes his way.

"I keep him alive with what I'm doing," he says, then motions to the locker stall beside his. "I feel him standing next to me all the time. It's hard to explain, but I just know he's close by."

Baseball was a childhood memory long before basketball.

"It was my father's love, and I loved it, too," says Jordan, who started T-ball at 6. "You looked forward to Saturdays. My parents never missed a game. Then we'd watch the 'Game of the Week' on television. My father rooted for the Atlanta Braves because it was the closest team. But Roberto Clemente was our favorite."

Jordan is not a kid anymore, as he so often is reminded. Suddenly, he is not merely one of the greatest athletes of our time but a 31-year-old Double-A ballplayer looking to buck the odds while he roams Clemente's right field or searches for a pitch to hit.

Under his Birmingham Barons uniform, he still wears the Carolina blue shorts that never have left him. But he yearns for the other reminders of basketball, the ones that won't allow him to be just one of the guys, to go away.

"I wanted to be the guy without any expectations, to just go out and have a good time, but I couldn't do that," Jordan says of his early days in baseball. "Regardless of what I did, I couldn't just mingle in. I was always above everybody when physically I wasn't capable of being above everybody. But when that happens, there's a natural competitive instinct to try to maintain a certain level."

For the first time in a long time, that isn't easy. He sits at the end of the Barons' bench, silent and alone. Not because he's anti-social, but because he studies the game like it is a new language he must learn to communicate.

These are the dog days of an Alabama summer. The humidity forms a permanent mist on your skin, the mosquitoes bite like catfish and the sweat rolls off Jordan's famous head like rainwater as he stoops to retrieve loose balls in the infield.

This is a far cry from Mayberry, but just as far from Chicago, and the scattered applause from the average nightly crowd of 6,000 and change makes no one mistake it for the Stadium.

But the thing is, it doesn't matter.

Off the field, Jordan's young teammates try hard to act cool, to have you believe this Michael guy is just another player. Yet they file by his locker in a seemingly endless stream asking for pictures or autographs, taking advantage of a clearly remarkable situation and stocking up, no doubt, for when he is no longer around.

Clearly, they are all amazed by the Jordan phenomenon.

One day, the team got off the bus after a trip to Huntsville and walked over to a nearby apartment complex for a pickup basketball game. Pretty soon, heads started poking out of doors and cars came screeching to a halt.

"People were standing outside with their phones saying, 'You won't believe this. Michael Jordan is playing basketball in the parking lot. Come on over,'" designated hitter Scott Tedder recalled. "Pretty soon, there were 100 people standing around."

The 6-foot-4-inch Tedder, who led his Ohio Wesleyan basketball team to the 1988 NCAA Division III national championship, found himself guarding you-know-who.

"He was a good player," says Jordan earnestly. "He averaged like 28 points a game in college, and he was shooting well. We were going up and down the court. He'd score, I score."

Jordan flashes a mischievous grin. "But when the game got close, every now and then I'd show flashes," he says. "I'd dunk the ball or block some shots. I'm just having a good time."

More and more, he can appreciate this outlook. Unfortunately, the fun only lasts as long as the game, as long as visits last from family and friends. The bad days most often occur when he finds himself alone with his thoughts.

"I spend a lot more days alone than I'm used to, and I do crossword puzzles now," he says. "I never did a crossword puzzle before in my whole life, but my father did. So now I do."

His father's presence is never far away.

"All the situations now, when I would normally ask his advice, I try to think of what he'd say and the things he'd tell me to make me laugh," Jordan says. "And I know exactly what he'd say, so I'll start laughing to myself.

"You have good days and bad days, but the thing about me is I try to think only of positive things."

And baseball—numbers and criticism be damned—is positive.

"There's still the hope and the faith in people that they do believe in you," Jordan says. "This is all a challenge. And as long as I know I have a challenge, I'm going to have a good time doing it."

There are still good days and bad days. But today's a good one.

Jordan Applies a Perfect Touch to One Last Masterpiece

JAY MARIOTTI

Chicago Sun-Times June 15, 1998

SALT LAKE CITY—Forgive our selfishness. But that is how he should exit, the way the curtain should fall, with a climax somehow better than anything he has produced before. If Michael Jordan chooses to return, we obviously would love to have him. Don't mistake the message.

Yet in the motion picture that is his life, shouldn't this epic moment linger as the lasting memory? The mental snapshot we download in the company of grandchildren? If anyone ever asks what the Jordan phenomenon was about, we can point to Sunday night and say one thing. There.

Watch. Admire. Revere.

It was better than The Sick Game. It was better than the swooping, scooping, reverse layup. It was better than The Shrug during the three-point spree, better than anything else that happened against the Lakers, Trail Blazers, Suns, Sonics, Jazz, Knicks, Heat, anyone in the sport he grabbed by the jugular vein a dozen years ago and never let go. This was the definitive MJ masterpiece because his team needed him like never before.

Scottie Pippen was barely able to walk, clenching his teeth through back problems that would have left most players in the hospital. Jordan himself was exhausted, having played more minutes than at any point in his career. They may not have won Wednesday night at the maniacal Delta Center. But now they won't have to. All because of Michael.

"Last year in the fifth game, I didn't think he could top that," said Phil Jackson, who pronounced the dynasty dead afterward, even while Jordan and Pippen did not. "But tonight, he topped it."

You thought Jordan had raised his legend to the highest of heights. But there he went in the final seconds, lifting ever higher, with doom lingering after John Stockton nailed a three-pointer with 41.9 seconds left. It took Jordan only 4.8 seconds to drive on Bryon Russell and cut the Utah lead to a point. That is when he rose above all, like a monster, overwhelming the scene. The MVP of a year ago, Karl Malone, wasn't fully aware as he set up near the basket with the ball. He was plotting his move, ignoring the blindside. Whoosh.

There was Jordan, with the tentacle of an octopus, slapping the ball away, making the steal that reminded us of his all-time prowess as a defender. At that point, we knew the ending: an easy jumper. The world watching, knowing it couldn't possibly miss. As the ball hung, it occurred to us that this was one hell of a famous final scene. When it swished through, it occurred to us that we could live with this as a beautiful finale to the greatest athletic career we have known.

And you know what? Jordan agreed.

While hedging on retirement, he sat at the podium, nodded his head and understood the dramatic flair at hand. If you retire, Michael, is that the way to go out?

"Yes. If that's the case, yes," he said. "As everything developed, my thoughts were very positive. The crowd gets quiet. The moment starts to become the moment for me. Things start to move slowly. I see the court very well, see the defense. I saw that moment. I saw the opportunity to take advantage of it. I never doubted myself or that moment."

As he smiled, Jordan was asked if he felt that would be the last moment, if the dynasty could be salvaged. He seemed doubtful.

"It is a feeling I will have eventually," he said of retirement. "It may be time for me to take a different turn. My life has to continue. Hopefully, I have put enough memories out there for people to know what Michael Jordan did, for kids to follow. I do have another life, and I'll have to get to it at some point in time. Right now, there are a lot of sympathetic feelings about keeping us together as a team. Some of the feelings may change."

Jackson, though, sounded like he was finished.

"The reality is, this is our last season together," he said. "Unless it comes out of left field, I don't expect us to come back."

Not singular. Plural.

Now it is left to historians and other contentious souls to debate the Jordan dynasty's place in history. With the Six-Pack, the Bulls one-up the Magic Johnson Lakers as the second-most successful NBA era. Some choose to malign them, saying the Bulls play in watered-down times when attitudes are lousy, players don't care about winning and no consistent

Western rival has risen to challenge them, like Larry Bird's Celtics challenged the Lakers.

Silly people.

The true magnificence of Jordan is this: No basketball champion ever has accomplished more with less. The other dynasties didn't have to contend, for instance, with salary caps and quick-fix free agency. Bill Russell had a deep, talented cast of seven Hall of Famers. Johnson had James Worthy, Kareem Abdul-Jabbar, so many others. Bird had Kevin McHale, Robert Parish, a bench. Jordan's teams have included palooka centers and a bunch of hangers-on fortunate to be in the league.

Truth is, had Jordan not dabbled in baseball, the Bulls likely would be celebrating their eighth straight title. No one could quibble with that. No one should quibble with any of it, really. "Every time you duplicate something, I think it's better the last time you do it because of how tough the road was to achieve it," Jordan said. "It's a lot more gratifying for me to win it now."

If this is goodbye, thank you.

So Long, Michael
It's Been Great
BERNIE LINCICOME

Chicago Tribune October 7, 1993

They already were sweeping up after Michael Jordan. In small clumps at the Berto Center, there was David Stern, the commissioner, and Jerry Reinsdorf, the owner, and Jerry Krause, the chief clerk of the Chicago Bulls.

Their duty was to explain the inexplicable, to try and fill with their inadequacy the huge hole that had just been left in their sport, in their franchise and in the heart of the town where they still would have to do business.

Jordan himself had left the building. This was no longer his mess or his concern.

His life was his own again.

They tried to put the best face they could on the bizarre and confusing. They understood, they said, and wished Jordan well.

To hear Reinsdorf tell it, he had practically insisted Jordan get on with his life. Reinsdorf said he always had thought Jordan was the Babe Ruth of basketball. Reinsdorf said he had changed his mind. Ruth was the Jordan of baseball.

The place was thick with such embellishment, the kind that usually requires a widow and an open bar.

The agent was there, too, of course, David Falk, and other assorted "endorsees," as Jordan called them, the corporate creatures who used Jordan's image for pay. All were poorer than they had been just moments before.

The media, local and national, legitimate and electronic, caught early airplanes and double-parked their trucks to be there. The air crackled with transponder coordinates, and the floor was a menace of cables and cosmetics.

There were fewer cameras, and certainly less makeup, at the surrender of Japan.

This went live, network and cable, and the messengers of the moment talked over Jordan on cellular phones to distant places. Yes, they said, he is quitting. Yes, they said, he has left the door open to come back. Yes, they said, it certainly is tragic.

Assorted accomplices in the Chicago Bulls' three championships were spotted among the great gaggle of media, explaining how they would carry on without Jordan, refusing to consider how they had gone so suddenly from being feared to being the Milwaukee Bucks.

Scottie Pippen, now the man, said he had dreamed of this day when Jordan's considerable shadow would be gone and the Chicago Bulls would be his to lead. It sounds worse than Pippen probably meant it to.

Phil Jackson, the coach, was more a phantom than usual, indulging no one's appetite for detail. It is understandable. Jackson now will have to work for a living.

For most of a very long night and half a morning, Chicago had waited for the punch line. On talk shows, in elevators, on public transportation, strangers shared a common disbelief the same way they had shared a common glory.

A city's life and pride has been so tied for so long to the achievements of one young man from North Carolina, this was like having surgery without granting permission.

Is Michael really leaving? Why? Why?

The answer, from the man himself, was that he had run out of challenges. To be 30 years old and to have done everything is an extraordinary dilemma to confront.

Red Kerr, the old coach and broadcaster, leaned on a cane from his hip replacement and said that he had seen every point Jordan had ever scored as a Bull.

Had we known this was a contest, maybe we all would have kept better memories.

By the time the place was empty and silence was nourishing the irrefutable truth, on the other end of town, the White Sox were about to try again to keep the sort of promise that Jordan had made trite.

His legacy is that winners are expected here. No team that follows will be permitted less.

Between the Sox and Jordan, being in Chicago Tuesday was like attending a wedding and a funeral at the same church.

All you needed was a dark suit and enough tears.

NEIGHBORHOODS

From the lakefront property along North Shore, where God would live if He had the money, to the gritty streets of its teeming urban areas, Chicago is, as has been said so often, a city of neighborhoods. Whether or not this is simply a polite way of noting how racially segregated it remains, there can be no doubt that for many fans where they were raised and where they live go a long way toward explaining their sporting allegiances.

It may also help explain the impassioned response to any changes, no matter how necessary to keep up with the times, in the city's major sports venues.

The battles over putting lights in Wrigley Field, and restricting access to the rooftops of the buildings across the street, were long and ferocious. The White Sox were one post-midnight legislative session in Springfield away from moving to Florida until it was agreed to tear down Comiskey Park and build a new stadium across the street. And despite the amenities of the United Center, there are basketball fans in Chicago who still mourn the loss of the Stadium, which one NBA coach said was the only place he had ever been where he could *feel* noise.

Here are some columns about the sense of place in Chicago sports. It should be noted that those by John Schulian and Rick Telander, which portray the battle against hopelessness in two of those neighborhoods, were written thirty years apart. The more things change . . .

K Town

JOHN SCHULIAN

Chicago Sun-Times March 13, 1981

Even in the loving glow of noonday sunshine, with March pretending it's May and the thermometer skipping toward 60, K Town has trouble wiping the sorrow from its face. On the West Side streets that gave birth to the neighborhood's name, on Kedvale and Keeler and the half-dozen others, there are too many boarded-up windows, too many burned-out houses, too many cars with flat tires or no tires at all. Stray dogs wander listlessly, ragged men kill time with bottles in brown bags, and the only sign of hope is a bouncing basketball.

Four kids cluster around it as they work their way up Karlov, stealing the sweet round treasure from one another and thrilling imaginary crowds with earth-bound dunk shots too magnificent for words. It is the classic ghetto dream—success in short pants—and though the dream too often evaporates after stealing from time better spent over school books, these pre-pubescent musketeers would never believe the warning.

How could they when they know what lies beyond the J&S Bar B-Q and the Greater Joy Baptist Church? How could they when, any minute now, they are going to stare across another of K Town's vacant lots and see the basketball court where Mark Aguirre learned to put one foot in front of the other?

Bryant Elementary School's baskets stood behind the house where he grew up, stood there singing a siren song that should have been irresistible, and yet Aguirre had his doubts. At 13, he was pudgy, withdrawn and wide-eyed, a combination that might have kept him inside were it not for the strength of the familial ties that bound the 1300 block of South Karlov. His grandparents catered to him, his aunts and uncles watched over him, and the most volatile of his cousins made him stop living with the nickname Laundrybag.

Ricky Scott was a playground swashbuckler in those days, and he didn't take no for an answer, particularly when he was asking Aguirre to be the 10th man in a pickup game. "Ricky didn't want to hear no excuses about me not playing good," Aguirre says. "He said, 'If you leave, don't ever come back and see me again.'" So Aguirre stayed and, unbeknownst to him, laid the foundation for his legend. Never mind that Bryant's metal backboards are now splattered with graffiti that declares the last gang to get a can of spray paint the ruler of this turf. After all the magic Aguirre exported to De Paul, there is no doubt who the king of K Town is.

He will lead the No. 1 Blue Demons into the NCAA playoffs Saturday just as he once led his elementary school team against Skip Dillard's on a court where the baskets had no nets. "We was bangin' heads, both of us playin' center, and I got 30 points," says Dillard, who followed Aguirre on the underground railroad to De Paul. "I think that was a real letdown to Mark, me beatin' him like that, 'cause even when he was younger, he was The Man."

There were rematches to prove that point, although rematches still seems too tame a word when you consider the circumstances. "Wars was more like it," Dillard says. "Man, we'd be out there 2, 3, 4 in the morning. One-on-one. Shootin', fightin', scrappin'. Every night, somebody would go home mad." They always returned, though, drawn by the spell they were spinning, the same spell Bernard Randolph so willingly fell under when the three of them found themselves in lockstep at Westinghouse High.

They are supposed to be Westinghouse's gift to De Paul—Aguirre, the All-America scoring machine; Dillard, the backcourt bombardier, and Randolph, the improbably funky sixth man—but their roots are deepest in their native K Town. They have watered its cracked concrete with sweat and blood, and brought joy to its sullen streets with their raucous, high-flying ways.

"The things y'all see at school ain't nothin'," Randolph says. "Man, when we was playin' over at Delano Playground—yeah, over on Pulaski and Wilcox—the stuff goin' on was so good you couldn't wait for the next day. Mark was doin' some things he wouldn't never do now. Now he don't want to get himself hurt and mess up with the pros. But when we was young, he didn't have no fear. Like . . ."

Randolph's eyes grow wide.

". . . like . . ."

And wider still.

". . . like taking off—I mean seriously taking off—from the foul line and doing a 360 and dunking over three or four dudes, man. I'm serious. It was beautiful, and y'all ain't never gonna see it."

The irony is that the only audience Aguirre, Randolph and Dillard could count on back then was the gangs that had made their younger days miserable. The Vice Lords and the Four-Corner Hustlers had treasured them as potential foot soldiers until it became obvious that basketball was their ticket to something more than K Town could provide. From that point on, the gangsters trod softly. Oh, they still might chase an enemy through a pickup game, waving knives and chains and guns, but in mellow times, they were content to drink their wine and smoke their reefer while they tried to believe what they were seeing on the basketball court.

It made K Town different, if only for a few hours at a time. For once, the boarded-up windows and the burned-out houses and the tire-stripped cars didn't weigh so heavily on the psyche. There was hope instead of hopelessness when the sounds in the night were jump shots, not gunshots. Someday the people on the outside, the ones who passed by on their way to better places, were going to hear about Mark Aguirre and Skip Dillard and Bernard Randolph. The outsiders were going to know that, however briefly, K Town was that rarest of things—the most beautiful place in the world.

Mark Aguirre became the first overall pick of the 1981 NBA draft by the Dallas Mavericks and was a three-time All-Star, averaging twenty points a game in a thirteen-year career. He won two NBA championships with the Detroit Pistons. Skip Dillard served four years of an eleven-year term for armed robbery in a series of holdups he said he committed to support a cocaine habit. Bernard Randolph spent time in a mental hospital and later seemed to have no permanent address. "He just shows up from time to time and then goes away," said an old friend. "Nobody seems to know what he is doing."

Roof Bums

RON RAPOPORT

Chicago Sun-Times July 22, 1982

Proceeding on the theory that the Cubs are best viewed from a distance, I crossed Waveland Avenue behind Wrigley Field and called to the ladies on the roof.

Come on up, they waved. I had no sooner climbed the steps, taken my seat and adjusted to the sight of baseball behind the left-field wall than I heard my five favorite words of the summer: "Would you like a beer?"

Trying not to let my gratitude appear too abject, I murmured an affirmative. Within minutes, the sun on my face was working like a drug. I leaned back, put my feet up and made a mental note to think up assignments for myself like this more often. It would take more than another Cubs loss to ruin this afternoon.

The brunet with the shy smile introduced herself as Rita. She lived in the building. The blond in the cutoff jeans said she was Jill. She was from next door. I never did get the name of the two other ladies in attendance. My reportorial instincts were fading fast.

Yes, they were Cub fans, Rita and Jill said. Yes, they spent as much time watching games from the roof as possible.

"It's a genetic deficiency," Rita said. "Recessive genes."

"I used to be a Bleacher Bum," said Jill, who grew up close to Wrigley Field, but not this close. "Now I'm a Roof Bum."

For a while, nobody said anything. Rita set the bag with the beer in it down next to me. The major sounds were the organ and the public-address announcer. The major sights were the left-field wall and, beyond it, the Cubs trying to set a National League record for force plays.

"It really keeps you a perpetual child living up here," Jill said at last.

"During that two-hour rain delay last Saturday, we sat up here with that big tarp back there over our heads," said Rita, as if that would prove the point.

"And when the rain was over, we snuck into the ballpark and watched the last inning from behind the dugout," Jill responded.

The apartments the roof people live in are seldom available on the open market. Family and friends tend to succeed each other, and newcomers quickly learn that the hovering presence of the ballpark adds a definitive rhythm to their lives. Jill and Rita, for instance, are teachers who often hurry home for the final innings during the school term.

"It's great to come on the roof and scream and yell during a game like you want to at the kids, but don't dare," said Jill. "In the winter, we get kind of tense. Sometimes, we come up and yell anyhow."

"Yeah," said Rita. "On Jan. 17, I'm coming up and yelling, 'Come on, let's get some runs!'"

"The best day is the first day you can hear the organist practicing, a few days before Opening Day," said Jill. "It's like hearing the ice cream man for the first time in the spring."

The first game of the season brings some headaches with it, though. The seats on the roof are at almost as much of a premium as the ones across the street. The building's landlord nearly started a rebellion this year when he suggested Opening Day guests be limited, but fortunately the controversy ended when snow kept the crowd down.

"We watched them shovel the field twice," Jill said. "And we moved the snow around the deck and put our beer in it. Then there was a great snowball fight after the game between the people down on the street and us up here."

Last season's strike affected the roof people more intensely than the average fan. Often, they would come out and cheer on the missing players as if baseball was still being played. Once, they sneaked into the ballpark and played a pickup soccer game.

"The kids used to be able to sneak in under the gate all the time," Jill said. "Before the Tribune took over, things weren't as tight. That's the worst part of the 'new tradition'—the fact you can't sneak in anymore. That and the trash compactor."

The latter is a new machine in the left-field concourse that loudly mashes the day's garbage, often until well past midnight. Nights on the roof looking at the stars above the dark and empty ballpark are not nearly as pleasant with the compactor masticating away.

Before the season opened, the roof people got a nasty scare when they saw workmen putting up a pole near the left-field foul line. The rumor quickly spread that it was part of a big scoreboard that would block the view and some of the workmen teasingly called out that their afternoons of free live baseball were coming to an end. Everybody breathed easier when the pole turned out to be support for a line that helps keeps the net behind home plate in place.

The seventh-inning stretch was faithfully observed, Harry Caray's fully kraeusened tones filling the air.

"Harry said he was going to broadcast a game from here some time," Jill said. "We're waiting. Like waiting for Godot."

We talked softly, lazily studying the figures below, when suddenly the peace of the afternoon was shattered. A Cub hit rocketed to the right-field wall, driving in three runs that would win the game. We were all on our feet, shouting at this rare display, forgetting for the moment the topic of only moments before.

"The last game of the year is always so sad," Jill said.

"It signals the ends of summer, the beginning of bad weather," Rita answered.

"Last year," Jill said, "my daughter cried."

The Sun Sets on Cubs' Illusions

BERNIE LINCICOME

Chicago Tribune August 8, 1988

On this date in history, or near enough, the only American president to ever leave office in disgrace gave up the world.

And Wrigley Field gave up its innocence.

Only a fool, or a Mets fan, would confuse which one contains the greater shame.

I will take a pass on the lighting of Wrigley Field. It is an easy choice. Whenever possible I avoid the soiling of virgins.

The great jangling street hustle that has preceded the event is worth neither the noise nor the souvenirs.

The loss of innocence is too precious to end up on a T-shirt. You do not strike commemorative coins for an execution. Maybe you do. This is my first.

This is not about night baseball, not about the Cubs, not about which way the wind blows after dark. Not about electricity.

This is not about property values or cable wars or corporate greed or common sense.

This is about dread and regret and the death of illusions. This is about fearing the world will be less tomorrow than it is today.

This is about wishes and memories and generations holding hands.

And all the logic and all the candlepower in the world will not illuminate it as something else.

The Cubs do not play baseball in a stadium. They play in a metaphor. Wrigley Field passed from being just a ballpark when, I'm only guessing, oh, when Pete LaCock was playing first base.

Or was that Peter Pan?

Wrigley Field is as ephemeral as Camelot, and as necessary.

It is the antidote to future shock, a reminder that the world got along perfectly fine without microwaves and spray paint and coffee whitener.

It is a shining sanctuary from the possible. And its occupants are living reminders that not only isn't winning the only thing, it isn't even necessary.

So rarely has the destiny of a sports franchise been as clear as that of the Cubs.

The Cubs are baseball's poster children, winsome and blameless. They never need to be forgiven for being as they are, for they cannot help it.

The Cubs are absolutely free of all expectations, unburdened by past excellence, immune from the urgency to prove they deserve to be adored.

The Cubs are as privileged as royalty, having done nothing to earn affection other than allowing it.

The Cubs have won a World Series. There are still a few witnesses alive to testify to it. The Cubs have won a pennant since the beginning of the nuclear age, if only by a few months. They have been models of restraint.

The Cubs are heartbreak-proof, no more capable of inflicting pain than statues in a park, one of their frequent disguises.

All of this is made tolerable only in the fairyland of ivy and bare skin, in the Cubs' own special world of Daylight Fantasy Time.

Night baseball at Wrigley Field eliminates one more lie, and we need lies. We need to believe in what is unreal, for truth kills imagination.

The truth is, you turn on lights to work. Recess never needed electricity.

The Cubs, our proxies, have lost the excuse of perpetual childhood, an amnesty possible only in natural, dependable light.

It is time to grow up.

Sunshine makes shadows; night makes secrets.

North versus South—the Twain Shall Finally Meet

DAVE HOEKSTRA

Chicago Sun-Times June 13, 1997

For the first time since the 1906 World Series, the Chicago Cubs will march down to Bridgeport on Monday to play the Chicago White Sox in a baseball game that counts. This is the equivalent of Gen. William Tecumseh Sherman's 1864 squeeze play on Atlanta, back during the Civil War.

And even then the Cubs were looking for a fourth starter. Despite the uncivil play by the Cubs and Sox this season, this week's series is serious business. North Side–South Side: It's a bottle of Merlot vs. a shot and a beer, a gelato up against the Rainbow Cone. It is a tale of two cities.

"The North Side fan carries the E-bola virus and has herpes," said Styx lead singer Dennis DeYoung, who grew up around 101st Street and South Michigan Avenue. "The South Side fan is intelligent, good looking and willing to leap tall buildings in a single bound." Except there are no tall buildings on the South Side.

The South Side is a passionate blues game called the Checker Board Lounge, eight blocks from Comiskey Park. The North Side is hot chicken wings at Yak-Zies, a block north of Wrigley Field.

"People complain they don't hear the real blues north," said Checker Board owner L.C. Thurman. "Like the down-home stuff with the harmonica. The real hoochie coochie stuff will be going on after the game."

The North Side is the hip-swinging Mighty Blue Kings. The South Side is the dignified charms of the late boogie-woogie pianist Jimmy Yancey, who lived on 35th Street. From 1917 until 1949, Yancey was also ground-skeeper for the Sox at old Comiskey.

The North Side is Richard Marx and Scott Turow. The South Side is Dennis DeYoung and Leon Forrest.

"Growing up, I would have rather been (former Sox center fielder) Jim Landis than Paul McCartney," said DeYoung, who is working on a musical, "The Hunchback of Notre Dame." "However, I've lost a little of that passion since the last strike."

At Wrigley Field, passionate fans sit on rooftops to watch the game. At Comiskey Park, fans pay to sit in the rooftoplike upper deck. Sox fans wait in line to go to Jimbo's tavern. Cubs fans wait in line to go to Bozo.

The North Side is the feisty attitude of rocker Liz Phair. The South Side is the soul of Mavis Staples, who has one of the hardest hitting vocal deliveries in rhythm and blues.

"The folks on the North Side are just as cool as the folks on the South Side," Staples said from her South Side condo. "They're just faster moving. There's more shops and boutiques. The South Side people are more down home and more down to earth, period."

Staples, 57, has lived on the South Side since 1953 when Pops Staples relocated his family from the West Side to 28th and Wabash. The Staples eventually settled at 70th Street and King Drive. Mavis Staples is a loyal Sox fan.

Loyalties run deep. The late Chicago mystery writer Eugene Izzi was so South Side, he often refused to cross over the Madison Street north-south boundary.

Chicago author Nelson Algren, didn't let geography stand in the way of his passions. He was a hard-core White Sox fan, although he lived in Wicker Park from the 1940s through 1975.

Algren died in 1981 at Sag Harbor, Long Island. But even in the White Sox' lean years of the late 1960s, he attended many games with his buddy, playwright Stuart McCarrell. Before games, they'd stop in for pasta at Tufano's, 1073 W. Vernon Park, on the Near South Side.

Chicago novelist-lawyer Scott Turow, 48, is a lifelong Cubs fan. But he closed the book on the team this year. Maybe that's why he's clicking on his next novel.

"I'm abstaining from all Tribune Co. activities until they spend more money on ballplayers," Turow said. "If a Cubs game is on TBS and WGN, I'll watch it on TBS. I have not watched one inning of the Cubs on WGN this year. And I'm a guy who used to live through spring training just waiting for the Cubs-Sox (city series that used to be played for charity). I'm that angry.

"Being a Cubs fan is deep within me. I've been through all the philosophical stuff about how losing is good for the soul. And a lot of that is true. But my father is 78, and if the Cubs don't do something dramatic, he's facing the prospect of having lived and died without ever seeing the Cubs win a World Series."

For Mavis Staples, though, the differences between the North Side and South Side go way beyond baseball.

With a good-natured laugh she said, "They're rich on the North Side with money. They're rich on the South Side with love."

A Space Invasion in Wrigleyville

CAROL SLEZAK

Chicago Sun-Times May 1, 2001

It was a day that made her wonder why.

Why does anyone live in this neighborhood?

Why are people such morons?

Why are the Cubs so lousy?

On most days, her Lake View neighborhood is a good one. The streets are quiet, the sidewalks safe to walk and, despite the recent arrival of the Asian long-horned beetle, the trees are plentiful. But a strange force invades the area when the Cubs play at Wrigley Field, a force that turns the neighborhood into chaos and normal people into jerks. The following is a true story about a Cubs game, a Lake View resident, a garage and a jerk.

"Now I've seen everything," the cop said from inside her patrol car.

The cop made a phone call. The cop was laughing. The Lake View resident was not amused.

"So this (jerk) just thought he'd help himself to my garage?" the resident said. "Isn't that, like, theft or something? I mean, what did he do, check every garage in the alley until he found an empty one? If he was hungry, would he have broken into my refrigerator? If he had to pee, would I have found him in my bathroom? What kind of person would do something like this?

"Can we put him in jail, officer? Please?"

The cop nixed the jail time.

"OK, then can we at least slash his tires?"

When the resident moved to Lake View years ago, street parking was pretty easy, even during Cubs games. But in recent years, it has become impossible—especially during Cubs games. So, being a reasonable person, the resident adapted. She leased a tiny garage in an alley near where she lives. She pays handsomely for the privilege. And the garage frequently sits empty because she would rather not navigate the narrow alley and its garbage bins and utility poles unless she has to. But on those days and nights when the Cubs play, the garage is a necessity.

Such was the case on the Saturday afternoon of April 20, when the Cubs were hosting (and playing patsy for) the Cincinnati Reds. The resident had to use her car for some errands and couldn't find street parking when she returned home. So she drove into the alley, put her car in park and got out to open the garage (which isn't equipped with an automatic opener and doesn't lock). Imagine her shock when she raised the door and saw a car inside. A strange car. A stranger's car. A big, green Ford. Driven by . . . no one she knew.

She looked for a note on the car. A "back in a minute" or a phone number or an explanation. Anything. She found nothing. She composed the nastiest note she ever had written on a scrap of paper, using words she never had used before. She stuck the note under the Ford's windshield wiper. It crossed her mind that the driver might have been scammed by an unscrupulous neighbor, someone pretending the garage was his to rent out for a game.

"Not my problem," she thought.

She turned off her car, left it in the alley with its emergency flashers on and ran home. She dialed the police hotline for Wrigley Field parking problems. (She confesses she was surprised that someone actually answered the hotline.) She explained the situation to the dispatcher—

hopefully keeping the curse words to a minimum, though she can't recall. The dispatcher said a patrol car would come by shortly.

"Yeah, sure," she thought. "And the Cubs are going to win the pennant."

But within minutes, a patrol car pulled into the alley. The kind and efficient cop behind its wheel ran a check on the Ford's license-plate number. She called for a tow truck, saying, "We gotta get this guy out of this lady's garage." The cop wrote out a fat ticket. Then she put the ticket under the Ford's windshield wiper. (The resident retrieved her note from under the wiper before the cop could read it.)

The tow truck arrived quickly, too. The tow-truck driver couldn't believe anyone could have the audacity to open a private garage, let alone park inside it. (The resident couldn't believe anyone could have maneuvered such a big car into such a tiny garage space.) The resident suggested they siphon the gas out of the green Ford before they towed it away. The resident suggested they form a neighborhood group, P.O.G., or Protect our Garages. The resident contemplated posting a "Beware of Angry Owner" sign on the garage door. The tow-truck driver and the cop ignored the resident's blathering.

The tow-truck driver got the Ford out of the garage with surprising ease.

"I'd love to see this guy's face when he comes back from the game," the tow-truck driver said to the cop.

"You should have seen my face when I found his car in my garage," the resident thought.

Their work done, the tow-truck driver and the cop left, still chuckling.

And the resident? Well, it took a while. But she can laugh about it now.

Really, I can.

Sox Fan Enters Lineup at Comiskey Park

MARK BROWN

Chicago Sun-Times April 23, 2002

Helen Deuerling was quite a White Sox fan, the type who seemed so permanently connected to her transistor radio that you might have thought it was a pacemaker.

She attended the first night game played at Comiskey Park in 1939. When the Sox held their Ladies' Day promotions, she and her daughter would ride three buses from the old neighborhood at 63rd and Pulaski to take advantage of the free admission.

Even after the Alzheimer's disease had robbed Helen's mind of nearly everything else, it left intact her sweet memories of Luke Appling and the White Sox of her youth doing battle with the dreaded Yankees of Ruth and DiMaggio.

When Helen died in February at age 86, it was only natural then that her family would want to honor the wish they'd heard her express so many times prior to her death: to make Comiskey Park her final resting place.

But the funeral home director told them the Sox would never approve.

So Helen's son came up with an alternative plan.

He noticed the White Sox had switched their annual Dog Day promotion from midsummer to mid-April to take advantage of the cooler temperatures.

On Dog Day, the Sox allow their fans to bring their pooches to the ballpark and parade them around the field before the start of the game. Then all the dog owners and their pets sit together in the bleachers during the contest. Amazingly, the dogs behave so well that this promotion has survived for several seasons.

Helen's son had never attended Dog Day, but he eagerly signed up for this year's event, which was held this past Saturday before the Tigers game.

He brought along his two Tibetan spaniels, Biscuit and Brandy, as well as about two dozen of Helen's friends and family members.

Accompanied by his own daughter, his sister and her daughter, Helen's son circled the field prior to the game with about 500 other dog owners.

And as they walked, you guessed it, Helen's family members surreptitiously scattered her cremated remains around the field.

The dog owners began their parade lap in center field and were supposed to stick to the warning track that separates the stands from the dazzling green turf, which was undoubtedly quite a temptation to the dogs.

Thousands of Little Leaguers and their parents make the same lap every summer, but I must say, it never occurred to me while I was making the trek with my boys that the guy in front of me might be sprinkling grandma underfoot.

It wouldn't bother me if he were, but it does give you pause. Let's hope Sox centerfielder Kenny Lofton isn't the type to get weirded out by that type of thing.

I had imagined Helen's son contriving some sort of contraption to sneak the ashes out the bottom of his pants legs like Tim Robbins dumping the dirt from his escape tunnel in "The Shawshank Redemption."

But it turns out he didn't have to go to that much trouble.

"It wasn't that difficult. It really wasn't," said her son. He didn't want his name used because he shares in a season ticket package and doesn't want to arouse the Sox ire. He didn't go looking for publicity either, but people have a hard time keeping quiet about these kinds of things, and I caught wind of it.

"We had the ashes in a variety of sport bottles, bags, things of that nature," he said. "So it wasn't too conspicuous."

His dogs are small, so he'd kneel down as if to pet them and empty a little bit of Helen here and a little bit of Helen there.

"Nobody's really paying attention to what you're doing," he said.

That makes sense. The people in the stands are watching the dogs, and the people with the dogs are looking into the stands, when they aren't glancing down to make sure they aren't stepping in something the doggies left behind. The dogs are checking out all those other dogs and wondering where to find that food they smell.

"We had the opportunity to get the ashes all over the place, not just one spot," Helen's son said proudly. "We even got some right behind home plate, not in the batter's box area, but in front of the screen."

188

When they were finished and returned to their seats, Helen's son and daughter had a strong sense that they'd done something good for their mother.

"Mom really would have liked that," said the daughter. "For her to be back at the ballpark, that's where she belongs."

Helen's son said he was never worried about getting caught.

"Even if they catch you, what are they going to do, prosecute you? The Sox have enough PR problems," he said.

And that's where the joke's on him.

Although they keep it quiet, it turns out the Sox routinely allow their fans to spread a loved one's remains on the field.

"We get about five to ten requests a year. We try to accommodate them the best we can," said Rob Gallas, the Sox' senior veep for marketing and broadcasting. "That's standard policy."

The ceremonies are usually arranged for when the Sox are out of town or during the offseason, he said.

"I wish (Helen's son) would have asked us. We would have made arrangements for him to do it under a little quieter circumstances," Gallas said.

Yes, but it sure makes a better story this way.

"If They Don't Have a Truce by Tuesday, Derrick Rose Day Will Never Happen"

RICK TELANDER

Chicago Sun-Times October 3, 2011

Derrick Rose is coming!

The long-awaited ceremony for "The Derrick Rose Renovation Project" will be held Tuesday at Murray Park, right on the basketball court that has been spiffed up this summer, with fresh paint and new baskets and white nets. Right on the court on which the 2011 MVP of the NBA played for years as a kid. "Man, he'd shovel snow off it in winter time," says his brother Reggie.

But the festivities next week don't mean much to Arsenio Williams.

Only last spring, Williams, a 6–4, 230-pound power forward who grew up on the same black with Rose, graduated from South Carolina State University.

Now, he sits in pain on his bed at Advocate Christ Hospital in Oak Lawn. There are bullet holes in him from his elbows to his ankles, a couple of them hidden by his green gown. He was shot seven times, but there are more than seven bullet holes, if you count exit wounds. And there is still a bullet in him, lodged in his right elbow and bulging slightly under the skin like a budding tumor.

"It was two guns," he says. "Something small, like a .22, and then"—he points at a larger scar—"I think a .380."

Williams was standing by his car near his house on Paulina Street, talking to some young men, when a car drove up and the occupants began firing. The alleged gang members were caught quickly by police, at whom they also supposedly fired. Six were arrested, three were charged with aggravated discharge of a firearm. Three of the detained were minors.

Williams is a group leader for Children's Home + Aid, a tutor for that national organization who visits schools "trying to de-escalate problems," as he puts it. That's what he was doing when he was shot, talking to teens, no doubt the actual targets, trying to get them to continue the peace treaty he had already negotiated.

"He was working to stop exactly that kind of violence he was a victim of," says Rebecca Clarkin, the vice president for external affairs for Children's Home + Aid.

And so three punk-ass fools who know nothing about life or dreams are charged with a lame felony and will probably be back on the streets some day soon. That Williams is not dead is like cutting an ace seven times in a row.

"They should call in the National Guard!" says his mother, sitting on the nearby chair.

"Mom," says Williams softly, shaking his head.

This isn't a foreign country or a hurricane or a concentration camp. This is us. Somehow we got here on our own.

"It was a 30-day peace treaty that I helped make happen," says Arsenio, whose right leg still has blood on the bandages. "Because I got shot, it's gonna be crazy out there. They were gonna squash it, no shootings, not even about drugs. Our turf—there's a gang called 'Small World'—goes from 71st to 74th, from Ashland to Damen. We're surrounded, and all these other gangs (he names them, but asks me not to print them) are coming after us." He looks down sadly. "If they don't have a truce by Tuesday, Derrick Rose Day will never happen."

Squash. Small World. Like something from Disneyland rides. And the thought strikes me: How could anyone—let alone perhaps the best basketball player on earth—have made it out of here.

"There was a lot of love in our neighborhood back then," says Williams. "And we had basketball. We had the game."

Here now walks Derrick Rose himself, coming out of the parkhouse, where he has been talking to reporters and signing basketballs. He is wearing black jeans, a gray sweatshirt and sneakers. He is almost 6–3 and he looks lean and ready to hoop.

Rose looks and sees an amazing sight. It is his pal Arsenio Williams hobbling on crutches into Murray Park from his house two blocks away for the first time since he was shot. They hug and then they text each other, and they'll get together when all this party hoopla is over.

It has been raining all day, but now it's clear and dry, with all these tents and big shots present at a park that never sees such pomp and ritual. Maybe things aren't as terrible as they seem. Oh, when I left Williams that night at the hospital I watched an ambulance take away a man who had been shot dead in the street at 76th and Wolcott, just a few blocks from the park. There were 40 cops there, in and around the yellow and red tape, a police helicopter overhead, snipers with rifles.

But what about the other people I met? I visited old Hershell Robinson a week ago and he had pneumonia, but he actually felt better than he had three months before. "Treyvaughn is doing good in school," he beamed about his grandson who had been shot in the belly. "The shooting thing drove a wedge between his mother and me, to be honest. But I have to agree with her about the incident. I just don't know what's going on. I don't. Who was the bullet for? There's no suspects. If I knew anything, it would help."

The kindly grandpa had coughed and covered his nose and mouth with a hankie. His voice was nasal and congested and he looked weak. Yet there was joy in him.

"On Tuesday he went to see the mayor, at City Hall, I think. All the gunshot wound survivors were invited. I think he enjoyed it. I think he did."

Derrick Rose speaks calmly to the kids, and he tells them, "When you look at me . . . just go out there and dedicate your life . . ." To something. To anything. Hold on.

Perhaps it's best to let Ivan Lee, the father of Murray Park's young supervisor, sum up, as he so eloquently did after the dignitaries were gone.

"It's a dirty diamond," he said of the park, the violence, Englewood, Chicago, the world. "There are many facets, and all are dirty. They need to be cleaned, one by one."

Then he asked, "Can we do that?"

SIDEKICKS AND AMATEURS,
FORGOTTEN MEN AND LOST TEAMS,
HUSTLERS AND CLOWNS

Michael Jordan had Scottie Pippen—Jordan never won an NBA title without him, in fact—Walter Payton had Doug Plank and Bobby Hull had Eric Nesterenko. It is not just the stars who make sports so compelling, but also those who complement them, who occasionally step forward for their own moments of glory, then move back into the shadows.

As the years go by, they, and sometimes even the teams they played for, can be forgotten altogether. But the writer who takes the time to hunt them down can often find something that reminds us why we cared about them in the first place.

That is what Tom Fitzpatrick has done with Lou Novikoff, what Bob Greene has done with Nesterenko, what Rick Telander has done with Doug Atkins, and what Bill Gleason has done with his memories of the Chicago Football Cardinals. David Israel, in contrast, gives us a hint of what is to come with an early look at Doug Plank, who would come to symbolize, and lend his number to, the "46" defense that would lead the Bears to a Super Bowl.

A few other characters show up in these pages, including Luther Lassiter, who works the shadows with his pool cue; Andy the Clown, who, on his own recognizance, brightened up Comiskey Park for years; and the mostly nameless hordes of varying ability and commitment who flock to the Chicago Marathon every year. And wasn't it clever of Carol Slezak to bypass the finish line and go where the marathon's action really was—the hospital tents?

Scottie Pippen Thrived in Jordan's Shadow

SAM SMITH

Chicago Tribune October 6, 2004

Scottie Pippen was old-school.

Not that he couldn't relate to today's NBA player. After all, Pippen was once arrested, he quit on his team, paid off for children born out of wedlock, demanded to be traded, tossed barbs at fans and management and threw the occasional chair.

Yes, Scottie Pippen could be a headache, migraine and otherwise—but mostly for the opposition.

Pippen, who officially announced his retirement Tuesday after 17 years in the NBA, was a unique player—willowy and long-armed, cat-quick, powerful and intelligent. He was the star who would be a role player, not that it always was his choice.

Like everyone else, Pippen wanted to be like Mike. Everyone wants to be the hero. It's even tougher when you're that close and cannot be.

Pippen was the ultimate supporting player, the perfect complement, the guy to defend the opponent's best and shut down an offense. When the Bulls finally won their first championship in 1991, John Paxson hit the big shots and Jordan made the highlight play, the switch-hands layup still shown as the symbol of that series. But it was Pippen who took away the Lakers' game, shutting down Magic Johnson and thus paralyzing the Lakers' offense.

It was Pippen over the years taking on a little point guard like Mark Price one night, going up against Charles Barkley or Shawn Kemp or Karl Malone the next. Whatever was necessary, even if he didn't shoot the ball, isolate and go one-on-one, do the things of NBA highlights and individual acclaim.

Pippen directed the Bulls' complicated triangle offense. While Jordan found the basket, Pippen found his teammates. Steve Kerr always said he enjoyed playing with Pippen more than any other teammate not only because of the way Pippen would get him the ball in good shooting position, but also because he knew when a struggling player needed a shot to boost his confidence.

195

Pippen set the screen, got the rebound, made the assist. Isn't the definition of greatness making your teammates better? Pippen did that as well as anyone with his versatility.

He allowed Michael to be Michael.

Jordan scored! The fans gasped! But Jordan never won until Pippen came along. Ah, the blasphemy!

It's clear it still grates on Pippen. Because of his various transgressions—his 1.8-seconds walkout in the 1994 playoffs, his migraine headache in the 1990 conference finals and his various rages—many believe he rode Jordan's coattails to six championships and status as one of the league's 50 greatest players.

"I've heard that numerous times," Pippen said Tuesday. "But as I stand here and look back, I don't think Michael had any championship trophies without me. That would be my answer to that question."

Jordan, truly, might not have.

Not to denigrate Jordan—and Scottie Pippen was no Michael Jordan—but Jordan needed Pippen as much as Pippen needed Jordan.

In his first three years with the Bulls, Jordan's teams never got out of the first round of the playoffs. In Jordan's fourth season—and Pippen's first—the Bulls advanced to the second round with a Game 5 victory over Cleveland. Pippen, in his first career start, was the star of that game with 24 points, five offensive rebounds, a game-high steals total and one key play after another. Coincidence?

Perhaps Jordan would have figured a way without Pippen. Perhaps not. Pippen was the anti-Jordan. Pippen didn't smile much and often didn't say the right thing. That's why his return wasn't exactly hailed here, and when he couldn't perform, many were quick to reject him again, his departing media appearance brief and unemotional.

But on the court Pippen, brought the ball up so Jordan could get his scoring place on the wing. Pippen defended big scorers so Jordan could roam the lanes and turn steals into breakaway layups.

One of the most famous shots of Jordan's career was that riser over Craig Ehlo to defeat the Cavs in 1989. It was Pippen who hit a pull-up three-pointer just before to give the Bulls the chance for the last play.

Jordan held the trophy in 1991 and cried on TV. He collapsed to the floor and cried when the Bulls won in 1996, he posed in 1998. Pippen was a witness like the rest of us, and sometimes it hurt.

Pippen's ambivalence toward Jordan sometimes defined him, a relationship of awe, jealousy and resentment. He would want to be like Mike. But then he would get too close to the flame and get burned by the heat of being Jordan.

Even Tuesday, Pippen could only acknowledge playing with "one of the greatest players to ever play the game."

Once Pippen tried it alone, in 1993–94 when Jordan retired for the first time, and he almost got it done. Almost.

He was the All-Star Game MVP with 29 points and led the Bulls to 55 victories, only two fewer than in Jordan's first final season. Who knows how far the Bulls would have gone against perhaps the weakest champion ever, the role player–loaded 1994 Houston Rockets. A late foul call against Pippen in the second-round series against the Knicks, one still fresh to Bulls fans and long conceded by NBA insiders to be erroneous, likely cost the Bulls the series against the Eastern Conference–champion Knicks. Phil Jackson often called that season his most satisfying with the Bulls. They all showed they could win without Jordan. And they liked the feeling.

Pippen leaves the game now, and given the glow from the bridges he has burned, it's not likely we'll see much of him again.

But it was truly a remarkable ride.

Eric Nesterenko and the Examined Life

BOB GREENE

Chicago Sun-Times

Sometimes, late in the night, during those hours when you know there is no reason to stay out and yet something keeps you from heading for home and sleep, you will see him at the end of the bar. Always he will be alone, with his thoughts and his memories.

For 16 years he was a star in this town. Now the name is starting to be forgotten, but the man is still here. Eric Nesterenko is 41 years old; his days of skating for the Chicago Black Hawks are over; his winters of traveling the world as a National Hockey League regular are all past. The sounds of the thousands calling his name from the distant reaches of the stadium are just a private echo.

Some nights you join him. He is good company. Nesterenko was always different, a reader of books in a professional world where most of his companions chose to pass the days in front of a television set. His athletic colleagues used to refer to him as an "intellectual," and even though they were speaking the word and not writing it, you could hear the quotation marks. His need to examine his life, to question the meaning of the fame and glory that had been his since he was a boy, made him a loner among the others, and he was made to know it every day and night of his working life.

Now the nights are different, and Nesterenko is still thinking about it, still wondering how it all came to pass. Sometimes he will look down at the bar and talk about it.

"The adulation you receive as a professional athlete is such an odd thing," Nesterenko will say. "To be made to feel that you are that important . . . when in reality you are just a kid, just a boy. I know that I was just a boy. I was 18 years old the first year I skated for the Toronto Maple Leafs. I had grown up in a tiny town called Flin Flon, in Manitoba, and I was truly an innocent young boy. And there I was every night in Maple Leaf Gardens, with 20,000 people screaming and shouting down at me, counting on me. The adulation . . . I was a virgin. I had never slept with a woman."

As Nesterenko talks, you sense that here is a man who has come to terms with his own weaknesses, his own limitations. He is not one to dwell on the peaks of his athletic career, the statistics and the numbers that now exist only on paper. Rather, he will be quick to turn to the other side of it—to the moments when a boy's doubts became a man's truths.

"The hardest thing in the world for any professional athlete to recognize is that he is not the best in the world," Nesterenko will say. "There are so few who make it to the major leagues of any sport. All of us were the very best in our schools, the very best in our neighborhoods. Until you become a pro, you just don't comprehend that this will change. It took me two or three years in the National Hockey League. Then one day, I just knew it was true: 'There are men here who are better than me. I can play my very best, I can play at the absolute top of my ability, and still there are men who are younger and much better. There's nothing i can do about it. It's a fact.' And that's when you start realizing what it means to get old playing a sport.

"Even now I see it. I work with teenagers, coaching them in hockey, and on several occasions a kid of 17 or so will skate into me and square off. He wants to fight. He wants to prove that he is man enough to fight with me. And I think to myself, someday he, too, is going to have to face it. You can't fool yourself forever. There are men younger and tougher and better than you are. That's what life is about."

Nesterenko will try to turn the conversation away from this. His interests are strongest when he is talking about a world not his own; he would much rather hear about a way of life he has never tried than discuss the years of his past. If you press him, though, he will tell you about it.

"I was never really with the rest of the players," he will say. "We got along well enough, but I always seemed to be on my own. For me the real fun of skating, the true joy of it, disappeared as soon as I started to get paid for it. There was never a moment in the National Hockey League that compared with the sheer joy I had as a boy skating outside in Flin Flon. That's something you can never recapture — doing it because you want to be doing it. Now, that is sport."

The hour will near closing time, and Nesterenko will know that it is time to head back to Evanston, where he lives with his wife and three children. But he will be reluctant to leave; there is something about going out into the night that keeps him inside the bar a bit longer.

"It's kind of funny," he will say. "I played in this town for 16 years, and I don't have one friend left here. I had two men who I could really call my friends, but they're both gone now. Do you know what I do for fun? I ski. I'm not very good at it; really not too good at all. But I'll go out there by myself to a place where there's snow, and I'll start down that course, and it will make me feel wonderful. Maybe not being good at it has something to do with it. I can't even tell you how fine it makes me feel. It's just me, trying to do something because I want to. It's like I'm back in Flin Flon again, learning to skate for the first time. It makes me feel like a boy."

Lou Novikoff
"I Am Dead and Only Waiting to Be Buried"

TOM FITZPATRICK

Chicago Sun-Times

The doorbell rang for a long time before a heavy-set woman answered. Her jet black hair was tied into a bun at the back and she was wearing an apron over her dress.

"Yes," she said. "Lou is here. Won't you come into the kitchen to see him?"

By this time a balding, barrel-chested man with a two-day growth of beard was making his way to the door, too. He was moving with that peculiar rolling gait common among circus bears and professional football linemen.

"And so?" Lou Novikoff inquired in a basso profundo rendered even more impressive by his Russian accent. (It was almost as though Akim Tamiroff were playing a cameo role.) "And so what do you wa-a-ant with me?"

Novikoff turned and signaled me to follow him into the kitchen. "Why are you here?" he asked. "Don't you know that what is past is past? I am dead and only waiting to be buried. I am ready for the grave. Are you? You had better be if you cross me."

From her position near the sink, Esther, his wife, clucked her teeth. "Louis," she said, "be nice, Louis."

Louis thought about that. Then he raised a glass of wine to his lips and polished it off. Suddenly, he got up from the chair and walked back into the living room. When he returned he was carrying a softball bat and a ball. He was one of the all-time great softball players, too, and it was only after making the switch from that sport that he became a $100,000 baseball property.

"Do you see that ball?" he said. "Take it out of the box and look at it. Do you see who signed it? That is the President of the United States, Lyndon B. Johnson. I got that when they put me into the Softball Hall of Fame. They wanted me to send my shoes to them, but I wouldn't do it. I had no shoelaces for them. It would have been a disgrace. I sent them my glove instead."

Novikoff sat there now, staring at the softball which had been handed back to him. His expression became contorted by the effort to hold back the tears that had appeared so unexpectedly on his cheeks.

"They are holding a benefit for me soon in Long Beach." he said. "They are holding it for me, the Mad Russian, the man who made them. They are holding it for me . . . and it makes me so ashamed."

He looked up at his wife, still standing near the sink. There were tears in her eyes now, too.

"Yes, Momma, that is right. I am ashamed. I am a man and this is what I have come to. All I have left now is pride."

The mood of depression vanished as quickly as it had appeared. Like a character out of Dostoevsky or Gogol, Novikoff was on his way back up.

"I am still a strong man," he said. "This is my family in this house and they are what I care about. We have much love here and because of that we are strong. What do I care about the rest? Next week we go to the benefit game and they will present me with my trophy. It will be a great day for us, and we will walk with our heads up. Isn't that right, Momma? Isn't that right?"

Mrs. Novikoff nodded nervously and managed a little smile while biting her lower lip.

"Yes, Louis," she said, "it will be wonderful . . . just like the old days with the Cubs."

Novikoff's eyes flashed again at that.

"What does anyone remember about the old days with the Cubs?" he said, almost shouting. "What does Leo Durocher know? But I know and I don't need Leo Durocher. You know who are my friends? George Raft is my friend, Joe E. Brown is my friend. With them as friends I do not need all these other people. 'Be proud. Lou,' George Raft told me. 'Be proud and never bend your knees to any man.'"

"But Louie," his wife said softly. "You haven't seen Mr. Raft since you played with the Cubs, and that was more than twenty-five years ago. And Mr. Brown is dead."

201

"That's right. Momma." Louis replied with a wily grin. "But remember it. If I ever really need a friend, George Raft will be there."

Novikoff spent four seasons with the Cubs during World War II and though he was a decent hitter—he batted .300 in 1942—his problems in the outfield shortened his career. Famous for his eccentricities, Novikoff was afraid the Wrigley Field ivy was poisonous and once tried to steal third with the bases loaded because "I got such a good jump on the pitcher." He died in 1970 at the age of fifty-four.

Doug Plank Leaves a Lasting Impression

DAVID ISRAEL

Chicago Tribune December 3, 1979

TAMPA—The big stars, the naturals, they do not always understand Doug Plank, the unnatural.

The stars, they cruised through high school, drove Cadillacs in college, and sauntered into the National Football League where the Mercedes were waiting, all deified and desired, flamboyant first-round draft choices with fabulous reputations.

Doug Plank, he struggled through high school, played second-string at Ohio State, and staggered into the NFL, all gritty and gutty, a 12th-round draft choice with no reputation at all.

Plank's problem was to make an impression when he came into the Chicago Bears training camp in 1975. Very quickly, he discovered that the only way to do that was, well, make an impression. In somebody's helmet, in somebody's chest, in somebody's back, in just about any obstacle that got in his way.

"Jack Pardee was a new coach in a rebuilding program then, and if the veterans weren't producing, he got rid of them," Plank said Sunday. "He loved people who hit and I wanted to be loved, so I went around hitting everybody I could."

Five years later, Plank has not quit. He still is the kamikaze pilot who completes his mission successfully and manages somehow to get home and to another assignment the next week. Jack Pardee is gone to Washington, and Doug Plank is now Neill Armstrong's beloved free safety, but that does not mean helmets, chests, backs, or goal posts are any safer if they get in Doug Plank's way.

Sunday afternoon, those helmets, chests, backs, and goal posts belonged to the Tampa Bay Buccaneers. The Bucs were supposed to be doing things like beating the Chicago Bears and winning the NFC's Central Division and celebrating with champagne and thinking about what it is going to be like, being the upstart team in the NFL playoffs.

Instead, they are sitting around at this very moment wondering how a Chicago defense managed to so thoroughly command the flow of the game that the Bears beat the Bucs 14–0, even while their offense averaged just 1.1 yards per pass, 3.1 yard per rush, and punted for 191 yards more than it gained.

What happened is that cornerbacks Allan Ellis and Terry Schmidt covered the sidelines flawlessly, while Plank and strong safety Gary Fencik took care of the middle tenaciously.

What happened is they discouraged the pass by intercepting five of them, and denied the run by cutting down most sweeps before they could develop, and dominated a game as few defensive backfields have.

They made the game's most compelling and dramatic plays. Dazzling broken field runs by Schmidt, Ellis, and Fencik, whose interception returns were the Bears' longest gains. Stunning hits and startling near-misses by Plank, who was unquestionably the most entertaining player on the field.

He was the game's little big man. He played with the ferocity of Butkus, the intensity of Nitschke, and the hostility of Schmidt. Sam Huff once bit Jim Taylor on the leg. Using his own body as a mobile skewer, Doug Plank tried to turn any number of Bucs—including Isaac Hagins, Morris Owens, and Ricky Bell—into football player-en-brochette.

It was not football by the gentlemanly Marquis of Queensbury rules that are in effect today, but Johnny Blood wouldn't have minded it, and it sure did discourage the Bucs from doing anything hostile to the Bears like scoring a point or two.

It was not free-safety play as we have come to expect it, the elegant, ball-hawking ballet of the lithesome Paul Krauses and Willie Woods and

Jake Scotts and Cliff Harrises and Jimmy Pattons, but it did make you pay attention when Plank's body went flying over a pileup or skidding into a tangle of players.

Apparently, some of the Bucs noticed.

"After the game, Ricky Bell complained to me about Doug," Gary Fencik said. "And a lot of other players were telling him that he better keep his head on a swivel. But the way Doug Williams was overthrowing his receivers, with a guy like Plank in the middle, they're going to catch their lunch."

And some of the Bears noticed, too.

"Please don't get me started on that subject," Alan Page said, when he was asked about Plank. "A lot of what he does is unnecessary."

Plank, however, does not believe that. He has knocked himself out 15 times, but no one else has. He has survived for five years with guys telling him to keep his head on a swivel—including some of his own teammates—and he plans to survive for many more. Playing this way got him here, and he figures it will keep him here.

"The thing I couldn't get out of my mind the whole game was that they had champagne waiting for them in the locker room," Doug Plank said. "That's what kept me going all afternoon."

Into helmets, chests, and backs.

And for Doug Plank, the unnatural, that was only natural. Even if the big stars like Ricky Bell do not understand.

Blood, Sweat, Tears, and Worse at the Finish Line

CAROL SLEZAK

Chicago Sun-Times October 25, 1999

"Better get him down, he's been throwing up all over himself."

This was where they came afterward. Often after completing the 26.2-mile course. Sometimes not. Sometimes nauseated, sometimes not. But always wrapped in their shiny silver Mylar blankets to ward off the chills. And always walking stiff-legged, like mummies. Those that were still able to walk, that is.

Some 200 yards south, you could see the rainbow of balloons over the finish line. But inside the fence that surrounded the medical compound, the Chicago Marathon seemed a million miles distant. The all-volunteer staff—doctors, nurses, students and the like—were all business.

Save for a quick tour beforehand, I wasn't allowed in either of the white tents inside the compound. The smaller tent was for physical therapy. The huge tent was for all other medical care. Inside it, some 100 cots lined either side of an aisle. I saw intravenous bags. I saw stethoscopes and other medical gizmos and crates filled with medical supplies. Out back I counted 10 ambulances, ready to go to whenever and wherever a runner might need help.

I also saw enough bananas to feed the apes at Brookfield Zoo for weeks. And I saw gallons of juice and coffee, although the coffee seemed to be more for hand-warming than drinking, thanks to a temperature in the 40s.

My guide, a non-medic, reminded me that the medical staff was there to heal.

"They don't need to be bothered by the likes of you," he said.

I nodded. When I initially tried to enter Fort Med I was told politely that only medical personnel were allowed inside. After learning an old Girl Scout badge for massage therapy didn't qualify me as medical personnel, I tried a different approach. Never underestimate the power of begging.

My guide, who has worked in the medical tent at many Chicago marathons, told me not to expect much action.

"Lots of chafing," he said. "Vaseline."

He brought me outside the medical tent and laid some ground rules.

"You can't talk to anyone," he said. "And you can't go in the tent. But you can sit outside the tent and watch the injured come in."

And come in they did. Not at first. By 8:30 a.m., word came that only two runners were down, and one had refused medical help. By 9:10, there were only seven slight injuries. But around 9:45, things started getting real. There were four patients in the medical tent, all with injured ankles.

And outside the compound, things were heating up, too.

A helicopter hovered. I surmised it was for television, to show the first runners crossing the finish line. But as it roared overhead and as the wounded became more numerous, I felt as if I were in an episode of "MASH."

Shortly after that, Khalid Khannouchi crossed the finish line in world-record time. And the medical staff became extremely busy. Some volunteers raced to the finish line with wheelchairs for those whose bodies wouldn't allow them to take one more step. Others waited by the entrance to lead the walking wounded inside.

Two elite runners walked slowly and stiffly into the tent, leaning heavily on the volunteers who were supporting them. The runners' mouths were covered with white crust. They looked like corpses. They were asked if they were OK. They could only nod.

A wheelchair participant rolled to a stop outside the gate. She sipped some liquid. Her eyes were glazed. She put her head down. She stayed that way, unable to move, for 20 minutes.

A dispatcher's voice was heard over a walkie-talkie: "A swollen ankle? Tell him to get on the drop-out bus. We can only handle medical emergencies now."

The dispatcher was heard again, this time to say that a runner was convulsing.

An unconscious runner, strapped to a board on a cart, was driven in.

A man with a bloody face was wheeled in. He held his arm and grimaced.

A man, supported on either side by volunteers, walked slowly to the tent. He was crying. "I'm just cold, I'm just cold," he whimpered.

A man, pale as tissue paper, was wheeled in, whispering, "Oxygen, oxygen."

A woman limped toward the tent. She stopped to pose for a victory picture. She smiled for her friend's camera.

In the next instant, she started sobbing.

And so it continued, a parade of pain.

There was no way of telling for certain if these folks, the ones who came from the direction of the finish line, had completed the marathon, but I suspect nearly all of them had.

On their faces? Exhaustion. Disorientation. But mostly, pain. Pain accompanied by glassy eyes.

A most disconcerting combination.

Yet I don't question why they ran the marathon. There's no bigger athletic challenge for the human body, or for a human being. I am wondering something, though.

Will they ever run another?

Darren Pang Measures Up as a Goalie

TERRY BOERS

Chicago Sun-Times March 6, 1988

The first time Montreal defenseman Larry Robinson saw Darren Pang, he turned to the Hawks' Doug Wilson.

"Where's the other half of your goalie?" Robinson asked.

The telling of the story turns the 5–5 Pang's smile to high beam. Even on this day when the Hawks have been put through a grueling practice, after which Pang can't find one of his socks, he is outgoing and pleasant, Mr. Tiny Bubbles.

"That has to be one of the better ones," says the 24-year-old rookie, who has become the Hawks' shot stopper as well as the darling of the Stadium crowds. "I've heard a lot of them."

That's no small wonder.

I can't help but think that Pang–"Spanky" to his teammates—looks more like a guy who should be getting a leg up for the sixth race at Sportsman's Park rather than someone who has been playing a winning game of Pang pong with the NHL's top guns.

Wouldn't you guess that every shot must look like a Mack puck coming at Pang?

But then people always have doubted Pang, dating back to the days when he became a goalie at 6.

"They used to score on me by shooting the puck over my head," Pang recalls. "I couldn't even jump up and hit my head on the (4-foot-high) crossbar."

Then there was one Betty Burrows, Pang's sixth-grade science teacher in Ottawa. Particularly disturbed by a Pang report that seemed to be written in an unknown language, she asked Pang what he intended to make of himself.

"I'm going to play in the NHL," Pang answered.

The flabbergasted schoolmarm had no reply.

"I don't think anyone had the heart to tell me they thought I was too small," Pang says.

Despite acquiring what Pang terms "a pretty fair reputation" in the Canadian junior leagues, he found himself undrafted by an NHL team at 18, his first year of eligibility, and again at 19.

The Hawks finally signed him as a free agent in August, 1984, although Pang says they had no intention of ever bringing him to Chicago.

"They thought they were going to get that Czech goalie (Dominik Hasek) at the time," Pang says. "But I was so happy to get a contract that didn't faze me one bit."

Pang made stops in Milwaukee, Nova Scotia and Saginaw, playing in just one NHL game, a 4–1 loss to the Minnesota North Stars in February, 1985.

"I was doing the little things wrong," Pang says, pun intended. "There's an adjustment period for every young goalie."

One of the many things Pang had to do was learn to stop being so "hyper" before games. As a kid, he was such a bundle of frayed nerve endings that he would spend the day firing pucks or tennis balls off the walls of his living room.

"My mother wouldn't say too much," Pang says. "But I'd be worn out by Christmas."

Another obstacle Pang overcame were the superstitions often associated with goalies.

Who'll ever forget former Hawk goalie Glenn Hall's penchant for throwing up before games?

Certainly not Hawk fans, who, in recent seasons, have found themselves following that same ritual after games.

"I'd worry about what I ate, how I ate it, how I'd drink my milk, which glove I'd put on first, how I'd tape my stick," Pang says. "I was headed for that rubber room and it had nothing to do with pucks."

That much done, it was the arrival of coach Bob Murdoch before this season that really opened the net for Pang.

Where Bob Pulford, a staunch traditionalist, had sizable concerns about Pang, Murdoch cared about playing a man short, but not a short man.

Pang has rewarded Murdoch's faith with a 16–16–1 record, a 3.63 goals-against average and a saves percentage of .898, third-best in the NHL.

"I'm pleased with the way things have gone," Pang says. "I'd like to play here 10 years."

So go ahead and say it.

Things are looking up for Darren Pang.

Pang's playing career with the Blackhawks lasted just two seasons. He later became a popular television broadcaster.

209

Doug Atkins
A Study in Pride and Pain

RICK TELANDER

Chicago Sun-Times January 1, 2007

KNOXVILLE, Tenn.–I drive slowly past the small red-brick house on the narrow, winding road in the hills outside town.

I pull into a driveway a quarter-mile farther on. A dog barks somewhere. It's a few days before Christmas.

The dog stops. Silence.

I turn the car around, drive past the house again.

I don't know.

The house has its curtains drawn. There are two old cars in the carport, one of them very old, I'm guessing 30, 40 years. Fins. Rusty.

There's a wooden wheelchair ramp that looks weathered and unused leading to the front door. A "No Smoking" sign in the front-door window. Two tiny American flags on the wall next to the carport.

No lights on. No decorations.

Doug Atkins, 76, the legendary Hall of Fame defensive end for the Bears, lives here.

"I don't want to see anybody," he had told me during one of our phone conversations. People had their minds made up about a lot of stuff, he said. Predetermined. The country was going to hell. No middle class. Only rich and poor.

I didn't need to ask which side he fell on.

"I'm doing OK," he had said. "I cracked my hip awhile back. Never got well since then. I can walk with a cane, but it's getting rough. I got sick, and I've been poisoned from some of the medicine they gave me—lead poisoning. They don't put out the truth about medicines. So many crooks in the country nowadays—politicians, oil companies, pharmaceutical companies, lobbyists. A lot of people are worse off than I am. But I don't need to see any reporters."

Everybody knows that football is a rough game, that the NFL is the roughness polished bright and turned into performance art, the brutality into religion, the cracking bones into the percussive soundtrack that suits our times.

But not many know the toll the game takes when the players themselves, the artists, have left the stage.

A shocking number of the men, starting sometimes well before middle age, begin to limp, then hobble, then stop moving much at all.

Dementia, mood disorders, osteoarthritis, surgery, more surgery, pain—the wheel of football repercussion spins and spins.

And often, the longer a man played—meaning the better player he was—the worse his debilitation.

Doug Atkins played 17 years in the NFL, the best 12 for the Bears.

In that time, the long-legged, hickory-tough 6–8, 260-pounder did things that hadn't been done before on the gridiron. A scholarship basketball player at Tennessee as well as an All-America football player, Atkins sometimes jumped over blockers like a hurdler vaulting rolling logs.

He went out for track at Tennessee and won the Southeastern Conference high jump, clearing 6–6. In the NFL, he went to eight Pro Bowls from 1958 to 1966.

All that talent came together on the football field like a rainbow palette.

George Halas, Atkins' coach with the Bears and the man who helped found the NFL, said of the giant from Humboldt, Tenn., "There never was a better defensive end."

But now there's the embarrassment the game has exacted.

Mike Ditka hosts a golf tournament each year wherein Ditka and sponsors earmark money for Hall of Famers in need.

Sometimes it's a payout for surgical procedures or medicine.

Sometimes it's a wheelchair ramp.

One time it was for a tombstone.

"It's pitiful," says Ditka, tearing into the NFL's stingy pension plan for old-timers, the NFL players union and all PR aspects of the league. "Rip 'em all. I don't care."

The league's frugal pension plan is complicated, but it's simplified nicely by the fact that the veterans die at a swift pace.

There's a new pension agreement being put into place, but as of last year, NFL players who had reached age 55 might typically get between $200 and $425 a month.

Enough for aspirin, for sure.

While the current Bears swagger down the road to success and the NFL wallows in money, the old men who helped build the brand suffer in silence, often lame, often nearly destitute, their pride too great to allow pity.

Atkins had mesmerized me when I had asked him, please, just for me, to detail his injuries.

The groin pull that tore muscle off the bone, leaving a "hole" in his abdomen. "My fault," he said.

The big toe injury. The broken collarbone. The leg that snapped at the bottom of a pile. ("I got to the sideline, and it didn't feel right.")

The biceps that tore in half, Atkins' arm hanging limply.

"It's just a show muscle," he said, explaining why he never got it fixed.

"I see these old football players," says Dr. Victoria Brander, the head of Northwestern University's Arthritis Institute, "and every joint is ruined— their toes, ankles, knees, hips, fingers, elbows, shoulders. The supporting structure in the joints is gone. Their spines are collapsed. I see one former star who is bent like a 'C.'

"But they are noble. They played their game because they believed in something. They were warriors. They never complain."

I have gone past Atkins' house four times now. I take a deep breath.

I dial his number on my cell phone.

His wife answers and gives him the phone. I just happen to be in the area, I say. Would he mind if I stopped by, maybe for a minute or two, on the way to the airport?

"Damn it, why do you all keep bothering me?" Atkins yells into the receiver. "I told you I was sick!"

And then the line is dead.

"These guys don't need much," Ditka will say later in barely controlled fury. "Your best players? Ever? Why can't the league give them enough to live out their lives in dignity? Is that so f—ing hard?"

I drive on, feeling terrible, feeling cruel. I never should've imposed on Doug Atkins. On his pride.

In the midst of our bounty, I feel lost.

The Chicago Football Cardinals
Fabric of a Champion

BILL GLEASON

The Daily Southtown

"We call them the Carpets because they get beat every week." (Wry comment by Joseph W. Gleason in a letter delivered to his son's foxhole in France, late autumn 1944.)

Actually, historically and hysterically, the name of the National Football League team was Card-Pitt.

This was a merger of two dismal teams, the Chicago Cardinals and the Pittsburgh Steelers, a consolidation made necessary by manpower demands of that spasm of history remembered as World War II.

Neither the Cardinals nor the Steelers had sufficient able-bodied players to field a decent team. "Merging made us twice as bad as we had been by ourselves," Arthur Rooney, owner of the Steelers, has said.

The Carpets were beaten 10 times that season. They played 10 games.

But the merger brought together two of the most fascinating characters in sports history. Rooney still is with us. Charlie Bidwill, owner of the Cardinals, has been gone much too long.

And so have the Chicago Cardinals. They played their last game in Chicago in 1959, moved to St. Louis, and now the owner of the Cardinals, another Bidwill, is talking about moving again.

You can find Cardinals fans even now—Chicago Cardinals fans, not St. Louis Cardinals fans—in taverns on the South Side and across the border in Whiting, East Chicago, Hammond and Gary.

You can find them, too, in South Bend and Mishawaka because so many legendary Cardinals came out of Notre Dame.

And Notre Dame gave professional football its first broadcasting analyst, Joe Boland, who had been an assistant coach for the Fighting Irish.

Notre Dame gave me—the Cardinals were my team and my father's team—Elmer Angsman.

Joe Namath, who likes to be liked, made a lot of enemies a few weeks ago, by knocking Angsman. And worse, by mispronouncing Elmer's name.

Doing color for television, but not doing it as gracefully as Boland did it, Broadway Joe pompously pontificated that Angsman could not do now what he did then.

What Elmer did then was run great distances on quick-opener plays. Namath, a nice man at heart, did not know what he was talking about.

Every time the ball was in Angsman's hands, every time, he was a threat to run downtown.

In 1947—mark that year now—Elmer was a halfback in the "Dream Backfield" with halfback Charlie Trippi, fullback Pat Harder, quarterback Paul Christman.

For Cardinals fans, that backfield was their dream because they had endured so many nightmares.

Charlie Bidwill shared those nightmares, but he didn't mind too much. Charlie also owned a piece of the Detroit Lions, a piece of the Chicago Bears. That's how the NFL was then.

While the war was on, while Bidwill and Rooney were laughing together as they watched Card-Pitt, Charlie gathered draft choices as squirrels gather nuts.

Appropriate because Charlie also gathered nuts. The postwar Cardinals may have been the most colorful NFL team of all time.

And they surely were the hardest drinking team. As one of the survivors said a few years ago, "We must lead the world in former NFL players who are in Alcoholics Anonymous."

Chester Noyes Bulger, tackle, insists that those Cardinals were the biggest, heaviest team ever.

The program weight for Angsman, one of the little guys, was 197 pounds. Fullback Harder was listed at 205, but he was very tough, and when the situation required, very nasty. And he probably weighed 225.

Those big, brawling Cardinals were Charlie Bidwill's surprise for the NFL and especially for his pal, George Halas, owner of the Bears.

After the war Charlie sprung his surprise.

Combining his squirreled-up draft choices with veterans home from the war, Bidwill had a potential champion.

But Charlie was not there to see his Cardinals win the league championship in 1947. He had died that spring of pneumonia. He was 51 years old.

This was the team South Siders had waited for since 1925, the first championship season.

In 1948 the Cardinals beat out the Bears again for the Western Division championship, but lost the title game to Philadelphia.

Had Charlie stayed around, the Cardinals might have become a dynasty. His successors destroyed his dream, and ours, and the nightmare years returned.

South Side fans blamed Halas for "driving the Cardinals out of town" after the '59 season. Halas, envisioning what television would mean for football, did want Chicago for himself, but there was more to it than that.

The Cardinals left because of bad management and apathy. Too many fans who loved the team rarely bothered to attend a game.

This is the 40th anniversary of that championship year. Some of us anticipated a celebration, a big party to reunite players and fans.

But nobody bothered.

It figures.

The Wimp at Work

BOB GREENE

Chicago Sun-Times August 19, 1971

The U.S. Open Pocket Billiards championships were about to begin, and the location was not a neighborhood pool hall, but a fancy downtown hotel. Many of the contestants were young, and they were dressed in colorful clothing like pro golfers. "No, I don't know where the Wimp is," the man from the tournament committee said. "I guess he's kind of a loner after all these years, and I hear he didn't even show up at the players' meeting last night. Usually he just stays to himself."

They weren't really thinking about the Wimp, who is known by that name in poolroom circles and whose real name is Luther Lassiter. The players were busy warming up in the Crystal Room of the Sheraton-Chicago. The room was bright, and it was just a few feet away from the Grand Ballroom, where the tournament matches were being played. The word was out that ABC television's "Wide World of Sports" program was coming later in the week, and the new breed of pool players were anxious at the thought of appearing on national television.

So many of them are new to this, are the kind of men who took jobs as salesmen and teachers during the week and play pocket billiards as a sideline. And while they were scurrying around the hotel, Luther Lassiter, age 52, pool player from Elizabeth City, North Carolina, was climbing out of bed in his room.

"I couldn't sleep last night," Lassiter said. "I'm getting a damn cold and it's going to take two or three days to break itself down. So I walked around the city. This town certainly has done some changing."

The only world he knows is pool. He has given up three-quarters of his stomach to an ulcer patch job and he has a bad gallbladder and his eyes are losing much of their ability to perceive depth. He has very little in common with the kind of situation where pool tables are in basements and suburban bowling alleys and championships are played in hotels for television audiences. But the tournament was offering $5,000 to the men's champion. So the Wimp was in Chicago.

In the main ballroom, the women were playing. Lassiter had no interest in a woman's pool tournament, especially one in which a 13-year-old girl was one of the strongest contenders. The ballroom had four pool tables set up, with risers on all sides for the paying fans. Scores were flashed up on screens behind each table.

It was not until the first round of men's competition had begun that Lassiter went downstairs. He took a look into the main room. A young guy named Pete Margo was winning his match. Margo was wearing two-toned shoes with raised heels, a dark blue shirt with a white tie, and a wide-lapeled windowpane-pattern jacket. Lassiter took one look and went over to the warm-up room.

He removed the cue from its ancient alligator-skin case and started to shoot. He looked wonderful. He wore a dark gray suit with pants that drooped over his shiny black tie-shoes. His white shirt was pulled out near the waist. A skinny blue brocade tie was yanked down enough for him to open his white shirt at the top. He chewed on an antacid tablet.

A man with a Polaroid asked to take a picture of the Wimp, and asked him to smile. He went on shooting pool. "Smile and laugh and giggle and you'll have a heart attack," he muttered as he circled the table. "Everyone knows that."

You did not have to know a thing in the world about pocket billiards to watch Lassiter work and realize what you were seeing. Old, yes. But the way he moved with the cue, effortlessly flicking the balls into the pockets, was poetry. His short-cropped white hair dully reflected the fluorescent lights. There may have been young men in the tournament who are better technicians at the game of pocket billiards than the Wimp. But one look at Lassiter and you never had to look for a pool player again.

"Most of the players 1 guess have jobs," Lassiter said as he knocked a ball into the side pocket. "Or they own pool halls. There are some of us who don't, though. I'm broke. I've won more tournaments by luck, and I'm still broke."

His people were beginning to gather. Milwaukee Lou and Cue Ball Kelley and the little men with cigars and gray skin who look like they have never seen the sun. Men who feel a little uncomfortable playing pool in a room where people have danced to orchestras on other nights.

He kept working, then went into the big room and sat to await his match. He was to play another old one, Richard Riggie, called "Socks" because he wears droopy white anklets in snappy shoes.

"He's a hard one for me to beat," said the Wimp. "He's a sly one, and he's even older that I am, but he looks 15 years younger."

The tournament was a double elimination affair, meaning that a man has to lose twice before being knocked out for good. But no one wants to lose in the first round because that means to reach the finals you cannot afford to make a single mistake from that point on.

The young players watched Lassiter respectfully as he waited. "I caught this damn cold on the plane," he said. "I wish I didn't have to ride those things. I hate to fly, the only time I want to fly is when I'm going toward heaven."

Lassiter went out and once again played a game of pool on 4 1/2-by-

9-foot table featuring a slate bed covered with a very fine-grade felt cloth. It took three hours, and he was behind much of the time; he finished it with a run of 16 to win 150 to 110.

He removed his rimless bifocals. "I guess I need new ones again," he said. "I'm not getting any depth perception at all. I just got a new pair six months ago."

The natural question was: If he couldn't really see the length of the table, what did he use to spot the balls?

"Forty years," he said. "I use 40 years of doing this."

There Were Lots of Clowns, but Only One Andy

RICHARD ROEPER

Chicago Sun-Times September 25, 1995

One afternoon in 1960, a fun-loving South Sider named Andrew Rozdil-sky showed up at his bowling league in a homemade clown suit, just for snicks. He had so much fun clowning around and cracking up his buddies, he decided to keep the outfit on when he went to a White Sox game that night at old Comiskey Park.

And thus Andy the Clown was born.

He was Chicago's clown. Every city had a Bozo, but only Chi-town had Andy the Clown. Stupid bowler hat, red nose blinking, face smeared with white greasepaint, pajama-like costume festooned with 508 polka-dots, and of course the voice:

"Go youuuuuuuuuuuuuuuuuuuuu White Sox!"

"Come aaaaaaaaaaaaaaaaaaaaaaahhhhhhhhhhnnnnnnnnnn Bud-deee Braaaaaaaaaaaadford!"

This was in the days when sporting events came without soundtracks and audiovisual displays, before the franchises felt the need to fill every single break in the action with canned music and furry-costumed gymnasts and wriggling cheerleaders and audience-participation stunts. (Well, the Sox did have a lot of that when Bill Veeck owned the team, but that's another story.) What was cool about Andy was that he just showed up, and the White Sox just sort of tolerated him. He wasn't a graduate of Mascot School, which is a real place.

For 30 years Andy rattled around the bowels of that ballpark like some wacky old uncle, filling the empty moments with his infamous bellowing cheers, posing for pictures with thousands of kids and hundreds of smirky, inebriated semi-adults, cheerfully acknowledging both the good wishes and verbal abuse.

Oh yeah, we liked to make fun of Andy the Clown, just as we always called those Andy Frain ushers "Andy," har de har har. You weren't a true Sox fan if you didn't engage in some light mocking of the Andys Frain and Clown.

If Andy knew he was sometimes the object of derision, he never let it bother him. He preferred to talk about the countless appearances he made at hospitals, and how people always lit up when they saw Andy the Clown.

He was harmless. He didn't hurt anybody.

When the White Sox moved into the new Bloomingdale's-style park, they told Andy it was a perfect time to retire, and they gave him a plaque. The next morning he was interviewed on Jonathon Brandmeier's radio program, and he shamelessly said he wished the Sox had presented him with something a little more memorable, "like a Zenith TV or something." Before the show was over, listeners had donated two television sets, a La-Z-Boy recliner, a watch for his daughter, service for a busted stereo, even an offer of trees for his front yard. (Andy declined; he already had a tree.)

A while later Andy was in costume for a pay-per-view New Year's Eve special at Steve Dahl's house. Midgets drunkenly cavorted around him as he embraced a stripper and helped bring in the new year.

In the first few years of the new park, Andy would occasionally show up, out of costume (except for the bowler hat) but still in character. He'd make himself known by launching into his famous bellow, amazing the fans with his elongated tributes to Frank Thomas or Robin Ventura, just as he had done with names like Pete Ward and Gary Peters in the 1960s. He'd also pose for pictures—if you tipped him a buck or two.

"The White Sox didn't like that," Andy told me in 1993, the day after the Sox had clinched the American League West championship. "They said I was welcome to come to the park as a fan, but not to ask for tips. What am I supposed to do? A clown's got to make a buck."

He didn't go to many games after that. But he kept on clowning, doing those appearances for hospitals and charities, making the red nose blink and filling the day with his big fun voice.

"I'm 76 years old, and thank God I'm in good health due to years of clowning," Andy said to me not long ago.

Last Thursday night, Andrew Rozdilsky collapsed in his South Side home. He died at Holy Cross Hospital. He was 77. If he ever gave you a smile when you were out at the old ballpark, send him a prayer or a good thought today.

THE REAL WORLD

Jimmy Cannon famously referred to the sports section as the newspaper's toy department, but there are occasions when the sports columnist must put the fun and games aside.

Sometimes, it is because of where he is. At the Munich Olympics, which are suddenly interrupted by an unspeakable act of terror. Robert Markus responded by driving to Dachau. Or at the 1989 World Series when an earthquake strikes. Ray Sons wrote three columns for the *Sun-Times* from San Francisco, each of them as brilliant as the one reprinted here. (Notice, by the way, that he never mentioned why he was in town.) Ray is also—and here I am speaking for many of us who worked with or for him—as nice a man as I ever met in the newspaper business.

Sometimes, it is because of where he has been. From his vantage point at the 1994 Winter Olympics in Lillehammer, Norway, the *Tribune's* Philip Hersh, one of only a handful of full-time Olympic sportswriters in the country, remembered an earlier Games in Sarajevo, which was then undergoing a merciless bombing and whose athletes were concerned with far more than winning medals.

Sometimes, it is because of where he is from. Skip Bayless was raised in Oklahoma City and when, several years after the bombing of its Federal Building in 1994 killed 168 people, his editor told him to go home and write about it, he went.

Sometimes, it is because of what he has done. Mike Imrem's tour of duty in Vietnam gave him a unique perspective on a Super Bowl being played as the Gulf War was about to begin.

Sometimes, it is because he needs a reality check after dealing with the egos and salaries of so many modern athletes. Bob Verdi traveled to South Bend to look in on the Special Olympics.

Sometimes, it is because athletes have something they want to tell him that is far removed from the games they play. Barry Rozner listened to the hair-raising stories of the Blackhawks' Sheldon Kennedy and Theo Fleury.

Sometimes, it is because he needs to pause and remember, which is what Taylor Bell did twenty-five years after the best high school basketball player in the country was gunned down on a Chicago street by a teen-ager who didn't know him.

And sometimes, it is because he feels the world is spinning out of control and, inadequate though it may be, he asserts the columnist's prerogative to try to come to terms with it on the printed page. That is what Rick Morrissey did after 9/11.

After he has finished, he moves on, sometimes grimly satisfied, often still despairing. There is another athlete to cover, another game to see. They will print another paper tomorrow. The toy department remains open for business.

Slaying of Israelis Recalls Nightmare at Dachau

ROBERT MARKUS

Chicago Tribune September 6, 1972

MUNICH, Sept. 5—I went to Dachau today. It is not what I had planned to do. Today was going to be a light day on the Olympic schedule, and we had planned to take a leisurely drive up Germany's romantic road through Augsburg and up to Rothenbert. We would see castles and sunlight through the trees and old churches with tall spires and cattle grazing in the lush grass.

But we turned on the radio and were plunged into a world of horror. The American Forces Network was telling of the insane murder by Arab terrorists of two Israeli Olympic team athletes in their Olympic Village quarters. So, when we came to where the road forks to Augsburg I kept the car pointed straight to Munich.

But halfway there I said to my wife, "We're not going to the village right now. We're going to Dachau." She didn't have to ask me why. In the 12 years between 1933 and 1945, when Dachau was transformed from a little country town to a dread place whose very name evoked terror, 31,951 prisoners died in the concentration camp there.

They were not all Jews, but they were all human beings, victims of the barbaric notion that murder is the final solution to any problem.

The main entrance to the concentration camp stands about eight miles from the building in the Olympic Village where the two Israelis were butchered just before dawn. It opens on an enormous gravel courtyard where it takes little imagination to envision a blizzardy winter morning with thousands of half-dead, half-naked men standing in ranks to answer roll.

On the right is a reconstructed barracks, built to accommodate 200 prisoners but in actuality crammed at its peak with 1,600. The crematoriums are beyond, and to the right of that and to the left stands what must be the world's most grisly museum, containing photos and memorabilia of that dozen years of infamy.

To tour the museum is to descend into hell with Roman Polanski as the guide. It begins peacefully enough, with photos of Hitler's rise to power.

Slowly the terror builds. There are pictures of prisoners at work, prisoners peering mournfully from their bunks, prisoners standing roll, prisoners tortured, prisoners murdered, prisoners committing suicide, gruesome medical experiments, and, one picture that tells it all, a mountainous pile of shoes taken from executed prisoners.

As I caught my breath and continued, I heard a man say, "This next room's even worse," and I told myself "it couldn't be," but it was.

There are pictures of the roundup of Europe's Jews and their deportation to extermination camps, ghastly scenes straight out of the newsreels of the summer of '45, of naked, skeletal corpses piled in grotesque heaps.

Then it hit me. It was a picture captioned simply: "On the Way to the Execution Chamber." It showed a young woman leading her four children down the road. Their faces were not visible but the smallest appeared to be about 2, a little girl, hunched forward against the wind, her mother's hand gently guiding her down the road to oblivion.

"I can't stand anymore of this," I said aloud, and I walked over into a corner and cried. My wife found me there and she was crying, too. We walked out into the sunlight and there were people talking, joking, laughing.

Maybe they have things in better perspective than I do. Maybe they know that was a long time ago, and people don't do that kind of thing to each other anymore.

Oh, but they do. It happened again this morning, the murder of the innocents, in full view of a world gathered for peaceful athletic congress.

It was one of the most infamous deeds committed in the annals of mankind. In ancient days, athletes were given safe conduct to the Olympic Games in times of war.

In the modern revival, the Games have simply been called off during the two World Wars. Never has a nation or a political force within a nation used the Games as a showcase for political terrorism.

It happened today, and the Olympic Games, which were too big to halt in 1936 when they were held in Berlin under Hitler's iron boot, have ground to a temporary halt.

I hope it is only temporary. Although the thought of going on is painful, the thought of giving in is unthinkable. It is unthinkable that a small band of murderers can disrupt the lives and aspirations of thousands of men and women, cancel plans that were a lifetime in the making.

For all the hypocrisy attendant to their celebration every four years the Olympics do offer a chance for men of every political persuasion to meet, compete, and mingle. I have seen Russians and Americans embrace each other after a competition, and East and West Germans warmly shake hands.

Let the Games go on, but for God's sake let the killing stop. Everywhere.

Eleven Israeli athletes and coaches were killed at Munich. Repeated requests over the years that the international Olympic movement honor their memory at the Games' opening ceremonies have been denied.

For Troops, Sports Provide a Strong Link to Home

MIKE IMREM

Arlington Heights Daily Herald January 27, 1991

TAMPA, Fla.—Clearly, an historic relationship has been developing between Super Bowl XXV and the Persian Gulf crisis.

Not so clear is what that relationship should be.

To play or not to play, that will be the question right up to today's scheduled 5:18 p.m. starting time.

The NFL's annual party was canceled. Peripheral affairs were scaled down. Heightened security turned this into a paranoid, guilt-ridden, war-haunted event.

Still, I remain steadfast that this Bills-Giants game should be played, mostly because it reminds me of the 1968 World Series.

I learned back then that home isn't just a place to a GI serving in a combat zone, it's everything—his goal, his dream, what he lives for, what he's afraid he'll die for.

In May of 1968, I was assigned to serve a year with the U.S. Army's 10th Psychological Operations Battalion in Can Tho, South Vietnam, 80 miles south of Saigon in the Mekong Delta.

Quickly it became apparent my primary links to home were mail call, reel-to-reel rock and roll tapes . . . and sports.

The Stars and Stripes newspaper was a treasure because it provided news from home on the likes of antiwar demonstrations at the Democratic convention, RFK's assassination . . . and sports.

Armed Forces Radio served a similar purpose by blaring the sounds of Credence Clearwater, the Doors, the Stones, the Beatles, Jimi Hendrix, Janis Joplin . . . and sports.

Sports, sports, sports.

Piped into us were the Army-Navy football game, the Rose Bowl, the Super Bowl, the World Series and selected other events.

They were in perspective more than any other time in my life, because listening from a war zone made it difficult to exaggerate the meaning of games.

But they were important just the same as entertaining diversions. If presidents believe in wartime that the continuation of sports is vital to Americans over here, just imagine how important they are to Americans over there.

Home was especially far away for guys like me, draftees who were as close to being real soldiers as Can Tho was to being Club Med.

I was a reluctant participant at best, scared to death for my life much like many of our people in the Persian Gulf are now.

Mostly, the Vietnam war for those of us on the back lines consisted of tense monotony, a drone of tedious assignments and numbing sameness.

It's hard for me to grasp this now, but back there in relatively secure Can Tho, it was almost a rush when the Viet Cong lobbed a few mortar shells our way and verified our existence.

October of '68 was halfway through my year's tour of duty, tucked between the anxiety of a new experience and the anticipation of going home.

Into this context burst the World Series.

The time difference between Midwest America and Southeast Asia meant the climactic seventh game started in the middle of the Vietnam night—2, 3, maybe 4 a.m.

I climbed up to the roof of our quarters and, in the dark, listened on Armed Forces Radio as Mickey Lolich outpitched St. Louis' Bob Gibson to win the world championship for Detroit.

It's impossible to explain how important that contact with home was. You had to be there, maybe.

Anyway, I imagine sports always have been comforting to Americans serving in foreign wars—including right now in Saudi Arabia.

It never crossed my mind back then, back there, that it was inappropriate for games to be played back home.

I just wanted to find out the final scores, argue with a buddy from St. Louis about whether the Cubs were better than the Cardinals and maintain that sports link to home.

Today I figure our troops in the Middle East want to debate the merits of the Giants and Bills, follow the Super Bowl on radio or TV and be reassured that sports still are here to come home to.

So this game shouldn't be canceled for our troops in the Middle East.

It should be played for them.

That's what the relationship between Super Bowl XXV and the Persian Gulf crisis should be.

They Teach You a Special Lesson

BOB VERDI

Chicago Tribune August 6, 1987

You drive here from a hot Chicago, and your car's air conditioning unit is spitting out blasts of warm blanks, and the toll gate jams just when you want to make some time, and you curse life's inconveniences.

It's not your day, you say, and then you see their faces, and you realize it's not supposed to be. It's their day, and it's their week, and if only they could have more days and weeks like these.

You come to the International Special Olympics on the University of Notre Dame campus expecting to feel sorrow for the 4,717 athletes, ages 8 to 83, from 70 different countries, but you wind up feeling humbled by the joy that pervades the place. You know that these people have been missing out on a lot of common pleasures since birth and will until they pass on, but you also realize that maybe you've been so swallowed up by running for airplanes that you've forgotten a few things, too, like what it means to hug someone for finishing eighth out of eight.

You walk into a hotel and there's a physically and mentally challenged kid in his track uniform scouring the lobby for any kind of souvenir that says Fighting Irish or Notre Dame on it. And you see the polite lady behind the desk give the kid a simple post card, and you see his eyes explode in glee, and even though he can't really say thank you, he can't say thank you enough. And you see the lady behind the desk, and you know that she's not tearing about the eyes now because she caught a cold.

You run into a Bill Hickey, who's the director of food services for the university and who has been serving up thousands and thousands of meals daily, and he tells you about the boy he met the other day, the boy from Ireland. Bill tells you that he asked the boy which part of Ireland he was from, north or south? And the boy looked at Bill and said, "What's the difference? We're all the same." And Bill wondered why they can't understand that back in Ireland, where the normal folk shoot at each other in the name of anger and politics.

And then you go out into the sunshine and realize what you've lost a handle on out there in the real world, the world of agents who lie and coaches who cheat and college presidents who sanction deceit and athletes who scream when their filet isn't cooked quite right. They staged an opening ceremony the other night, you're informed, and these athletes lined up at 5 o'clock in the broiling temperatures and weren't excused until 11 because ABC wanted to produce a delayed tape that was smashing, which it did and which it was, one night later.

Imagine, a guy from the network was saying, what it would have been like asking real athletes, the normal millionaires, to stand still that long for anything, except perhaps a free car or another commercial endorsement? But the kids, ages 8 to 83, gladly sweated it out in the bowels of the stadium, probably because they aren't dumb enough to complain. They've been sheltered, after all. They haven't learned how to hate or how to be ungrateful or how to practice hypocrisy. And in lieu of drugs, it seems, their narcotics are fresh air, love and companionship.

Mind you, Donna Sue Montgomery, 37, from Kentucky, came to win the 25-meter walk. But when the first-place time was announced as 6.7 seconds, and hers came over as 1 minute 41 seconds, it didn't seem to matter. She got into her wheelchair with a smile and headed over to receive her medal or ribbon, it didn't matter which. They all earn something, including David Diekow of Alaska, who had to be propped up by a volunteer—on vacation time—to accept his prize for fourth and the red rose, which the kid held high in a quivering hand. More than a sporting event, the International Special Olympics is an event, period.

You see a youngster dribbling a basketball toward the basket, an unmolested layup, a sure thing, and then you see him stop short to pick up a fallen opponent from the floor. The two points could wait, but not a helping hand. You see Geary Locke, 23, a local lad, crying because he finished third in his heat, crying because he figured his dad deserved a victory. His dad was Bill Locke, who, perhaps more than anyone else, brought the Games here. But Bill died of a massive hemorrhage three years ago, and Geary wasn't so sure Dad would be proud of him now.

"But I know his father is," said June Locke, Geary's mother. She was there Sunday night when Geary climbed the stairs of the stadium and lit the flame with the torch and said, "Dad, this is for you." And June Locke was there when Geary stopped crying Wednesday, which was when Sargent Shriver, the president of Special Olympics International, presented Geary that very torch to keep.

It was then that June Locke started to cry, because she's a special parent behind a special child. But there are lots of them, lots of special parents. You don't hear any of them shouting to kill the umpire, and you don't hear any of them browbeating a coach to get their son or daughter into the game, and you notice that even the reporters here have developed manners, keeping their microphones and ink-stained elbows out of each other's faces and away from participants' chins.

Must be that this isn't reality with all its attendant cynicism and cutthroat mentality. Must be that this is different, a friendlier spot than the Persian Gulf or the Iran-contra hearings or even the other Olympics, the one where amateurs take steroids to build their muscles and quiet cash to build their trust funds. Must be that this is purer than all the other forms of athletics that call themselves genuine.

"My son Chris is 16," says Sue Coffman, the Area Two Coordinator for Special Olympics, a woman who is doing it on adrenaline this week. "Like any mother, I wish that he was born normal. I wish that it didn't take him six years to learn how to tie his shoes. These children, many of them come here not only to compete, but to develop their sense of responsibility, to be able to tell time, to be able to pack their belongings, to be able to live in a dorm or with a strange family that has taken them in.

"Yes, I wish he was born normal, because every parent of a challenged child wonders down deep what will happen to them, who will take care of them when we die? Will they be okay? Will society look down on them, or will society, through events like these, learn to appreciate them? I wish, yes, but also I would not trade my Chris for any child on Earth. He's so good-hearted and so kind, and he was given to me by God for a reason. If it wasn't for Chris, I would never have gotten involved in something so wonderful as this. And, besides, you look at these kids smile and you wonder . . . what is normal?"

And you drive back to a hot Chicago, and you look through that toll gate now, because you are asking yourself the very same thing. Exactly who is handicapped here? Them or us?

An Earthquake That Brings Out the Best in So Many

RAY SONS

Chicago Sun-Times October 22, 1989

SAN FRANCISCO—Filip Isack, a stockbroker, was spending his third day as a volunteer in the Red Cross earthquake disaster center.

"I'm washing away all my sins," he said, "all the bad stocks I recommended."

The second-worst earthquake in our country's recorded history demonstrated anew the bonds that unite the human family.

As a Chicago dweller, I know we urban people can be unspeaking, cold, oblivious to others. Until disaster strikes.

After days of touring the quake devastation here and in Oakland, I can only pray we Chicagoans would be as kind to each other as the people here in the face of such an emergency.

The stories are legion.

Libbee Bell, an office manager, told me a stranger gave her and a friend the use of his apartment when they were left temporarily homeless.

Two days after the quake, an elderly woman ran up to Stuart Strother, a young resident of the area, embraced him and offered profuse thanks.

He had found her sitting in the dark street outside his apartment building in an area of collapsing buildings in the Marina district that terrible night.

She cried: "My daughter! My daughter!" Answering her pleas, he had dashed into her home to search for her daughter. It was a futile trip, because the woman was deranged by shock and did not remember her daughter was not home.

But the futility didn't diminish the selfless risk Strother took for her.

It would be easy to dismiss lightly the losses in the Marina district. It is an area of stylish homes, most built in the 1920s, that look like frosted cakes. Some, overlooking the Golden Gate Bridge and San Francisco Bay, surely were worth $1 million. Strother, who sells recording equipment, paid $1,000 a month for his one-bedroom apartment.

How can you feel sorry for people of such affluence, especially when you know they chose to live in houses built on sandy landfill that would quiver like gelatin in a major earthquake?

You can feel pity when you realize hundreds of these people are elderly and have lived here most of their lives. They bought these homes when they were cheaper, needed many years to pay off the mortgages, and now have lost everything.

President Bush flew over the Marina Middle School in a helicopter on his tour of the destruction Friday. If he had landed in the schoolyard of what has become the Marina district's main shelter, he would have seen a spectacle reminiscent of the Atlanta railway station in the film "Gone with the Wind."

Hundreds of temporarily homeless stood four to six abreast in a line that stretched more than 200 yards. They waited for hours to be issued cards they could use to pass police checkpoints to reach their homes.

The lucky received green cards that permitted them to go home and stay in structures engineers had judged safe. The less lucky received yellow cards that permitted them only an escorted visit of 15 minutes in which they would be allowed to rescue their most valuable possessions from homes set for demolition. If your card was red, you could not go home. Your doomed house was too risky to enter.

Volunteer Christine Carpenter, a law student, walked along the line, distributing cans of juice. Her 5-month-old baby was strapped to her back. She was spending every day in such kindness.

Why?

"Because I feel very lucky to be alive, and our house is fine."

Inside Marina Middle School, 400 people had spent the night, sleeping on donated sleeping bags. The Red Cross fed them.

Next to the long line of those waiting for the cards that would spell out their housing fate, the Salvation Army had set up racks of emergency clothing and bedding donated by San Franciscans. Anyone who needed it could just take it.

Major Charles Strickland, officer in charge, told them: "Help yourself. Don't be greedy."

Among the needy was Cynthia Morton, from a public housing project near Fisherman's Wharf. She stuffed bags with replacements for the clothing of her four children, ruined when pipes had broken and flooded their apartment.

Next to the school, a plumber had parked his truck and erected a sign offering free emergency repairs.

Cecelia McDonnell, handling public relations for the Red Cross, thought she understood why people were so generous.

"Everyone lives on the (San Andreas) fault," she said. "Everyone knows something is going to happen to California. Everyone volunteering realizes it was sheer luck they were not seriously affected."

Heartening as was all this service in relief of a catastrophe, I couldn't help but wonder why we didn't act like this all the time.

Remembering Sarajevo

PHILIP HERSH

Chicago Tribune February 11, 1994

LILLEHAMMER, Norway—It was in the oppressive heat of a Barcelona summer that the memories of a Sarajevo winter came flooding back.

The link between Barcelona in 1992 and Sarajevo in 1984 had nothing to do with climate and everything to do with the warmth generated by an outpouring of joy, the joy felt by the citizens of both cities at welcoming the world to their Olympic coming-out parties.

Barcelona was emerging from nearly a half-century of oppression by the late Spanish dictator, Francisco Franco. Sarajevo was hoping to be remembered as more than the site of the assassination that triggered World War I.

In nearly two decades of covering sports around the world, never have I felt so privileged to have this job than at the Summer Olympics of 1992 and the Winter Games of 1984. To have shared the passion of both cities for the Olympics made every waking hour into something special.

By the time of the Barcelona Olympics, though, some of the joy had dissolved into ineffable sadness over what was happening in Sarajevo.

Then the Serbs' siege of Sarajevo was only 4 months old. Now it is nearing the 2-year mark. Now, on the 10th anniversary of the Sarajevo Olympics, the sadness overwhelms anticipation of what will follow Saturday's opening of the Lillehammer Olympics.

Standing in the figure-skating venue at Hamar, waiting for the next absurd development in the Tonya Harding soap opera that consumes U.S. journalists' attention, one is haunted by the pictures of the burned-out Zetra Arena in Sarajevo. Next to the building where Katarina Witt and Scott Hamilton dazzled the world is a playing field turned into a cemetery.

Mt. Trebevic, site of the 1984 Olympic bobsled run, is a mortar emplacement from which the Serbs lob down shells on the city. The shell that killed 68 people in Sarajevo's central market Saturday could have come from Mt. Trebevic.

At the time the carnage was taking place, Bosnian bobsledder Igor Boras was on his way from Sarajevo to Lillehammer. He lived 100 yards from the central marketplace, did mock bobsled starts in the debris-strewn hall of a gutted government building and finally got out of Sarajevo when an armored personnel carrier took him to a United Nations relief flight heading to Italy.

Boras, who turned 26 Thursday, probably will not go back in the foreseeable future, although his parents and girlfriend remain in Sarajevo.

"The only wish of my mother is that she see my back, see that I was getting out," Boras said. "She doesn't want to see me without legs, without hands."

In Lillehammer, Boras joined nine other members of the first team to represent Bosnia-Herzegovina in the Winter Olympics. It is a team made up of Serbs, Croats and Muslims. Wednesday, they raised the flag of their newly independent country at the Olympic Village.

"I saw burned-down Sarajevo in front of my eyes—so many graves of the people who have died in the flag," cross-country coach Abdulah Panjeta said during the ceremony.

I try to see the Sarajevo of Feb. 8, 1984, when a light snow was falling in the ancient marketplace downtown, a place where cultures and centuries blended into a harmonious flow. The opening ceremonies were underway across town, and a journalist who chose to spend those hours wandering the snowy stillness of the souk caught occasional glimpses from the TV sets flickering from every shop through the late afternoon darkness.

The transcendent image was of a city at peace with itself and the world that had come to visit for the next 15 days. Each of us would leave with a story or several about the kindness of a new Sarajevan friend—the person going in an opposite direction who turned to pick up someone waiting for a bus that was very late, the woman in the pizza parlor who joked that the picture of ice cream on her shop window was "communist propaganda," the stranger who hugged you during the awards ceremony for alpine skier Jure Franko, Yugoslavia's lone Olympic medalist in 1984.

Sarajevo was then capital of a republic in a unified Yugoslavia, which was never so much a country as a tenuous political union, which would soon splinter under the weight of centuries-old hatreds. Sarajevo has become the focal point of all that hate.

"It is like the Middle Ages," said bobsledder Boras. "No water, no gas, no electricity. You have nothing."

When faced with the bounty in the athletes' dining room at the Olympic Village, Boras felt something akin to nausea, an emotion so strong he had to walk around between bites of food. Luger Verona Marjanovic said she felt almost ashamed to be at the Olympics while others were starving and dying at home.

At Barcelona, the International Olympic Committee first asked for the historical notion of an Olympic truce to be revived during the Games. Another such truce was to begin last Saturday, the day of the terror in Sarajevo's marketplace.

Historians have shown that the idea that wars were stopped by the Olympics of ancient Greece is largely a myth. Yet the modern Olympics, for all their commercialism, politics and fractiousness, provide what is likely the largest and longest peaceful contemporary assembly of diverse and often feuding peoples.

Most Norwegians don't think much of the IOC, according to a recent poll. They are also angry at the Greeks for being sanctimonious about their Olympic flame, refusing to allow its merger with the Norwegian Olympic flame being carried on a 75-day, 7,500-mile torch relay around this country.

Those irritations disappear in the torchlight. I saw that while running one of the relay legs outside Oslo last Friday. As I passed the Olympic torch to the next runner, several Norwegians reached in to light their own torches with the flame created by rubbing sticks together Nov. 27 at Morgedal, Norway.

As the final group of last Friday's runners followed the torch bearer up a snowy road past the hillside gravesite of triple gold medalist Sonja Henie, the zero-degree air was warmed by applause, the darkness pierced by the flickering flames of the torches held by spectators.

In Sarajevo, on Feb. 8, 1984, the snowflakes were like flames in the streetlights, when the Olympic cauldron was being lit to burn for 15 days. There is snow in Sarajevo again, but no streetlights left to transform it to something magic, the magic that can occur when briefly, ever so briefly, the Olympics carry the torch for humanity.

Oklahoma City
"Part of My Hometown Died"

SKIP BAYLESS

Chicago Tribune April 17, 1998
I didn't want to come back here. Not now. Not because of Timothy McVeigh and Mickey Mantle.

My editor strongly suggested I return to my hometown. He made me realize that most people remember where they were when two things happened: the Kennedy assassination and the Oklahoma City bombing. Now, eight blocks and three years from the worst terrorist act on North American soil, a state-of-the-heart ballpark has risen from the psychological rubble.

Oklahoma City is calling this $32 million park its "Field of Dreams." The pride this city feels in this park—undoubtedly the country's prettiest and classiest minor-league facility—is drawing people back downtown and finally helping them forget the blood and stench and severed body parts of 168 victims, 19 of them children.

Yet I was surprised to hear that the park is being dedicated to Oklahoma native Mantle. I knew Mantle all too well. Mantle never embraced Oklahoma. Just as surprising, many of Mantle's Yankees teammates, from Yogi to Whitey to Moose, made the trip without compensation for Thursday's opening-day ceremonies. LeRoy Nieman was on hand to capture the moment on canvas.

Just go, said my editor. Go and see and feel.

I resisted.

I left Oklahoma City for good when I was 18, and I wanted to remember it as it was before an agent of evil from somewhere up near Buffalo changed it forever. I wanted to cling to my memories of listening to Harry Caray do St. Louis Cardinals games . . . of playing YMCA baseball for the Mayfair Chipmunks, the most feared team in town . . . of filling shoeboxes with trading cards and filling my mouth with those nasty, flat, brittle pink pieces of trading-card gum . . . of doing wheelies on Schwinn Stingrays and licking Dairy Queen Dilly Bars before they melted down your hand.

I didn't want to see the YMCA in which I spent so many hours—the one left boarded up after the blast.

Oklahoma City was a great place in which to grow up. Thankfully, there wasn't much to do but play sports and enjoy the simpler pleasures. Terrorist bombs exploded in places called Belfast and Beirut.

Once I left Oklahoma City, it became my once-a-year haven. Every July I escaped back to my childhood for a week and went to minor-league games at wonderfully out-of-date All-Sports Stadium. I sat in the right-field bleachers the night that park opened, April 19, 1962, and I never wanted to see it die.

On April 19, 1995, at 9:02 a.m., part of my hometown died. Timothy McVeigh blew apart 168 people and permanently injured or devastated many more. This wasn't an act-of-God tragedy caused by the tornadoes that come sweeping down Oklahoma's plains. This wasn't even one madman shooting one president.

To get even with "big government" for the Waco "massacre," McVeigh considered bombing federal buildings in Phoenix or Omaha or Kansas City. But the Murrah Building at 5th and Harvey in Oklahoma City was the easiest target because it was virtually defenseless. McVeigh didn't know one soul in that building. But he did know there was a day-care center.

A day after the bombing, sports columnist Berry Tramel wrote in the Daily Oklahoman, "This made you wonder if throwing a ball or bouncing a baby, chasing a pup or grilling a burger would ever be the same."

237

The reaction will never be the same when I'm asked where I'm from originally. Now, people say, "Oh, the bombing. Did you know anybody? Is everything OK?"

Sadly, it took this tragedy to put Oklahoma City, whose metro population is more than 1 million, on the national map.

No, says Kirk Humphreys, it wasn't the bombing. It was the way Oklahoma City responded to it. Humphreys is Oklahoma City's new mayor and my boyhood friend.

"When the bomb went off," he said, "there was a sense nationwide of, 'Oklahoma City? If it can happen there, it can happen anywhere.' This was an attack on unprotected working people and children, and Americans everywhere thought of it as an attack on them personally.

"I'll never say the bombing was a good thing for Oklahoma City, because the city suffered an unrecoverable loss of hundreds of millions of dollars, not to mention the dead and crippled. But we had rescue workers come here from all over the country who couldn't believe how much people did for them and how they were treated like heroes. We feel better about ourselves than before because we know we have uncommon moral fiber, and we got to show it to the nation."

When asked where I'm from, the one reason I've always cringed is Oklahoma's downtrodden legacy. From the Trail of Tears to "The Grapes of Wrath," Oklahomans developed an inferiority complex. That was one reason Mantle moved to Dallas soon after signing with the Yankees at age 18. He was raised in Commerce, about three hours north of Oklahoma City on the Kansas border, and he couldn't wait to escape.

That fact didn't escape many Oklahomans, who balked at a proposal to name the new park for Mantle. It's now called the Southwestern Bell Bricktown Ballpark—The Brick for short—and Mantle would have preferred that. Mantle once told me that one reason he drank so much was he never could understand why "so many people treat me like a god just because I played a damn game."

Mantle's weakness was that he sometimes felt too intensely. Mantle would have been touched by how Oklahoma City responded to the bombing. Mantle gladly would have been there Thursday night, more to honor Oklahoma City than to let it honor him by unveiling a 9-foot statue of The Mick swinging from the heels.

One reason so many ex-Yankees came for free was because Oklahoma City deserved it. Without the bombing, that wouldn't have happened. Without it, Oklahoma City wouldn't now be so proud of itself.

Thursday night about 15,000 jammed The Brick—a miniature of the Texas Rangers' Ballpark at Arlington—to reach back and ahead. They celebrated the many baseball stars this state has produced: Mantle, Johnny Bench, Warren Spahn, the Waners, Pepper Martin, Carl Hubbell, Allie Reynolds, Bobby Murcer, Darrell Porter. They cherished springtime, the crack of the bat, rebirth.

I was glad I was there. Oklahoma City will never be the same, and maybe that isn't all bad.

Remembering Ben Wilson
"We Must Rise Up and Seize Control"
TAYLOR BELL

Chicago Sun-Times November 14, 2009

The mayor of Chicago called for an end to the violence, the senseless killing of children and high school students. So did the Rev. Jesse Jackson, city officials and school administrators. The tragic story was highlighted on local and network TV news. Newspapers editorialized about it.

That was 25 years ago. It seems nothing has changed.

Even today, people who saw Wilson play wonder how good he might have been and where he would have gone to college. Nobody knows for sure. But before Bob Hambric, Wilson's high school coach, died in August, he told a friend that Indiana was the youngster's choice.

Wilson remains a legendary figure in Chicago high school basketball. As a junior, he led Simeon to the Class AA state championship in 1984. He was so good and so charismatic that future NBA star Nick Anderson opted to transfer from Prosser to play with him. After receiving national attention, Wilson was acclaimed the No. 1 player in the nation going into his senior season.

Then he was killed. On the eve of Simeon's 1984–85 opener, a gang member shot him while he was walking with friends outside the school. His funeral attracted thousands of mourners. Jackson eulogized the fallen hero. The community was devastated.

Wilson is remembered to this day. Former Simeon star Derrick Rose wore Wilson's number during his high school career in tribute to his memory.

But what happened then and what is happening now has convinced longtime educators that nothing has changed. In fact, they believe things have gotten worse. There are more gangs, more drugs, more budgetary issues and more cutbacks. Fewer kids are participating in sports, fewer after-school activities are available, parents and communities are reluctant to get involved and coaches aren't as committed as they once were.

Rodney Hull, who played with Wilson on Simeon's 1984 championship team, said he is appalled at what is happening in the public school system because, in his view, nothing is changing for the better. One high school principal documented 1,100 fights in his first year.

"We are putting out a good crop of kids from elementary school, but we lose them when they walk into high school," said Hull, who has served as principal at Nicholson Elementary Math and Science in the gang-infested Englewood community for the last nine years. "We need people with fresh energy who want to do something. We must have activities to draw kids in. We can't release them to the streets."

Hull has changed the dynamics at his school. When he arrived, there were 17 teacher vacancies, gangs were everywhere, parents were nowhere, students fought all day, there was a high absentee rate and teachers were intimidated and couldn't wait to find another job.

Now, Hull said, gangs aren't operating in the school, there is no graffiti, no fights have been documented in two years, teacher retention is high, kids are learning and test scores are up.

"I hold on to my kids," he said. "I keep them in school all the time, until 6 p.m. And when they have problems, I go to their houses. We can do some things, but the clergy and politicians have to get away from it. We don't need people in front of a camera, we need to do work off-camera instead. From a school standpoint, police are reactive, not proactive. The proactive part has to start in the schools and at home with parents."

Roy Curry and J.W. Smith are retired after serving for 40 years in the Chicago Public Schools as football coaches and administrators. They saw how it was and see how it is. They have suggestions about how to solve the problems, but they aren't optimistic that positive steps will be implemented. In fact, they are downright discouraged about the future of the system.

"It hasn't changed in 25 years," Curry said. "We've got to learn how to control our communities. We don't have control; the gangs run them. The communities must rise up and seize control. The priority is to get rid of gangs, but that isn't a police priority now. As long as it is black-on-black crime, that's OK with the police. We know who the gang-bangers are, but no one says anything. Twenty-five years from now, we'll be talking about the same thing."

Smith, who founded a very successful elementary school football program while serving as the CPS' executive director of sports administration, now calls for a universal pre-school program to give kids supervision and direction and get them involved in positive activities.

"If I had a pile of money, I'd put it in universal pre-school," Smith said. "Send all kids into pre-school at age 3 or 4. Give them an early appreciation for learning—arts, health, music, sports, math, English. They also can learn about character and how to react with other students."

Smith pointed out that educators long have understood that juvenile crime peaks from 3 to 7 p.m. So it is imperative that the park district, YMCAs, schools and government agencies come together to provide more after-school activities for kids.

"It is difficult to take a high school junior or senior and make changes," Smith said. "We're missing the boat by misappropriating the funds we have. We can have schools for the elite, but those who came up with only a mother in the home and no male image need to be put in an environment where they learn and appreciate education.

"Otherwise, we're headed back down to a situation that caused Wilson's death."

From the Depths of Darkness, Theo Fleury and Sheldon Kennedy Find Light

BARRY ROZNER

Arlington Daily Herald December 25, 2011

In this, the December of the human soul, a mammoth searchlight shines on the darkest tales our species can tell.

It is a cold and barren Christmas this year for sexual-abuse victims in sports, their pain only extended by their bravery.

That is the excruciating contradiction of their feat. By coming forth and revealing the torture they endured, they will suffer publicly until the depositions, hearings and trials end months and years from now.

But the healing can only begin when the truth is set free in the face of those they fear will doubt them, and they must know that the world hears their cries.

"They need to know we believe them, and they need to know they did the right thing," says Sheldon Kennedy. "They need to know it's not their fault and that the world will support them."

"They have to stick together and not allow themselves to be victimized all over again by the system," says Theo Fleury. "Obviously it's not going to be easy to experience this again, but they can have a huge impact and make an incredible difference in the world if they can get through it."

Getting through it. Right. Probably sounds reasonable to anyone who hasn't suffered the abuse Kennedy and Fleury did as children, raped by the same junior coach, Graham James, who pleaded guilty in 1997 to 350 counts of sexual abuse.

It was Kennedy's decision to go public that brought the scandal to the surface and put James in jail, and Fleury's revelations years later that put James back in prison.

"A victim fears that no one will believe them," Kennedy said. "Between that and the incredible power an abuser has over the victim, it keeps victims quiet."

Kennedy was raped hundreds of times by James, his junior hockey coach, beginning at the age of 14 and continuing for years.

By the time James was sent to prison in 1997, Kennedy's life had spiraled out of his control. His NHL career (107 points) was never what it could have been, and by the turn of the century he had given up on hockey, marriage and life.

He hit the sexual-abuse trifecta: drug abuse, alcoholism and thoughts of suicide.

"For so long you think it's your fault and you live in fear," says the 42-year-old Kennedy. "The fear grips you. It was like, 'Oh, my God, what if no one believes me?' That was my fear."

Kennedy remembers the devious ways in which James would keep the abuse secret, how he told others Kennedy was a troubled child who needed special attention, explaining why Kennedy had go to James' home for "tutoring" several times a week.

And all the while Kennedy wondered why those who suspected something terrible never did anything about it.

"Pedophiles thrive on our ignorance and indifference as a community," Kennedy explained. "They have complete control, and because of that victims' biggest fear is confronting their abuser. The victim has been hammered into believing it's their fault, and they prey on a child's guilt, destroy their self-esteem and manipulate. It's devastating."

Kennedy and Fleury were held hostage by a coach who controlled everything about their lives and hockey futures, which a junior coach could destroy in an instant.

Say a word and that's the end of your NHL hopes. Say anything and you'll be sent home, labeled as a troublemaker.

Suffer the terror, stay quiet and eventually reach the NHL, turning a Canadian boy against his true love, hockey, raging against the game and life, instead of at the man who ruined their lives, stole their innocence and turned them into drug addicts.

242

By the time Fleury made it to Chicago in 2003, he was at the end of a career that saw him play more than 1,000 games and collect more than 1,000 points, but it is in the games missed, the seasons forfeited, that you wonder if Graham James also stole Fleury's ticket to the Hall of Fame.

It is in the 1,840 penalty minutes that you understand more about the 5-foot-6 Fleury, and it is in the games he played intoxicated that leave you wondering how great he could have been if a man hadn't stolen his sanity.

It is within that infamous brawl with Blackhawks and bouncers at a strip club in Columbus during his last months in the NHL that you understand a man possessed by decades-old demons can't always find the bottom, no matter how desperately he screams he wants to get there.

"When I was in Chicago I was pretty much done," says the 43-year-old Fleury. "To go from there, one of the lowest points of my life, to where I am today, it's an absolute miracle."

Neither Fleury nor Kennedy wants their story to be one of pity. It is gut-wrenching and sad, but there is also hope.

Fleury wrote *Playing with Fire* in 2009, revealing that he also had been raped by James. The book became a best-seller in Canada and led to new charges against James, who has since pleaded guilty to sexual assault and will be sentenced in February.

Fleury, meanwhile, has become an advocate for sexual-abuse victims, and developed a career as a public speaker.

"I'm clean, but it's one day at a time," Fleury says. "I'm here to help others, to speak out and make sure people know there's help for them.

"It takes a brave man to take on a monster, but there's strength in numbers and they can support one another. The best healing that is done is when you have a group of men sitting around talking about their sexual abuse.

"To have your innocence taken away and then to fight back, it's an amazing journey. They can get there with help from all of us."

Out of his personal hell, Sheldon Kennedy co-founded Respect Group Inc., which trains hundreds of thousands of coaches every year, a program that Hockey Canada has made mandatory for every one of its coaches.

"Maybe something good like that can come out of all these headlines, where people have the tools to recognize and act instead of being bystanders," Kennedy says. "We want to empower youth, coaches and parents,

243

and change the imbalance of power, take the power back from those who use it against children. Take the initiative as an organization and mandate that everyone has to have the training."

Men like Kennedy and Fleury do not pretend it is easy to come forward, tell the truth, face their accusers and clean up their lives, but that is precisely why they tell their stories.

"I didn't want to be a victim anymore. I wanted to get on with my life," Kennedy says. "It takes years of hard work and the lifelong scars don't go away, but once you take the power away from the abuser and give it back to yourself, you have a chance.

"I got sober and I got my life back. It's an everyday process of checks and balances, but I feel good and there are positive things in my life."

On this Christmas, Kennedy's wish is that all who have suffered can find that peace.

"Children come into this world with so much love, and with abuse they are robbed of the ability to love," Kennedy says. "It's an attachment disorder. Emotionally, you shut down and never let anyone close. You can't love or be loved.

"But I'm proof that there is a way back. I'm proof that there is life after abuse. I'm proof that one day the men we have heard so much about lately will be able to live again. That's my wish for them."

When Silence Is the Only Answer

RICK MORRISSEY

Chicago Tribune September 16, 2001

My God, this is football weather, cool and crisp and full of promise. Summer has stopped sweating, and if you close your eyes long enough, you can almost feel the white stubble of winter starting to come in on the breeze.

The star quarterback is rumored to be going out with the sorority beauty queen again or else she's breaking up with him for the fifth time. Nobody seems to be quite clear on the details. The college mothers' club is putting on a bake sale outside Gate S, and the ladies are all complimenting Edna on her apple pie, which, most of them later say could have used some more nutmeg, but that nobody's perfect, even if Edna thinks she is.

Everyone's excited because the coach told the men at the Elks Club fish fry he expects 10 victories this season, but to keep it to themselves because the players don't need their heads to get any bigger than they already are. But word gets out anyway, because Frank tells his son, Fred, a reserve wide receiver on the team, and everyone knows Fred can't keep a secret or his hands on the football.

I'm staring down Ashland Avenue in Evanston on Saturday morning, at a college football stadium rising grandly to meet a gray sky. I'm seeing what I want to see, a world that never was and never will have the chance to be, and I don't care about anyone else's 20–20 vision. I'm seeing Northwestern the way I want to see it, sport the way I want to see it, the world the way I want to see it. You might want to try it too. Keep your finger pressed on the rewind button, right past Sept. 11, 2001, as if it never happened, and keep going right into the sweet stupor of a concocted year in the 1950s.

The problem, you'll find, is that Sept. 11, 2001, refuses to leave the premises and, worse, keeps pounding its shoe on the table. As much as we want to pretend Tuesday's terrorist attacks didn't happen, as much as we'd like to make the dust and bricks of the World Trade Center and the Pentagon rewind back to wholeness, like a genie being sucked back into the bottle, the emptiness here has its own thoughts on the matter.

There is, as far as the sports world is concerned, nothing. We, as a nation, aren't very big on nihilism. We have 500 channels to choose from, and all we have to do is run a net through the air, and normally we can catch a game to our liking.

But not on this day, not on this weekend. Tuesday's attacks led the NFL, Major League Baseball and big-time college football to shut down this weekend. Northwestern vs. Navy is a memory that won't exist.

We're a funny people, we Americans. We work hard, but we live a disproportionate amount of our lives for our games. We take sides, choose different teams, wear our colors proudly. It's Cubs vs. White Sox and father vs. son, a house gently divided. We're a diverse people, too, in so many more ways than skin color or religious beliefs. We're so diverse that we rarely agree on anything.

We agree that the games don't seem to mean so much anymore.

The consensus, almost to a man, woman and child, is that we have seen hell. You can hear that consensus in the wind Saturday as it whistles around the walls of Ryan Field and causes the ropes to clang off a flagpole. It's called silence. It's not complete silence. It's not a monastery's silence or a library's silence. It's the silence of introspection, of shared loss, of respect.

You want to know what quiet is? Quiet is going to Sluggers sports bar in Wrigleyville on Saturday afternoon and hearing Paul Simon singing loudly on a video on a big screen. Paul Simon is on a big screen because there are no sports to take up the space. He's a replacement player.

We're looking to each other now. Illinois-Louisville is nowhere to be seen on any of the screens, but the casket holding the body of Rev. Mychal Judge, who was killed while giving last rites to a firefighter, is being shown on one of the TVs in the bar.

It's two hours before the Cubs would have played the Pittsburgh Pirates, and Sluggers, down the street from Wrigley Field, is close to empty. This is unprecedented, general manager Zach Strauss says.

"This place is normally packed before a game," he says. "And afterward it's a zoo. But not today, and that's OK. I didn't think they should play the games. We'll make it up down the line."

The sports world in this country will start its engine again Monday. It's the right time, but I can't tell you why that is. It just is. It's the right time for America, clothed in black, to put on a baseball cap. It doesn't mean we've stopped mourning, just that we're moving on, forcing one foot to move in front of the other. We've already gone back to work. Now we're going back to play.

I don't know if it will ever be the same again, if sports will continue to provide the same joy and retreat. I hope it will, but I suspect we have a hard, arduous journey ahead. We'll find out if sport is, indeed, the great escape.

In a little less than a week, we have watched our national obsession go into a lock-down mode, and many of us have thought it was the right and respectful thing to do. That's the adult view of life, but I don't remember any of us consulting with children on the matter. They still need to laugh and be kids.

And so I stop at a park to watch a baseball game for 9- and 10-year-old boys and girls. The weather has decided to cooperate. It's baseball weather now, sunny and warmer. I see a throwing error on a ground ball turn into what will certainly be called a home run by the time the player gets to the dugout. It's so much fun that you almost forget for a second. The important thing is that you believe with all your heart that the kids have forgotten for a few hours.

Inside my car, I turn on one of the sports radio stations, which has become all news, all the time because of the bombings. I turn it off.

I sit back in my car and I think of how well Northwestern's game went Saturday, of Navy's valiant effort, of words that I'll write to describe it. I see the sorority beauty queen put her head on the quarterback's shoulder. I see him put his arm around her and know that everything is all right.

I see, too, that I was wrong. I see now that you can't rewind what has happened, can't make the airplane stop from slicing into the tower, can't hit a button and hear the shrill warble of tape going backward. You can't escape, not now.

I see people coming together, helping each other when I thought nothing could ever make this country an army of one. I see firefighters and police officers covered in ash and looking like ghosts, and I see them rescuing people. I see people rolling up their sleeves to go to work, to get back to this business of living, and I see people rolling up their sleeves to give blood.

These are the days of miracle and wonder.

It's not so bad, this silence.

BATTLES WON AND LOST

The fight to integrate baseball did not begin in the few years leading up to Jackie Robinson's arrival in Brooklyn. It was pursued for many decades, as Al Monroe's deliciously sarcastic column in the *Chicago Defender* in 1933 attests. And nobody pursued the battle with more dedication and passion than Wendell Smith.

Smith was "the most talented and influential of the black journalists" of his generation, wrote Jules Tygiel in *Baseball's Great Experiment*, and Smith's colleagues in the black press agreed. His notes columns in the *Pittsburgh Courier*, which he joined in 1937, were indispensable for fans, players, and executives alike, and there was very little going on in the Negro Leagues he didn't know about.

Smith was particularly close to Robinson—he was intimately involved in the details of his signing with the Dodgers and ghosted his first autobiography—and had his own experience with discrimination when his application to join the Baseball Writers Association of America was rejected because he worked for a black newspaper. When he joined the *Chicago Herald-American* in 1948, he became that organization's first black member.

Though baseball was integrated by the time he came to Chicago, Smith found another indignity to campaign against—the conditions black players endured in spring training—and again he was on the winning side. Two of his columns from *Chicago's American* on this issue are reprinted here, one that shows Smith's devotion to the cause, the other his humanity.

The Mike Royko column that appears here was written the day Robinson died, while Mike Downey took advantage of the White Sox's appearance in the 2005 World Series to try to correct an injustice suffered by a Sox player eighty-five years earlier.

Jeannie Morris and Melissa Isaacson offer before-and-after columns on the revolution in women's sports—Morris pointing the way toward the future less than six months before Title IX was adopted, Isaacson applauding one of the women who reaped that law's benefits almost thirty years later.

Morris, who was among the first women sports reporters to work in daily television anywhere in the country, got her start when her husband, Bears receiver Johnny Morris, was asked by *Chicago Today* if he would write a column for the paper. "I can't write," he said, "but my wife can."

"Until then, my only job since quitting college had been birthing and rearing four kids," Morris says. "I sent *Today* some samples and got hired at $50 a week. But they didn't dare put me on the sports page. My column appeared in the women's section and was titled, 'Football Is a Woman's Game, by Mrs. Johnny Morris.' Eventually, I earned the right to be called Jeannie."

Look Who's Beating the Cubs Now

AL MONROE

Chicago Defender September 16, 1933

Officials of the American and National Leagues would have profited had they attended the all-star game played at Comiskey Park Sunday afternoon between Race players of the East and West. They would have seen a game run off in clock-like fashion. They would have seen a substitute second-sacker commit three errors and receive encouragement from both players and spectators instead of boos which are familiar when such things occur in National and American league parks.

They would also have seen 20,000 at Sox Park while fewer than 12,000 saw the Cubs beat Philadelphia twice on the north side of Chicago.

But what your correspondent wished them to see most was the brand of ball played. I should have liked for Bill Veeck, president of the Cubs, strictly a lily-white organization, to watch shortstop Dick Lundy, pitcher Bill Foster and first baseman Oscar Charleston perform. It was Veeck, you know, who not that long ago laughed loudly when asked about chances of Race players performing in the National league.

Then, too, it wouldn't have been bad for Mr. Veeck to have witnessed the sight of owners Robert Cole and Gus Greenlee congratulating The Chicago Defender for giving the fans the line-up of the two teams despite the fact that programs were being sold in the park. This might have shamed Veeck for his act in changing the numbers of his players daily to thwart the attempt of one daily paper to give the fans at the Cubs park a lineup of the players for two cents.

The Philadelphia team beating the Cubs while the all-star game was being played on another side of the city naturally meant good business for both attractions. But Veeck is noted for his adeptness for taking advantage of coincidence.

We made frequent visits to the press gate to see what officials of the league were attending the game, and, believe it or not, there were seven men whose names you see in the metropolitan press rather often. Even Andy Lotshaw, the trainer of the Cubs, was on hand, although his team was playing a synthetic doubleheader with the Philadelphia club.

Frankly, major league ball gave your author quite a laugh Saturday when the Cubs and Philadelphia played 13 frames before the issue was decided in the visitors' favor. I have never quite understood why the North-siders would attempt to go through an extra-inning battle without inserting a single pinch hitter for a pair of rookies that had been at bat five or six times with not even a threat of a hit when such men as Hendrick, Grimm, Campbell and Koenig were occupying the bench. And the Cubs wanted to win this one so badly.

The Bill Veeck referred to here was the father of the future White Sox owner. While considered enlightened on racial matters for his era, he was powerless to effect any real changes. A decade later, his son would be in the forefront of the battle to integrate baseball.

"We Are Tired of Staying in Flop Houses"

WENDELL SMITH

Chicago's American January 23, 1961

Beneath the apparently tranquil surface of baseball there is a growing feeling of resentment among Negro major leaguers who still experience embarrassment, humiliation, and even indignities during spring training in the south.

The Negro player who is accepted as a first-class citizen in the regular season is tired of being a second-class citizen in spring training.

With spring training only four weeks away, this problem looms large on the baseball horizon. It may not explode into a national controversy this year, but soon it is going to be a major issue if steps are not taken to bring about a solution.

Moving cautiously and anxious to avert becoming engulfed in a fiery debate over civil rights in baseball, the Negro players already have made plans to take the following steps.

1. Meeting with their respective club owners and discussing the issue.

2. Placing the problem in the hands of their player representatives.

3. Selecting a spokesman, preferably a former Negro player, to explain their position to baseball's top executives.

The Negro player resents the fact that he is not permitted to stay in the same hotels with his teammates during spring training, and is protesting the fact that he cannot eat in the same restaurants, nor enjoy other privileges.

At the moment he is not belligerent. He is merely seeking help and sympathy, and understanding, and a solution.

There is concrete evidence, however, that his patience is growing short. The owners have been handling this touchy problem with kid gloves. But the day is near when they must face it forthrightly.

This has not been a sudden or spontaneous development. The resentment over so-called separate but equal facilities in the South has always been present.

It wasn't until recently, however, that Negro players felt they were well enough established to tackle the situation. Not until, in fact, they had achieved first class citizenship in the north . . . in St. Louis, Philadelphia, Chicago, and Baltimore where they once had similar problems.

Now that they have won that battle, now that they are permitted to eat and sleep in the same hotels with their teammates in the North, they are turning southward to correct the evils they encounter there.

"We think we should enjoy equality the year around and intend to get it," an outstanding Negro player told this writer recently. "We are tired of staying in flop houses and eating in second-rate restaurants during spring training. If we are good enough to play with a team, then we should be good enough to share the same facilities and accommodations as the other players both in spring and summer."

The Negro player particularly resents the fact that he is compelled to secure his own accommodations while his white teammates enjoy the luxury of the most elegant hotels during spring training in the south.

This attitude is especially true of the Negro player who is married and must bunk his wife and children in comparative hovels during the spring.

Ironically, this battle for first-class citizenship first started in the North. When Robinson joined the Brooklyn Dodgers in 1947, he was not acceptable in hotels in St. Louis and Philadelphia. When the Dodgers played in those cities he stayed in Negro hotels.

The Dodger management subsequently moved the club from the Philadelphia hotel which barred him to one where he could stay.

There also was a problem here in Chicago. The hotel here where the team stayed for years accepted Robinson reluctantly his first season. The next year the club moved to another hotel which had no objections to his presence.

The last bulwark of resistance was the Chase hotel in St. Louis, which refused Robinson, Roy Campanella, Don Newcombe, and other Negro players until the 1954 season and then accepted them afterward with reservations.

When the Dodgers threatened to move elsewhere, the management rescinded its "no Negroes" policy. Robinson, who had been staying with his other Negro teammates at a Negro hotel, leaped at the "opportunity."

Campanella and Newcombe, however, refused to move because they objected to the limitations which the hotel placed upon them.

"We have a terrible time during spring training," one of the Negro bigleaguers told us. "We have to find places to sleep and eat by ourselves.

"We played an exhibition game in one town, for example, and afterward couldn't find a decent place to eat. We couldn't eat in the same hotel with the other players and there wasn't a decent Negro restaurant in the town.

"We went to a store and bought a loaf of bread and some cold meat. We didn't have a place to stay, either. So we walked around the streets and ate the bread and cold meat like a bunch of vagrants.

"That was quite a sight, believe me—about $250,000 worth of precious baseball talent walking down the street eating bread and cold meat in the broad daylight."

There will be approximately 100 Negro players training in major league camps this spring. The Negro players with the White Sox will not be able to stay with their teammates in Sarasota, Fla. They will have to stay in the Negro community under conditions that leave something to be desired.

The Negro members of the Cubs will be a little more fortunate. They will be accepted along with the other players at the hotel where the team stays in Mesa, Ariz. However, when the club hits the road and plays exhibition games in Texas, for example, Ernie Banks, George Altman, and other Negro players will have to scout around for places to stay if the team stays in the town overnight.

It is such conditions and circumstances as described above that Negro players are preparing to fight in their own quiet way.

They are not soliciting the aid of the National Association for the Advancement of Colored People nor any other such group.

They realize, of course, that the owners are not responsible for their plight. But there is a definite feeling among them that many conditions could be improved in the South if the owners would exert their influence in the towns where their teams train. One Negro told this writer:

"Major league clubs not only spend thousands of dollars in the cities where they train, but they are responsible for luring millions of dollars to those towns in tourist trade. Very few towns would be willing to lose that revenue if the owners threatened to move their clubs to California or other places where there aren't so many racial restrictions. This situation can be worked out. It must be worked out. We are tired of being shunted around in the spring. We want to live respectably the entire year, not just part of it."

Baseball owners are sympathetic, of course, but they are also extremely cautious about the situation. In a sense, they can hardly be blamed. The South is currently rebelling against enforcement of mass integration. It is the most explosive issue in the nation today.

255

Taking a Stand and Paying the Price

WENDELL SMITH

Chicago's American April 5, 1961

SARASOTA, Fla.—Meet the loneliest people in Sarasota, Fla.—Mr. and Mrs. Edward Wachtel.

They are the proprietors of the DeSoto motel, the eight-unit establishment where the Negro members of the White Sox have been living during spring training.

The official headquarters for the Sox is the Sarasota Terrace hotel which refused to accept the black players—Minnie Minoso, Al Smith, Juan Pizarro, Stan Johnson, Floyd Robinson, Winston Brown, and Frank Barnes.

Mr. and Mrs. Wachtel came to the rescue when President Bill Veeck and Secretary Ed Short of the Sox were desperately searching for suitable quarters to house the seven Negro players.

The Wachtels, bitterly opposed to any form of segregation or discrimination, volunteered to take in the rejected players.

They are paying a heavy social penalty and taking a daring risk for their benevolent and courageous stand against the deep-rooted bigotry which exists in this southern town of 45,000 people.

As soon as it was learned that the Wachtels had consented to accept the players, the proponents of segregation here launched an attack of harassment upon the kindly couple which has been relentless and frightening.

The motel is situated in the heart of a white neighborhood. It is a neat, rambling green and white construction located on route 301, the town's main thoroughfare.

Ed Wachtel purchased the establishment when he moved here with his wife five years ago for $90,000. He was a prosperous realtor in New York before he came here to live what he expected to be a quiet life of retirement.

His decision to accept the Sox Negroes, however, has created great turmoil and probably has made him the most disliked individual in the community.

Scorned by their immediate neighbors as well as some civic leaders, the Wachtels are living a lonely and desolate life.

They are paying a heavy toll for advocating and practicing racial integration in a middle class neighborhood which has been tightly restricted previously.

However, the 60-year-old motel owner shrugs off the penalties which have been inflicted upon him and his wife with a benign indifference. He says:

"I accepted these young men in my motel because I do not believe in segregation. I am fighting it here in Sarasota in my own quiet way. I have created a lot of ill-will among people who once were my intimate friends, but that is the price a man must pay sometimes for doing what he believes is right.

"These ballplayers have been perfect gentlemen and I am honored to have them as tenants. There isn't a neighbor around here who can point an accusing finger at them and say they have not lived an exemplary life since they moved into the motel six weeks ago."

Those who have objected to the Negroes in the motel threatened Wachtel and his wife with bodily harm almost daily. He says:

"When it was first discovered that I was going to accept these players, people called us all hours of the day and night and demanded that I refuse them.

"They warned that if I didn't, they would bomb us out. We received calls from men who said they were members of the Ku Klux Klan and that they were going to burn a fiery cross on my front lawn.

"There were calls from merchants who said they would refuse to serve me in their stores. All but one or two of my neighbors quit speaking to me. Naturally, my wife and I were frightened. I informed the sheriff of the bombing possibility and for the first two weeks they kept a close watch on the place.

"However, I think the community is beginning to accept the fact that this isn't such a bad thing after all. I receive only one or two daily threats by telephone now, and the police no longer consider it necessary to guard the place around the cloak.

"I think this has been a good thing for Sarasota. It has enlightened a lot of people and proven that integration can work. In fact, I understand that the owner of the Sarasota Terrace will accept all the White Sox players next spring, regardless of race.

"If that is true, then I am especially happy. I will feel that I have contributed something in my small way toward the betterment of mankind and helped to bring this community one step closer to real democracy.

"Not everyone here is opposed to what I am doing. The mayor, Ed Marabella, and most of the members of the chamber of commerce silently approve of the idea. In time, Sarasota will be a better city for it."

Meantime, Mr. and Mrs. Wachtel are living a life of isolation. They are alone, chastised and tormented by hostile Sarasota citizens, but they are not yielding in their determination to make this a better community for all people, regardless of color.

The following season, the White Sox bought their own hotel in Sarasota. Their players never lived in segregated housing again.

When Jackie Robinson Came to Wrigley Field

MIKE ROYKO

Chicago Daily News October 25, 1972

All that Saturday, the wise men of the neighborhood, who sat in chairs on the sidewalk outside the tavern, had talked about what it would do to baseball.

I hung around and listened because baseball was about the most important thing in the world, and if anything was going to ruin it, I was worried.

Most of the things they said, I didn't understand, although it all sounded terrible. But could one man bring such ruin?

They said he could and would. And the next day he was going to be in Wrigley Field for the first time, on the same diamond as Hack, Nicholson, Cavarretta, Schmitz, Pafko, and all my other idols.

I had to see Jackie Robinson, the man who was going to somehow wreck everything. So the next day, another kid and I started walking to the ballpark early.

We always walked to save the streetcar fare. It was five or six miles, but I felt about baseball the way Abe Lincoln felt about education.

Usually, we could get there just at noon, find a seat in the grandstand, and watch some batting practice. But not that Sunday, May 18, 1947.

By noon, Wrigley Field was almost filled. The crowd outside spilled off the sidewalk and into the streets. Scalpers were asking top dollar for box seats and getting it.

I had never seen anything like it. Not just the size, although it was a new record, more than 47,000. But this was twenty-five years ago, and in 1947 few blacks were seen in the Loop, much less up on the white North Side at a Cub game.

That day, they came by the thousands, pouring off the northbound Ls and out of their cars.

They didn't wear baseball-game clothes. They had on church clothes and funeral clothes—suits, white shirts, ties, gleaming shoes, and straw hats. I've never seen so many straw hats.

As big as it was, the crowd was orderly. Almost unnaturally so. People didn't jostle each other.

258

The whites tried to look as if nothing unusual was happening, while the blacks tried to look casual and dignified. So everybody looked slightly ill at ease.

For most, it was probably the first time they had been that close to each other in such great numbers.

We managed to get in, scramble up a ramp, and find a place to stand behind the last row of grandstand seats. Then they shut the gates. No place remained to stand.

Robinson came up in the first inning. I remember the sound. It wasn't the shrill, teenage cry you now hear, or an excited gut roar. They applauded, long, rolling applause. A tall, middle-aged black man stood next to me, a smile of almost painful joy on his face, beating his palms together so hard they must have hurt.

When Robinson stepped into the batter's box, it was as if someone had flicked a switch. The place went silent.

He swung at the first pitch and they erupted as if he had knocked it over the wall. But it was only a high foul that dropped into the box seats. I remember thinking it was strange that a foul could make that many people happy. When he struck out, the low moan was genuine.

I've forgotten most of the details of the game, other than that the Dodgers won and Robinson didn't get a hit or do anything special, although he was cheered on every swing and every routine play.

But two things happened I'll never forget. Robinson played first, and early in the game a Cub star hit a grounder and it was a close play.

Just before the Cub reached first, he swerved to his left. And as he got to the bag, he seemed to slam his foot down hard at Robinson's foot.

It was obvious to everyone that he was trying to run into him or spike him. Robinson took the throw and got clear at the last instant.

I was shocked. That Cub, a hometown boy, was my biggest hero. It was not only an unheroic stunt, but it seemed a rude thing to do in front of people who would cheer for a foul ball. I didn't understand why he had done it. It wasn't at all big league.

I didn't know that while the white fans were relatively polite, the Cubs and most other teams kept up a steady stream of racial abuse from the dugout. I thought that all they did down there was talk about how good Wheaties are.

Late in the game, Robinson was up again, and he hit another foul ball.

This time it came into the stands low and fast, in our direction. Somebody in the seats grabbed for it, but it caromed off his hand and kept coming. There was a flurry of arms as the ball kept bouncing, and suddenly it was between me and my pal. We both grabbed. I had a baseball.

The two of us stood there examining it and chortling. A genuine major-league baseball that had actually been gripped and thrown by a Cub pitcher, hit by a Dodger batter. What a possession.

Then I heard the voice say: "Would you consider selling that?"

It was the black man who had applauded so fiercely.

I mumbled something. I didn't want to sell it.

"I'll give you ten dollars for it," he said.

Ten dollars. I couldn't believe it. I didn't know what ten dollars could buy because I'd never had that much money. But I knew that a lot of men in the neighborhood considered sixty dollars a week to be good pay.

I handed it to him, and he paid me with ten $1 bills.

When I left the ball park, with that much money in my pocket, I was sure that Jackie Robinson wasn't bad for the game.

Since then, I've regretted a few times that I didn't keep the ball. Or that I hadn't given it to him free. I didn't know, then, how hard he probably had to work for that ten dollars.

But Tuesday I was glad I had sold it to him. And if that man is still around, and has that baseball, I'm sure he thinks it was worth every cent.

High Time for Bud Selig to Pardon Buck Weaver

MIKE DOWNEY

Chicago Tribune October 20, 2005

Bud Selig, I have a favor to beg of you.

A request, really. A plea. An appeal to you as a decent, honest, red-blooded American who happens to be in charge of our national pastime. You are the commissioner of baseball. You have clout. You have influence. You have say-so.

How would you feel about being truly brave? About becoming a hero to the people of Chicago—and to one Chicago man's family in particular—here in a town that hasn't won a World Series for 86 years?

Grant amnesty to Buck Weaver.

The grave marker at Mt. Hope Cemetery, just off 115th Street, reads this way:

Husband

George D. Weaver

1890 — 1956

And that's it. Nothing else. Not a word about how Ty Cobb called him the greatest third baseman of his day.

Not a word about his .333 batting average in the 1917 World Series as the White Sox took the championship.

No mention of how he hit .324 in the 1919 Series and played each of its eight games error-free.

Of how he never took a dive or took a dime.

Of how he was banned for life by the commissioner anyway.

Of how he was guilty of nothing except not being a snitch on his friends.

Of how he was the only one of the eight "Black Sox" defendants to ask for a separate trial.

Of how catcher Ray Schalk spoke during the case and for years thereafter of "the seven" Sox teammates who were crooks.

Of how the trial judge, Hugo Friend, reportedly instructed the jury that he would overturn a guilty verdict in Weaver's case (and his alone).

Of how 14,000 Chicago fans signed a petition in 1921, pleading for Weaver's reinstatement.

Of how until his death in 1956, Weaver was the only one of the "Eight Men Out" who remained here in Chicago—and the only one who maintained his innocence to the end.

Bud, this one's up to you.

I am asking on behalf of George Daniel Weaver's descendants, who cannot for the life of them comprehend baseball's 80-plus years of persistently, maddeningly blind justice. They have all but given up hope.

"When you're family, as I am, you're biased of course," Buck's niece, 78-year-old Pat Anderson, told me this week. "But you can't understand why someone else could be so obtuse.

"Some of these commissioners, it's like they put a brown paper bag over their heads."

I ask also on behalf of Dr. David Fletcher, a man still very much devoted to this cause. He is president of the Chicago Baseball Museum and the man responsible for ClearBuck.com, a Web site dedicated to the Sox player's receiving of a full pardon for a crime he didn't commit.

Acquitted by a jury, Weaver was banished by Commissioner Kenesaw Mountain Landis for attending a meeting at which the "fix" was discussed and not telling anybody about it. In other words, for not being a rat.

"If you want to compare it to events just of the last few weeks, just look at the reception Rafael Palmeiro got after he said a teammate gave him a drug," Fletcher said.

The disgraced Palmeiro was abandoned for good by the Baltimore Orioles not after his suspension for steroids but after he said teammate Miguel Tejada had given him a B-12 vitamin that might have been responsible for his positive drug test.

To ask a baseball authority to be lenient with a Palmeiro (for drugs) or a Pete Rose (for gambling), well, let's just say I would be ashamed to do that. Some punishments do fit some crimes.

But in the words of Buck Weaver himself, a man who did nothing except to say nothing: "There are murderers who serve a sentence and then get out. I got life."

Bud Selig, commute this innocent man's sentence.

Be a hero to the late Marge Follett, who died shortly after coming to the 2003 All-Star Game hosted by the White Sox to personally beseech you to exonerate her Uncle Buck.

Be a hero to the late Bette Scanlon, a longtime reporter for the Sun-Times who was raised like a daughter by Buck Weaver for 16 years after her own dad died.

Be a hero to Pat Anderson, who used to walk her uncle to work at a drugstore on the South Side, who never heard him speak of the 1919 World Series, whose own husband is 83 now and would love to get the news that the good name of Buck Weaver has been resurrected at last.

I don't know about you, Bud, but all my life I have wanted to do one really good thing.

Correct an injustice. Right a wrong. Do something of merit, something magnanimous, something more than watch a man catch a ball or report a score. You can. You have the power.

And what a gesture it would be on your part, to let Chicago have a World Series back in town and have a World Series hero back, all in one fell swoop.

Anderson says she would fly in from Missouri in a blink of an eye for that World Series celebration.

"I'm not a drinker," she told me. "But I think if that did happen, I would really go hang one on."

Bud, the first round would be on me.

Buck Weaver remains on major-league baseball's suspended list.

Crystals on Top of an Iceberg

JEANNIE MORRIS

Chicago Today February 11, 1972

Confess, now. Haven't the girls—spinning, schussing, and whizzing over the ice and down the slopes in Sapporo—thrilled you every bit as much as the men have?

The beauty of the Olympics puts me in mind of the multitudes of women who have been and will be denied the rewards of sport and competition because of archaic systems and outdated prejudices still prevalent in this great, upbeat super-culture of ours.

Olympic gold medalists Dianne Holum and Ann Henning are the lovely exceptions who prove the rule. Suburban Northbrook takes its speed skaters in both genders—and takes them seriously.

But there are many other excellent female athletes who surround us. In addition to the lonely self-discipline required to achieve a high level of competence, most have had to fight FOR training and facilities and AGAINST resentment,

Take Mayor Daley's Youth Foundation Track Club. Our city should be very proud of these girls, led by four-time Olympian Willye White. Most have grappled their way to the surface from Chicago's poorer neighborhoods only to practice—and succeed—in obscurity.

They earn no money, little glory, and certainly do not attain the special social status enjoyed by the men. The girls run for the love of sport.

The MDYF girls, the Northbrook skaters, Janet Lynn and others have found the support they needed *outside* of our schools.

Hinsdale Center School boasts a wealth of female athletes, led by swimmer Sandy Bucha. Don Watson, coach of Hinsdale's perennial state championship men's team, says Sandy could compete on any men's team in Illinois.

School administrators, already pressed for funds, do not fancy stretching budgets to spend as much money on girls as they do on boys.

Coaches and men's P. E. personnel are naturally hesitant to give up dominance of gyms, pools, fields, and locker facilities.

Yet that alliance may be fighting a losing battle. Last spring, following legal action and experimental studies, the New York State Board of Regents made it official—girls can now play on boys' teams in noncontact sports.

At Skyline College in San Mateo, Cal., one-thousand students recently signed a petition seeking to end "male Chauvinism" in sports.

At the NCAA meetings in Florida last month delegates were told by Joanne Thorpe of Southern Illinois University that many college administrations "are still in the uninformed state of believing that women exist only to perform the supportive tasks in athletics of cheering, drilling and waving pom-poms."

Mrs. Thorpe is director of women's P. E. at SIU and also director of the Association for Intercollegiate Athletics for Women, which she intends to keep very separate and make very equal.

A 34-year-old female marathon runner, Pat Tarnawsky, looked back on her youth and her sport and put it this way: "We're not out for a lark. We're not even merely dead-serious. We are out—each in her own way—to get back something that an over-repressive, overprotective society took away from us."

And, looking ahead at a woman's life in our times, Ms. Tarnawsky continues, "Our society has refused to recognize how badly women need the sanitizing, mind-bending experience of high-stress sports like long distance running. And it does its best to keep women fretting on the minimal levels, wallowing in affluent ease."

A bill, introduced by Rep. Harber Hall (R., Bloomington), which forbids exclusion of students from intramural or interscholastic athletic programs solely on account of sex has cleared the House and awaits action in the Illinois Senate. It is sure to lend a push in the right direction.

The lovely young women in Sapporo are but crystals on the top of an iceberg.

From Too Tall to Scaling the Heights

MELISSA ISAACSON

Chicago Tribune May 6, 2001

She looks out among the young faces in the crowd and, almost always, Kelly Kennedy can see herself.

It might be the way they slouch their shoulders or drop their heads, or maybe it's just a certain look in their eyes that tells her exactly what they are going through. Usually, she's right.

Kennedy's is not necessarily a dramatic story, as stories go. She did not battle a life-threatening illness or endure family tragedy or financial hardship.

Hers is simply a story about a kid who found sports and found herself. It is worth telling because her feelings, as isolating as they were, are universal, cutting through sports and gender, although one suspects girls can relate more easily.

Kennedy was 6 feet 2 inches tall her freshman year at Barrington and, by her estimate, 40 pounds overweight. The double whammy for adolescent girls, who want only to fit in.

"It was one of those things where I felt like I stood out, and I did," she says. "A lot of people teased me about being so tall. It was something I definitely did not embrace back then."

She had tried out for the volleyball team twice in middle school and didn't make it. She wasn't much interested in basketball. Through her parents' urging, she tried volleyball again and, thank goodness for freshman B teams everywhere, found her niche.

"My first year was so hard, I don't know how I made it," she said. "When

I started they literally had to show me how to run, I was so awkward. I had to go to practice an hour a day before I started just to figure out my body, how to get my hands up to block a ball."

As she learned how to play volleyball, something else started happening as well. Her grades improved and so did her entire outlook.

"People started wanting to be around me," she said. "When you have high self-esteem, it rubs off on other people. Once it hit me, I started feeling so much better about everything, about myself, that there's more to life than being popular."

Anyone who still questions the impact of Title IX and every knucklehead who still resents the law that gave girls equal opportunity in sports 30 years ago, made girls freshman B teams possible and gave girls like Kelly Kennedy self-esteem and direction should be forced to face a situation like the one Bill and Pat Kennedy did.

"Kelly was falling apart," Bill Kennedy said. "She was being teased in high school because she was tall, and she became so upset she put weight on. She walked into a room all hunched over. She had no self-esteem. Volleyball literally changed her whole life."

By her senior year, Kennedy was a top club player and coveted college recruit bound for the University of Wisconsin, where she eventually became a three-time first-team All-Big Ten selection, an All-American and a member of the school's all-century team.

On Sunday, as a member of the U.S. Professional Volleyball League "Dream Team," Kennedy will compete in the Millennium Cup at Allstate Arena, an event to be televised nationally on Fox Sports Net.

Eight-team league play will start in January. Women like Kennedy have elected to put off a variety of careers—six say they have turned down job offers of $60,000 per year up to $135,000—for the experience of getting the upstart league going, a job for which they will be paid from $30,000 to $40,000.

"This is something I want to do for the future of volleyball," Kennedy said. "It would be really cool to look back in 10 to 15 years and say I helped start this. Up until a couple of years ago, there weren't a lot of people or things in sports little girls could look up to. When I was little, I looked up to Walter Payton and Michael Jordan.

"Before, a lot of girls wanted to be in movies or magazines. But now there are great female role models in sports. There are other options and realistic goals."

Kennedy knows this for sure because, as she says, she made herself an athlete by sheer will and the grace of a physical stature she once hated.

"I talk to a lot of kids and I can just tell I was the same way when I was younger," Kennedy said. "The girls who are really tall who you can tell are real uncomfortable with it, I just want to say, 'Stand up straight. Don't slouch.' I want to tell them just to stay with it, to fight through the doubts."

Bill and Pat Kennedy are thankful their daughter did.

"Our belief is that if we raise our children with self-esteem, they will be successful in life," Bill Kennedy said. "And I don't mean monetarily, but to like yourself. I saw my child's life change when she found that."

"For me, I had to do something and I finally found my niche," Kelly said. "And what a great niche it is."

FROM THE HEART

After all the time they spend talking to athletes, managers, coaches, executives, and fans, there are occasions when sports columnists must interview themselves. Call it nostalgia, therapy or working through inner demons, it puts me in mind of something Philip Roth is reputed to have said: "Nothing bad ever happens to writers. It's all material."

Alas, Lacy Banks is here to tell us differently. Lacy and I worked together at the *Sun-Times* and I think it is fair to say that nobody was ever in his company, or talked about him in his absence, without smiling. I also think it is fair to say that there was never another sports columnist remotely like him.

Lacy was an ordained Baptist minister who said, "God bless you" instead of hello, preached in Chicago churches, referenced the almighty in his columns and sometimes prayed with the athletes he covered. He also had a beautiful singing voice that he would use, uninvited, in front of startled but delighted strangers, and, invited, at weddings.

And then Lacy was struck down by his own version of the trials of Job. The column reprinted here describes them and it should be noted that he hung in and hung on, writing and smiling all the way, for four more years. Several hundred people, including some of the athletes he covered, attended his funeral and Chicago mayor Rahm Emanuel called him a trailblazer in his field.

Sun-Times writer Diane Simpson was moved to give a harrowing account of her battle with eating disorders as she followed the highly charged national debate that, in 2005, reached all the way into the White House, over whether to end life support for Terry Schiavo, who had long been in a vegetative state after suffering massive brain damage. With all due respect to Rick Telander and David Haugh, who played football in college, Simpson, who was a member of the 1988 U.S Olympic rhythmic gymnastics team, is surely the most accomplished athlete ever to write about sports on a regular basis for a Chicago newspaper.

As for Jack Griffin, he loved writing about fishing and his family about as much as he loved writing about the Chicago Bears. In the column reprinted here, he indulges all of those passions. Other mothers and fathers make memorable appearances in columns by John Kuenster, Phil Arvia, and Carol Slezak, while Greg Couch ponders the recent change in fortune that has overtaken Chicago sports fans and Skip Bayless remembers when he was young enough for baseball to be the center of his universe.

Then there is John Schulian, who was a sports columnist, first at the *Daily News* and *Sun-Times* and then at the *Philadelphia Daily News*, for several decades before moving to Los Angeles where he had a lengthy career writing for television. But Schulian left behind a distinguished body of work in sports, one that he has added to with many fine magazine articles over the years, and his colleagues, myself among them, will tell you he is on the short list of the very best sports columnists of his generation. His "Summer's End" column is Schulian at his finest and it strikes me as a proper ending for a collection that began with Ring Lardner.

God Is My Primary-Care Physician

LACY J. BANKS

Chicago Sun-Times May 6, 2008

Welcome to the story of the adventure of the healing process that I am undergoing.

My blog will take you with me as I go from serious sickness to, I hope, miraculous recovery, by the grace of God and the aid of God-gifted doctors and nurses.

First, let me describe our outbound point of origin. Last month, destiny dealt me a triple dose of trauma. Doctors at the University of Chicago and Northwestern hospitals examined me over a two-week span and diagnosed three big problems:

—Brain cancer, which might require surgery.

—End-stage congestive heart failure, which definitely requires a heart transplant.

—Prostate cancer, which also definitely requires surgery.

Any one of these diagnoses is enough to drape a man with doom and gloom. But the Lord has seen fit to visit me with all three.

I am a 64-year-old black man, a Sun-Times reporter for 35 years, a Baptist preacher for 55 years.

I have a family history of congestive heart failure, which killed my oldest and youngest siblings, my father and an aunt, and of prostate cancer, which killed three uncles.

Now, it's my turn to tangle with both of those terrors, and brain cancer, too.

Each diagnosis hit me like a proverbial ton of bricks, drove me to my knees in prayer, made me tell my wife and children, to their despair, and motivated me to surf the Internet and question doctors to see what information they could share.

Many doctors prefer that their patients be simple, silent and totally surrendered to whatsoever they suggest.

But it's my life at stake. I already underwent a cardiac triple-bypass in 2001—when I was sawed open, had three ribs broken and had a plastic surgeon fail to stabilize my sternum, or breast bone, with experimental

271

titanium plates. The latter required me to undergo a subsequent serious surgery three months later to have the plates replaced with the standard steel sutures.

Since then, I have been determined to make sure I communicate more closely with my doctors, ask as many questions as possible, talk to as many patients as possible and get as much published information as possible to enable me to know exactly what it is that doctors say I have, what options are available, how they compare in effecting a cure—and how much time do I have for ME to make the decision as to what will be done.

In other words, I have promoted myself to being CEO, as best I can, of my medical dream team, where, first and foremost, God is my primary-care physician.

I invite your feedback after each posting. I am most eager to hear from people who have recovered from similar medical issues, or are still dealing with them, or are caregivers for someone else who has dealt with them.

I cordially invite you all to watch God heal me.

Right now, I actually feel good. I take 10 different pills a day, run at least a mile on my treadmill, eat responsibly, don't do anything strenuous and get plenty of prayer and rest as I also schedule the surgeries that I feel are in my best interests—unless God postpones them with a cataclysmic healing.

It's going to be one of the strangest, most exciting and—I hope—enlightening tales you'll ever read.

I Cannot Escape the Compulsion to Be Thin
Even though I Know It Could Kill Me

DIANE SIMPSON

Chicago Sun-Times April 15, 2005

Terri Schiavo died two weeks ago after more than a decade and a half on life support. But the truth is she began to die many years earlier.

I know this because I could die at any time for the same reason she did: from desperate, repeated attempts to lose weight driven by psychological forces so strong that neither I nor anybody else can control them.

In 1988, I was a member of the U.S. Olympic rhythmic gymnastics team. Last year, I was inducted into the USA Gymnastics Hall of Fame. I have been a gymnastics commentator on network television. My husband and I have a beautiful 5-year-old daughter. I have a good job doing media relations for a large nonprofit medical organization in Chicago's suburbs. Last Thursday, I turned 36 years old.

I have also battled eating disorders similar to those that led to the brain damage that put Schiavo in what doctors called a "persistent vegetative state" for so long. I continue to fight that battle every day of my life, a battle that can be so overwhelming that when Schiavo died I actually felt jealous. At least her battle was over, I thought.

Let me tell you what it's like to have a serious eating disorder like Schiavo. It starts at about four or five in the morning when, if I have slipped back and become what my doctors call "symptomatic," I am hit by my structural coronary artery spasm. It feels like a large brick falling off a ledge and landing on my chest. "My God," I think, "I'm dying," and I wonder if I should wake my husband. I pop a Nitrostat pill instead.

It continues when I get up and step naked onto the scale that I should throw away. It results in broken bones, multiple surgeries, endoscopies, colonoscopies, bleeding gastritis in my stomach lining, gastric and colonic polyps, damage to my nervous system, concussions from repeated fainting episodes, bloody diarrhea, impacted fecal matter that results from dehydration, hypothermia, pancreatitis, the removal of my gallbladder and diseased bile ducts that pinch my sides whenever I eat any fat. There are also the burned bridges among friends and loved ones—the aftershocks of years of starvation.

Eating disorders are relentless, wicked, suffocating. No matter how much treatment I receive, no matter how much money my husband and I spend, no matter how many speeches I give to young athletes saying "don't make the same mistakes I did," I cannot escape the compulsion to be thin. Even though I know I could die at any moment.

I will not tell you what I weigh. If you met me, you would think I am too thin for a woman who is a shade taller than 5-feet-7. I think I am fat. Last month, when I was inducted into my high school Hall of Fame, I wore a black backless Calvin Klein dress. In preparation, I pumped iron, starved myself and lost seven pounds in four days. I was dizzy from hunger the entire evening.

That was nothing, really. As an elite competitive gymnast, I sometimes lost 20 pounds in three weeks—close to 15 percent of my body weight—even though the heart palpitations this caused scared the wits out of me.

Between 8 million and 9 million Americans suffer from eating disorders, which account for the highest mortality rate of all psychiatric conditions. Many of these deaths are from suicide.

Eating disorders took the lives of the singer Karen Carpenter and world championship gymnast Christy Henrich, who once asked me how I stayed so thin. An eating disorder also claimed Amy, a lost girl with hollowed-out eyes and an empty soul with whom I shared a hospital stay for a month. My doctor said Amy wasn't going to make it, and he was right. I sometimes wonder what he thought about me.

Soon, I will take Alexis to the store to buy a dress for her graduation from kindergarten. I hope that I can muster the will not to try on something in a girls' size 12 for myself. Just to see if it fits.

Diane Simpson later discovered her eating disorder stemmed from a birth defect that led to severe intestinal damage and Celiac disease, a condition that injured the lining of the small intestine, as well as from multiple abdominal surgeries after the birth of her two children. With the support of her family and doctors, she says she is now "healthy most of the time."

Fishing with Mother
Strangled Chicken for Dinner

JACK GRIFFIN

Chicago Sun-Times August 8, 1971

My mother can catch a catfish and bait a hook, although she could never kill a chicken, except by accident. I know these things to be true, because I grew up around her.

A long time ago, during the summer, we went fishing every Sunday, my mother, my dad and I, and later my kid sister. Usually, it was to Indian Creek, which looked much larger when I was a boy than it did when I became a man.

It was a pleasant place, with many great trees hanging over the water and shading the banks, and it was suitably populated with catfish.

My mother would get liver from the corner butcher for bait and my dad dug the nightcrawlers and I snatched live crawdads out of the creek for additional bait. Sometimes, I remember, we would go to one of the dust bowl lakes on the Kansas prairie. And occasionally my father would get very daring and we would drive all the way to the Lake of the Ozarks, where once we had to live in a cave because there were no cabins.

Another time, and I am sure it was the Lake of the Ozarks, we lived in a tent, and it was very hot, and there were very many mosquitos, and that's where my mother killed the chicken accidentally.

She and my Aunt Effie had rustled two live chickens off some unsuspecting farmer's ranch and brought them to the tent. But there they hit the cul de sac.

Neither my mother nor my Aunt Effie could bring herself to kill either of the chickens. They debated this at great length while each was holding a chicken by the neck.

It was getting close to supper time and each was protesting she could not kill the chickens. It was then they discovered both chickens were dead. They had accidentally strangled them during the long debate. But they cooked them anyway, and they did not taste any the worse for the experience.

I had a dog named Chub. I always thought he was a Russian wolfhound, or at the very least a German shepherd. But actually, he was only a scuffy little mongrel.

But he was a lovable little guy, and he dearly liked to go fishing, and we always took him with us. Once Chub ate all the liver, which did not please my father, but we never left him at home.

We went even when it rained, and nobody minded. We went even if we had not caught any fish the Sunday before, because catching fish wasn't all of the trip.

But mostly the sun shined, and usually it was very hot. There were no cooling boxes then. My father would stop outside of town at an ice house and get a 50-pound cake which he put in a galvanized tub.

Around the ice, mother would put the milk and the soft drinks and a volatile homebrew my father and Uncle Fred made in the basement. About half the homebrew would explode before we got to the fishing hole. But dad and Uncle Fred anticipated this, and always put in twice what they needed.

Mother made all sorts of wonderful things, starting with fried chicken. And sometimes she put in homemade root beer, if dad wasn't using the crock that week for homebrew.

If we ran short of supplies, mother would buy milk from a farmer for a nickel a gallon, and eggs went at about the same rate. Sometimes we had homemade bread.

I hardly remember making a trip without blowing a tire or two on dad's car. Sometimes, we ran out of gas, but people were gentler then, and there was always someone to help.

I don't think we had much money then. But I was very young, and I never thought about such matters, or cared. But I do know we had a lot of fun.

My mother is visiting this week. I get to see her only about once a year, and I thought you wouldn't mind that I gave her the column this Sunday.

I Was a Bears Baby, Too

GREG COUCH

Chicago Sun-Times January 25, 2007

The other day, we saw the story of Chicagoan Colleen Pavelka, who had her child's birth induced so it wouldn't conflict with her husband's enjoyment of the Bears-Saints game. She was hailed as wife of the year.

Unique. Well, that wasn't the first time something like this happened.

My mother did it, too. I was born Dec. 29, 1963, and the night before labor was to be induced, my parents called the doctor and put off my birth until after the Bears game. They beat the Giants that day to win the championship. Then I was born, and Chicago's long sports slide began.

To me, it was some sort of cruel joke from the gods, born hours after a title and not seeing another one for 22 years. Life as the Chicago sports jinx.

Twenty-two years old. Zero major championships, forcing myself to care about Karl-Heinz Granitza, the shootout and the Chicago Sting. The '85 Bears were the first champion.

City of Champions—ha!

Bears quarterback Rex Grossman complained that the Chicago media are a bunch of glass-half-empty people. Look, Rex: When I was a kid, having Chicago sports as a glass even half-empty would have been a dream come true. All that losing brought the city together in a strange way.

Chicago is a different place now, with mixed-and-matched expectations based on age. I looked up all the winners of the Super Bowl, World Series, NBA Finals and Stanley Cup, starting with Da Bears in January 1986. And guess what?

Chicago is the City of Champions.

Ha! One title from the Bears, six from the Bulls and one from the White Sox in that time. That's eight titles. No city has more, though New York is tied. If the Bears beat the Colts in the Super Bowl, then Chicago stands alone.

277

If you're 25 years old, then you are defined by championships (except from the Cubs, who are defined by goats). But Chicagoans from their mid-30s to early 50s can't put the words "City of Champions" and "Chicago" in the same sentence without adding "Ha!" on the end.

On average, Chicago has been winning a major title roughly every two and one-half years. How can today's punk kids possibly appreciate this?

They figure that if the Bears lose, another title will come in a couple years. To me, you can't take championships lightly because another one might never come.

Put it this way: If the Bears beat the Colts, I'll feel bad for Chicago kids born that night.

Today's 25-year-olds grew up watching Michael Jordan fly. Their first memories are of the Fridge in the Super Bowl.

Mine are of my dad and a Cubs game at Wrigley Field. It was 1969, and by summer's end, my dad went to get a haircut, and his barber, a young man, was bald! He had lost his hair in a bet with a Mets fan.

Remember, Jordan hadn't made baldness stylish yet. This was pure horror to a kid.

The Cubs' collapse of 1969 turned a Norman Rockwell moment into this: Kid. Chicago sports. Losing. Horror.

It all equated back then.

Following Chicago sports was about the Cubs' collapse, about the South Side Hitmen not making it. It was sneaking a transistor radio under the covers to listen to the Hawks blow Game 7 to the Canadiens, or watching highlights of the Bulls blowing the final minutes of Game 7 to the Lakers. Turnover, turnover, turnover, and not being able to stop it.

By the time the Bears next made the playoffs, in 1977, they lost to the Cowboys 37–7. When they finally got their first first down, some Bear spiked the ball in celebration—and was penalized. At least, that's the memory of a glass-half-empty guy.

Last week, Chicago historian Rich Lindberg said the 2005 champion Sox haven't surpassed the 1959 World Series losing Sox in fans' hearts.

That's because today's Chicagoans take championships for granted.

Advice: If the Bears win, don't do that. Today, baldness means MJ and the City of Champions. To some, baldness and Chicago sports means horror!

Remembering the Land of Enchantment

JOHN KUENSTER

Chicago Daily News October 7, 1964

You called us at 5 a.m., just as you said you would.

It was still dark out, and even a "young pup" could sense it was going to be a cold October day.

The rest of the family was still sleeping. The house seemed deathly still, more noticeable, perhaps, because the traffic in it was usually pretty heavy.

The only noise that could be heard was the coffee percolating on the kitchen stove. It smelled good.

We sat down at the table, the two of us, as though we were conspirators about to embark on some secret mission

In truth, it WAS the beginning of a big adventure together.

You had cooked up a batch of oatmeal and had said: "Eat some of this . . . it'll warm you up and stick to your ribs."

We ate the oatmeal, but it was tasteless. Our mind was on the big adventure—our first World Series game together.

We don't remember much about the trip to Wrigley Field, but we do remember waiting in line for bleacher tickets.

We waited on Sheffield Ave., and recall looking in wonderment at hardy souls who had been in line all night long.

We remember, too, the temporary bleachers that had been erected so they extended outside the ball park.

Finally, we got our tickets and we sat in the right field stands. The fans were noisy and boisterous and packed together like sardines.

But, we didn't mind. We were in . . . in the land of enchantment for an 11-year-old kid.

We watched the Cubs work out, and we watched the Tigers.

The Tigers, you said, had a fine ball club.

"See," you said, "there's Mickey Cochrane and Charlie Gehringer and Billy Rogell and Tommy Bridges.

"Bridges is very good," you said. "He has a wicked curve ball."

"Will he pitch today?" we asked.

"No," you said. "They have a fella named Crowder. Alvin Crowder. He's good, too.

"There," you pointed. "There's Tex Carleton warming up. He's going to pitch for the Cubs."

The game started. We don't remember all the details, but we do remember some of them.

We remember the Tigers scoring the winning run, on two errors—one by left fielder Augie Galan, and the other by shortstop Billy Jurges.

"They are usually excellent fielders," you said.

We remember Gabby Hartnett hitting a home run. It headed our way.

"Here it comes!" you shouted. "Maybe, we can catch it!"

We didn't. The ball landed a few rows in front of us.

The Cubs lost, 2–1.

The trip back home has been lost in memory, and we don't recall too much about the many other games we later saw together.

But, we remember that first one.

And now when baseball comes alive over the prospects of another World Series, we think back fondly to that happy day in 1935 when a skinny, redheaded kid saw his heroes in the flesh for the first time:

Jurges, Billy Herman, Galan, Lon Warneke, Stan Hack, Frank Demaree, a teenager named Phil Cavarretta . . . and even Charlie Root who was an ancient 36 then.

It all seems so long ago . . . that wonderful time when life was simple and baseball its mainspring.

Thanks, dad, for the memories.

Wishing for Dreams That Can't Come True

SKIP BAYLESS

Chicago Tribune September 19, 1998

I wish I was 8 years old right now. I wish I lived in or around Chicago and that I loved the Cubs as much as I loved peanut butter and jelly. I wish I was living and dying with this team as only a kid can.

I wish memories were being formed on the blank slate of my mind that could grow warmer and larger by the summer. Memories of Sammy Sosa's furious uppercuts and Kerry Wood's blazing fastballs and Rod Beck's swinging arm and Mickey Morandini's flying hair and Mark Grace's game-winning hits. Memories from what has the feel of the most memorable Cubs season since, who knows, cavemen roamed the Earth in 1945.

Wrigley hasn't changed since then, but I have. I have witnessed too many "greatest" games and "miracle" finishes. Now I wouldn't give you the price of my newspaper for the next Sammy Sosa home run ball. But at age 8 . . .

Like Christmas, memorable baseball seasons are mostly for kids. The reason Sosa is enjoying this one so refreshingly much is because, as one clubhouse observer says, he's "a 29-year-old 12-year-old."

If only I could have defied my parents' orders to go to sleep the other night and snuck a little radio under my pillow. When I was 8, we called them transistors. I wish I had been listening in the dark around midnight—the latest I had ever been awake on a school night—when Sammy hit the grand slam that beat San Diego.

I wish I had come flying out from under the covers yelling, "Sixty-three! Sammy hit 63!" I wish I had been grounded without TV for a week, then snuck over to my friend Larry's house Friday afternoon on the way home from school.

I wish I had thrown pillows at Larry's TV as the Cubs' bullpen blew it again. I wish one of the coolest insults I could lay on my friends was to say, "You're worse than Terry Adams." I wish I had nightmares about manager Jim Riggleman signaling for a new pitcher—for Adams or Felix Heredia, who scared me worse than the wicked witch's flying monkeys in "The Wizard of Oz."

I wish I hated the Mets worse than I did turnips and that I hated their manager, Bobby Valentine, worse than getting stuck with a needle.

I wish watching the Cubs battle the Mets in the wild-card race was like riding the biggest roller coaster I had ever been allowed to ride. I wish I could feel the highs and lows as only a kid can—and that I could completely forget them as soon as Larry and I resumed our continuous game of back yard home run derby.

I wish, when I was 8, I hadn't had to wait until the next morning to run out in my pajamas and snatch the newspaper off the lawn so I could see who won and lost and hit home runs. Now I'd just flip on ESPN before bedtime. Now I could watch many of Sammy's and Mark McGwire's at-bats live.

I was 10 when, on the way home from peewee football practice, I heard on the car radio that Roger Maris had hit No. 61. Unfortunately, I heard it the next day. I didn't see any grainy black-and-white highlights of Maris' liner into the right-field bleachers until I was an adult.

Oh, to be 8 now, to know instantaneously what had happened, to watch postgame interviews live on my bedroom TV. Oh, to have been able to see Sammy say live Friday afternoon at Wrigley, "Last night was a great moment for me when I saw my mother at my house."

Oh, to wear a No. 21 Cubs uniform top and to amaze my friends with a perfect impersonation of Sammy at the plate: tapping the umpire and catcher on the backs of the leg with my bat handle, digging in with my right foot, "blessing" home plate with three taps of the bat's barrel end, locking into my stance with my hands held away from my body, bat pointing skyward, hopping twice as I watched the ball soar toward the seats, baby-stepping before touching each base, sending heart-tap kisses to my mother . . .

Oh, to stick a pillow under my T-shirt and practice in the mirror being Rod "the Shooter" Beck, swinging my right arm as I took the sign from my catcher.

Oh, to have my Mom tell me, "No, you can't let your hair grow as long as Mickey Morandini's."

If only I didn't know that a stunning number of Cubs smoke cigarettes. If only I didn't know that lots of baseball old-timers consider the newfangled wild-card race as sacrilegious as wearing earrings in the clubhouse. If only I had been just young enough not to understand the last baseball strike and just old enough to love Harry Caray almost as much as I did my grandfather.

If only my father could announce that, for my birthday, he was taking me to Sammy Sosa Day Sunday at Wrigley. If only he and I could sit in box seats, sharing popcorn and perhaps the greatest sports memory of my life.

That Stinging Sensation
This One's for You, Dad

PHIL ARVIA

Southtown Star October 17, 2005

ANAHEIM, Calif.—That champagne stings when it gets in your eyes.

Yeah, that's it.

Forget about the fact that, in my office at home, I have two ticket stubs from the 1959 World Series, given to me by my father, who went to that game with his father. Forget about the fact that those two tickets rest in a frame, sandwiching a stub from the last game at old Comiskey Park, a game my mom and dad went to and I covered. Forget about the fact that I'm going to have to get a bigger frame now.

That champagne stings.

So forget about the fact that dad and grampa took me to my first White Sox game in 1968, when I was 5, and . . .

Oh, forget this.

The fact is, the White Sox are in the World Series, and at least one guy in the raucous postgame clubhouse had to bite his lip, take a deep breath and hope no one noticed how much he wished he could have been sharing the moment with the White Sox fans he misses the most. Especially the one who told him he didn't need to throw a curve when he was 10 years old, because his fastball had "natural movement."

"I feel the same way," said Frank Thomas, whose father passed away in

2001. "As all these milestones come, I think of my father. He was instrumental in me playing. He was the one that pushed me. Not having him here is tough on me. I know what his goals were for me. As we get closer to them, of course—I know what you're feeling, man."

Isn't it what a whole bunch of fathers and sons are feeling right now?

The White Sox are in the World Series.

Is "in" enough? Not knowing what is coming, I can only answer that it was enough to make those 46-year-old ticket stubs among my most cherished possessions.

The White Sox are in the World Series.

Not even their opponent is certain yet. But the opportunity for memories is an absolute. Let your kids stay up late to watch, and if they sleep through homeroom, so be it.

The White Sox are in the World Series.

The first person to celebrate that fact with Ozzie Guillen in the visitors' dugout at Angel Stadium was Ozzie Guillen Jr. Father kissed son on the cheek.

"We have a ritual," the namesake said. "Every game, after every clincher, I give him a hug. I'm the first one to congratulate him. I told him a long time ago, if they ever got to the postseason, I was going to be right there next to him to congratulate him."

Baseball does this, even in families where headlocks pass for hugs.

"It's not weird at all," Junior said. "It's the relationship I have with my dad.

"It's something that bonds you. When you have a love for the game and you get to cheer for the same team as your dad, it's a bonding experience. You get to go through the hardships and the good times together."

Sunday was a very good time.

In the clubhouse, Jermaine Dye was in the middle of it, ever so slightly calming the bedlam screaming, "Hey!" and thrusting the American League Championship trophy toward the ceiling. He held it aloft and waded into a mosh pit of teammates, he and the trophy disappearing in an omnidirectional bombardment of champagne.

We are not promised the experience again. A lot of folks have been waiting 46 years for their second taste of the Sox in the Series. Some of us have waited all our lives for a first.

The White Sox are in the World Series.

"It means a lot," general manager Ken Williams said. "It means that all the people who have written me letters, all the feelings I've gotten from White Sox people, generations of people, 40-, 50-, 60-year fans, somewhere right now, they're celebrating with us and partying, and that gives me a great feeling.

"My secretary Nancy's father died a few weeks back, my grandfather died a few weeks back—and they would have loved to have seen this. But how many other generations of people, White Sox fans, have died between the last time and this time they'll see their team in the World Series?

"For me, I feel honored to be able to be a part of it."

The White Sox are in the World Series.

And Ozzie Guillen Jr. will be in the dugout for every pitch of it.

"When I have my kids, I hope they love the game of baseball," Junior said. "I think my dad's been very fortunate we love the game as much as he does."

I think you have too, kid.

A Short Walk Down a Long Corridor

CAROL SLEZAK

Chicago Sun-Times June 21, 2009

I can't remember the last time I spent Father's Day with my dad. But I'm headed east on I-94 to visit him today in Detroit. I haven't even bought him a present. I guess my company will have to do.

Hopefully I'll be good company and we won't argue about politics, which we tend to do whenever we're together. That would be bad form on my part this time, not only because it's Father's Day, but also because he's not feeling so great. He has been stuck in a rehab facility for about a week, after having been stuck in a hospital for a week, after suffering a heart attack that left him very weak.

You don't know my dad, but chances are you know someone like him. He was an excellent athlete. Seriously. You had to have a really good shot to beat him in a game of H-O-R-S-E. If he had been able to play regularly as an adult, he would have been a scratch golfer. He was a fast-pitch soft-ball pitcher with a curve that would put Sandy Koufax's to shame. Man, was that thing impossible to hit. He had a smoking fastball, too. Back in the day, they called him "Fireball George." My glove hand still aches at the thought of catching him in the backyard.

My dad probably wouldn't admit this, but he's a feminist at heart. He grew up in an era when girls didn't play sports and assumed he would have a few sons to share in his passion. But when he ended up having six daughters and no sons, he adapted. He played sports with his daughters.

And he made it seem like the most natural thing in the world. He always made time for a game of catch, H-O-R-S-E or 21 when anyone asked. Because a few of us were really into sports, we kept him busy. And he always made it fun.

I can't remember the last time I played catch or shot baskets with my dad, but I do remember going to the driving range with him when I visited a few summers back. After watching my swing, he said, "Don't quit your day job, honey." He thought that was funny. To his credit, when I was a kid, he dished out only hugs and encouragement, never criticism.

For the last few years, my dad's memory has been giving him fits. But despite struggling to recall many things, some things seemed cemented in his head, including the fact that I'm a sportswriter. My mom and sisters joke that I'm his favorite daughter because of my job. Last week, he asked my sister Karen to print my columns from the Sun-Times' Web site and bring them to him at the rehab facility. I call that unconditional love.

Because of everything he's going through, my dad hasn't been keeping up with sports the way he used to. But I'm sure we'll talk about them when I see him. When it comes to conversation with my dad, there's basically sports and conservative politics—and I've promised myself to stay away from the latter topic. Instead, I'll ask him what he thinks about Sammy Sosa. We'll talk about the Detroit Tigers. And I bet we'll commandeer the TV at the facility to watch the U.S. Open.

I figure most dads and kids will be doing pretty much the same thing, wherever they are. Talking sports, that is. Or watching sports. Because that's typically what dads and their kids do when they're together, and why should Father's Day be any different?

I'd be lying if I said this was going to be a typical Father's Day for me, though. I can't say I'm looking forward to seeing my dad under these circumstances. I know that people get sick, that parents age. I realize the days of my dad slinging a 60-mile-an-hour fastball past me are long gone. Intellectually, I get it. Emotionally, I'm not buying it. I have an urge to play catch with him, to challenge him to a game of H-O-R-S-E, to watch him hit golf balls at a driving range. That said, I will settle for watching him take a short walk down a long corridor.

Chances are, you know someone like my dad, a man who loves sports but loves his family even more. If that sounds like your own dad, you're a very lucky person.

Lucky like me.

Summer's End Recalls Memory of a Faded Dream

JOHN SCHULIAN

Chicago Sun-Times September 24, 1983

Up ahead, you could see a full moon sandwiched by thick, wet clouds. Beneath them glowed the lights of Chicago, turning the soggy heavens red-orange and proving that this ribbon of highway actually led somewhere.

Another country radio station faded into oblivion inside the car, so you pressed a button and came across the White Sox, summer's golden children at play on a night made for antifreeze.

Their presence should have been a comfort at 70 miles an hour, just as it had been since they used June as their launching pad to glory. But now the Sox were bidding adieu to their regular season at home. They weren't going to return to Comiskey Park until October's playoffs, and the thought left you feeling as empty as a farewell at a train station. Summer was over.

All you could do about it was punch another button on the car's radio, punch another button and hope you would hear the Police singing "Every Breath You Take." For that was the song that provided the background music for the last three months, lingering in your mind whether you were mowing the lawn or trying to describe the cosmic significance of the infield fly rule. The melody haunted you, the lyrics left you wondering about the residue of your own tilling and threshing. And, like a lot of other things this summer, that hadn't happened for a while.

Maybe you have to go back as far as the days before baseball finally defeated you, days of keg parties and a curveball pitcher who lay down next to a stereo speaker filled with the Rolling Stones' voices and begged his kid brother to turn the music louder. The season was over by then and the unraked diamonds had started turning hard under the fading sun. Every morning, the chill sunk a little deeper and lasted a little longer, and you began to realize how impossible it is to hang on to summer and all the things it represents.

No team you played on would ever be the same, no chance for a professional contract ever as good, no friendships ever so unencumbered. And that was what mattered to a catcher with a strong arm and a weak bat, a kid who hid inside a game and thought it would always sustain him.

Even on the night he graduated from high school, he tried to flee what scared him most for the safety that the Salt Lake Bees provided. But before he got to his $1.50 seat, before he even got out of the auditorium where he had received his diploma, there was lipstick on his cheek and a pretty girl saying, "Now you can go."

Funny how long a kiss can last. Ask the man who got it now and he will tell you that summers should have such staying power. For he would think about it from time to time, smile and wonder about the girl who didn't dance off into that happy night before she had made sure he was remembered. And when it came time for the 20th reunion this summer, when he flew back to the place that used to be home, he wondered if she would remember her own kindness. He looked for her and found only a mutual friend with bad news: "She's very sick. I understand it's terminal."

What do you do then? Do you write a letter, or do you pray? Do you retreat into the silence that has become your comfortable enemy, or do you hope that the next knock on your door brings a smiling face and laughter that tinkles like chimes in an ocean breeze? Do you see your own life reduced to what the poet Yeats called "day's vanity and night's remorse," or do you borrow from Tom T. Hall, the hillbilly songwriter, and tell someone dear, "You love everybody but you"?

The questions pile up, but there are never enough answers to clear them all away. Ten years ago, you couldn't have imagined such a predicament. You knew everything then—knew it and said you knew it and expected the world to know you knew it. Perhaps it is only age that brings stupidity.

Summer certainly suggested as much. Whether you were gazing out at Lake Michigan or laboring over your prose, your mind kept drifting away from the business at hand. For too many hours, neither the splendor of Floyd Bannister's left arm nor the foot in Dallas Green's mouth held the appeal of life's complexities. It was time to consider what you had let get away from you, and how, and why. The process was as unsettling as the gray taking over your beard and the lines growing deeper around your eyes.

"I don't know," you kept saying. "I just don't know." It was an all-purpose reply for a summer that raised new questions almost daily. It could also, however, be tiresome. "This is the place for you," a friend said, passing a senior citizens' center. And you couldn't keep from laughing. You feigned anger, too. But down deep, you thanked God there was someone who cared enough to remind you that the sun always comes up in the morning.

It shows its face later and later now, though. You can't ignore that. The leaves on the trees have already started to turn, and even if the White Sox go on to win the World Series, there won't be many more trips to Comiskey Park. The days are growing short, and more and more you cling to the brightness that Ron Kittle, the rookie free spirit, brings to them. "Here's my bat," he said to a team trainer after two hitless nights. "Take its temperature." What a pleasure to find someone who knows where to get answers.

But when they aren't to your questions, the answers are only for enjoyment, not enlightenment. They serve the same function summer did this year as you spun your wheels for week after week, searching for something you hesitate to define and eventually heading back to the garage empty-handed. The answers made you forget the storm front, but by the time you got home it was starting to rain again.

Phil Arvia began covering the White Sox for the then-*Daily Southtown* in 1993. He became the paper's sports columnist in 1995 and sports editor of the *Southtown Star* in 2007. His work has been honored with two Peter Lisagor Awards and awards from the Associated Press Sports Editors, the Illinois Press Association, and the Illinois Editors Association.

Lacy J. Banks (1943–2012) was the first black sportswriter at the *Chicago Sun-Times*. An ordained Baptist minister, he covered Michael Jordan's entire NBA career. Upon his death, his colleague Fred Mitchell of the *Chicago Tribune* wrote: "He talked about God, he talked about his family and he talked about Michael Jordan. In that order."

Skip Bayless began his career as a feature writer and investigative reporter at the *Miami Herald* and *Los Angeles Times*. At twenty-six, he became the lead sports columnist at the *Dallas Morning News*, then was hired away three years later by the rival *Dallas Times Herald*. He transitioned into TV, eventually helping lift ESPN2's *First Take* into a ratings success. He still writes columns for ESPN.com.

Taylor Bell covered high school sports for the *Chicago Daily News* and *Chicago Sun-Times* for thirty-three years before retiring in 2001. A member of the Chicago Journalism Hall of Fame, he now writes about the preps for CSNChicago.com, Comcast Sports Net Chicago's website. He is the author of four books.

Terry Boers has been a sports radio talk show host on WSCR, "The Score" since 1992. He joined the *Chicago Sun-Times* in 1980 and covered the Chicago Bulls from 1982 to 1995. He was a *Sun-Times* columnist from 1988 to 1991 and won the prestigious Peter Lisagor Award for column writing in 1989.

Mark Brown is a local news columnist for the *Chicago Sun-Times*. Roger Ebert called him the "best local columnist since Mike Royko," and *Chicago Magazine* recognized Brown in its Best of Chicago. Noting that was a few years ago, Brown says he subscribes to the Satchel Paige philosophy: "Don't look back, something might be gaining on you."

Warren Brown (1894–1978) was a writer, columnist, and sports editor for several Chicago newspapers in a career that lasted more than fifty years. He was much in demand as an after-dinner speaker, often appeared on national radio broadcasts, and is credited with calling Red Grange "The Galloping Ghost" and for saying, before the 1945 World Series between the Cubs and the Detroit Tigers, "I don't think either one of them can win it."

Dan Burley (1907–62) was the sports editor of the *Chicago Defender*, the theatrical editor of the *Amsterdam News*, and a war correspondent during World War II. As a pianist and composer, he performed with such musicians as Duke Ellington, Cab Calloway, Lionel Hampton, Fats Waller, Billie Holiday, Ella Fitzgerald, and Louis Armstrong.

John P. Carmichael (1902–86) was called "the home run champion of sportswriters" by Ted Williams and "one of the all-time greats" by Bill Veeck. His column, "The Barber Shop," ran in the *Chicago Daily News* from 1934 to 1972.

David Condon (1924–74) wrote the *Chicago Tribune's* "In the Wake of the News" column for twenty-seven years and was known in equal measure for his gifted writing, his wide circle of friends, his ever-present cigar, and his practical jokes. "Dave was mischievous, a character out of 'Guys and Dolls' and 'The Front Page,'" said former *Tribune* sports editor George Langford.

Greg Couch is a sports columnist for FoxSports.com. Previously, he was an award-winning columnist at the *Chicago Sun-Times* and a national columnist at AOL Fanhouse and *The Sporting News*. His work has been featured twice in *Best American Sports Writing*.

James Crusinberry (1879–1960) joined the *Chicago Chronicle* in 1903 and worked for newspapers in St. Louis and New York before joining the *Chicago Daily News*, where he was that paper's first full-time sports editor. While working for the *Chicago Tribune* in 1920, he reported extensively on the Black Sox scandal. He later became news director of CBS in Chicago.

Steve Daley (1948–2011) started writing freelance sports articles while working as a bartender in Washington, DC, where he met editor Dave Burgin, who hired him as a sports reporter in Palo Alto, California. At the *Tribune*, he was a sports columnist, television critic, and political correspondent before becoming a political consultant in Washington.

Mike Downey was a paper boy, proofreader, obit writer, police reporter, columnist, and sports editor for suburban Chicago newspapers, all by the age of twenty. Later, he became a *Chicago Sun-Times* sports and entertainment writer. He wrote sports and metro columns for the *Detroit Free Press* and the *Los Angeles Times* before returning to Chicago to write the "In the Wake of the News" column for the *Tribune*.

Charles Dryden (1860–1931) began working for the *Chicago Daily Tribune* in 1906 and "probably deserves to be called the father of modern sportswriting," according to Stanley Woodward, the legendary sports editor of the *New York Herald Tribune*. Hall of Fame baseball writer Fred Lieb said he "towered over the baseball writers of his day and since as Mark Twain towered over contemporary humorists."

Tom Fitzpatrick (1928–2002) became a sports columnist for the *Chicago Sun-Times* subsequent to winning a Pulitzer Prize in 1970 for a series of articles he wrote after following the members of a radical antiwar group as they rampaged through Lincoln Park and the Near North Side and clashed with police in the "Days of Rage" protests.

Hugh Fullerton (1873–1945) worked at the *Chicago Tribune, Chicago Herald,* and *Chicago Herald-Examiner,* where he developed a national reputation after predicting the underdog White Sox would beat the Cubs in the 1906 World Series. He was a founding member of the Baseball Writers Association of America and proud of the role he played in discovering and promoting Ring Lardner.

Bill Gleason (1922–2010) spent more than sixty years writing sports in Chicago, twenty-five of them as a columnist for the *Chicago Sun-Times.* Born and raised on the South Side, he was an unabashed fan of the White Sox. With Ben Bentley and Bill Jauss, he helped created the popular radio program *The Sports Writers,* which later became a syndicated television show.

Joe Goddard covered the Cubs and White Sox for the *Chicago Sun-Times* for twenty-seven years, was a two-time runner-up for the National Baseball Hall of Fame's J. G. Taylor Spink Award, and wrote over two hundred Sunday "What's Up With . . ." columns. He had a baseball field named after him in a summer teenage baseball league he founded near his home in Palatine, Illinois.

Bob Greene is a contributing writer to CNN.com and the author of more than thirty books. He wrote an award-winning column at the *Chicago Sun-Times* and the *Chicago Tribune* for more than thirty years, was a regular commentator on the ABC news program *Nightline,* and wrote the best sellers *Hang Time: Days and Dreams with Michael Jordan* and *Good Morning, Merry Sunshine: A Father's Journal of His Child's First Year.*

Jack Griffin (1917–76) a sports columnist for the *Chicago Sun-Times* for more than thirty years "loves to put words together," said the judges of one of the many contests he won. Asked to list his special interests, Griffin said, "Fishing, fiction writing and wandering around in as wild a country as I can find." A collection of his columns, *Grif,* was edited by his son, Woodson Jack Griffin.

David Haugh spent ten years as sports columnist at the *South Bend Tribune* and four years covering the Bears before becoming the seventeenth columnist to write "In the Wake of the News" for the *Chicago Tribune.* Haugh was an All-Mid-American Conference safety and Academic All-American at Ball State University.

Philip Hersh has been the Olympic sports writer for the *Chicago Tribune* since 1984 and has covered sixteen Olympics and reported from some fifty countries. Previously, he wrote about baseball and other sports for the *Chicago Daily News* and the *Chicago Sun-Times.* A German publication, *SportIntern,* has ranked him among the hundred most influential people in international sport eleven times.

Dave Hoekstra has been a *Chicago Sun-Times* staff writer and columnist since 1985. He has written books about the Farm Aid movement, travel, and country music. His latest book, *Cougars and Snappers and Loons, Oh My! A Midwest League Field Guide,* is about minor-league baseball in the Midwest.

Jerome Holtzman (1926–2008) had a lengthy career at the *Chicago Sun-Times* and *Chicago Tribune*, during which he invented baseball's save rule and was known as the "dean" of that sports' writers. He wrote or edited more than a dozen books, including the classic oral history *No Cheering in the Press Box*. After retiring from the *Tribune*, he was appointed the official historian of major-league baseball.

Mike Imrem has been a sports columnist at the *Daily Herald* in Arlington Heights, Illinois, since 1978. He has covered twenty Super Bowls, including a Bears' victory and Bears' defeat; nine World Series, including the White Sox's victory in 2005; all six Bulls' championship victories; and two Blackhawks' appearances in the Stanley Cup Finals, one a defeat and the other a championship.

Melissa Isaacson is a columnist for ESPNChicago.com and was a columnist for the *Chicago Tribune* and the paper's principal beat writer for the Chicago Bulls during their championship years in the 1990s. She has covered virtually every major sporting event. Her most recent book is *Sweet Lou—Lou Piniella: A Life in Baseball*.

David Israel was a sports columnist for the *Chicago Tribune* from 1978 to 1981 and went on to a career in Hollywood as producer and writer of television dramas and made-for-television movies and miniseries. In 1984, he served as the director of the Office of the President for the Los Angeles Olympic Organizing Committee and later as the president of the Los Angeles Coliseum Commission.

John Kass has been a reporter and columnist for the *Chicago Tribune* since 1983. His honors include the Society of Professional Journalists' Sigma Delta Chi national award for general column writing, the Scripps Howard Foundation's National Journalism Award for commentary, and the Press Club of Atlantic City's National Headliner Award for local interest.

John Kuenster (1924–2012) began writing about baseball for the *Chicago Daily News* in 1957 and left in 1969 to become editor of the venerable publication *Baseball Digest*, a position he held for more than four decades. "Obviously, it's something I enjoy a great deal," Kuenster said. "As they say, it beats working for a living."

Paul Ladewski worked at the *Daily Southtown* for thirty years. He became the paper's sports editor and sports columnist, won the Peter Lisagor Award, and, in 2005, was named the top sports columnist in Illinois. He is currently executive director of the Chicago Baseball Museum, which serves as a repository for Chicago baseball lore and is in the process of securing a permanent location.

Ring Lardner (1885–1933) wrote more than fifteen hundred "In the Wake of the News" columns for the *Chicago Tribune* between 1914 and 1919. He is considered one the greatest American authors of the early twentieth century

Bernie Lincicome wrote the "In the Wake of the News" sports column for the *Chicago Tribune* for seventeen years. He survived a pie in the face, a broken collar bone, and the clubhouse rage of a naked, wet, and all-over pink Don Zimmer, all in the name of journalism, a lot of it on deadline, at least half of it before the laptop computer, and too much of it without press parking.

Jay Mariotti spent seventeen years as a columnist at the *Chicago Sun-Times*, where he was known for his challenging opinions and passionate approach to sports-writing. For eight years, he was a regular panelist on ESPN's popular daily TV program *Around the Horn*. In 2011, his book, *The System*, a raw and revealing look at his life and career, was published by Amazon and Kindle Publishing.

Robert Markus wrote sports for the *Chicago Tribune* for thirty-six years. Reversing the usual order, Markus's first full-time assignment was as a columnist, a job he held for eleven years. Later he covered the Cubs, White Sox, Blackhawks, Notre Dame, Illinois, Northwestern, and twenty Indianapolis 500s. In 2011, he published a retrospective of his career titled *I'll Play These*.

Al Monroe (1901–66) worked for the *Chicago Defender* for thirty-five years, serving as sports editor, entertainment writer, and correspondent in New York and Los Angeles. He gained a reputation as the *Defender*'s "man about town," and his friends said "he knew everybody and everybody knew him."

Jeannie Morris began her journalism career as a columnist for the *Chicago Daily News* where she wrote many articles and columns as well as *Brian Piccolo: A Short Season*, the best-selling biography that was the inspiration for the film *Brian's Song*. She won eleven Emmys for sports production at CBS sports in Chicago and is coexecutive producer of *Adventure Divas*, which unites women in adventure travel around the world.

Rick Morrissey has been a sports columnist at the *Chicago Sun-Times* since 2009 and was previously a columnist at the *Chicago Tribune* for nine years. Morrissey has been named an Associated Press Top Ten columnist six times. His latest book, about Ozzie Guillen, is *Ozzie's School of Management*.

Brent Musburger, a sports broadcaster for ABC and ESPN, has long been one of America's most versatile and omnipresent sports commentators. He began his career in journalism at the *Chicago American* after graduating from Northwestern and covered the Bears and the White Sox before being named a columnist.

Dave Nightingale (1935–2007) joined the *Chicago Daily News* copy desk in 1961, spent six years covering the White Sox, and was a sports columnist for the paper from 1973 to 1978. He then covered baseball for the *Chicago Tribune* before becoming national correspondent for the *Sporting News* in 1981.

Westbrook Pegler (1884–1969) was one of America's most widely read sports-writers during the Golden Age of Sports in the 1920s. He then turned to political reporting, for which he won a Pulitzer Prize for articles on union racketeering, and wrote columns that were reviled in many quarters for their mixture of personal invective and right-wing politics.

Don Pierson covered the Chicago Bears for the *Chicago Tribune* from 1969 to 1988 and covered the NFL at large from 1988 to 2007. He is a winner of the Dick Mc-Cann Award for long and distinguished pro football reporting presented by the Pro Football Hall of Fame. He collaborated with former Bears coach Mike Ditka on *Ditka: An Autobiography.*

Richard Roeper has written a column that covers politics, media, and popular culture for the *Chicago Sun-Times* since 1987. For eight years, he was the cohost of the nationally syndicated movie review program *Ebert and Roeper* with *Sun-Times* film critic Roger Ebert. He has written eight books, on subjects ranging from urban legends to Hollywood flops to the Chicago White Sox.

Mike Royko (1932–97) wrote columns for the *Chicago Daily News*, *Chicago Sun-Times*, and *Chicago Tribune*, where he established himself as a unique voice in American journalism. He won the Pulitzer Prize for commentary in 1972. Among his books is the classic *Boss: Richard J. Daley of Chicago.*

Barry Rozner has been a sports columnist for the *Arlington Daily Herald* since 1997. He has won the Peter Lisagor and Associated Press writing awards and among his books is *Second to Home* with Ryne Sandberg. In 2011, he was inducted into Northern Illinois University's Northern Star Hall of Fame and in 2012 he was given the school's Distinguished Alumni Award.

I. E. Sanborn (1866–1934) covered baseball for the *Tribune* for more than twenty years and was considered one of the best-informed and most intelligent sportswriters of his era. A Phi Beta Kappa graduate of Dartmouth, he was a founding member of the Baseball Writers Association of America. In ill health after his retirement to Canandaigua, New York, he committed suicide with a gunshot to the head.

John Schulian was a sports columnist for the *Chicago Daily News*, the *Chicago Sun-Times*, and the *Philadelphia Daily News* before moving to Hollywood where he wrote for a number of television shows and was the cocreator of *Xena: Warrior Princess*. His work has been collected in several books, including *Sometimes They Even Shook Your Hand: Portraits of Champions Who Walked among Us.* With George Kimball, he edited *At the Fights: American Writers on Boxing* for the Library of America.

Diane Simpson covered high school sports for the *Chicago Sun-Times* for ten years. A winner of more than twenty international rhythmic gymnastics medals, she was a member of the 1988 US Olympic team and was inducted into the USA Gymnastics Hall of Fame in 2004. She is a member of numerous US Olympic Committee panels and was manager of athlete relations and communication for Chicago 2016.

Carol Slezak grew up in Detroit where her career choices ranged from being a fashion designer to playing point guard for the Pistons. After abandoning her career as an attorney, she joined the *Chicago Sun-Times* as a sports columnist in

1996 and spent the next thirteen years writing about the absurdity and corruption, as well as the valor and inspiration, she found in sports.

Sam Smith covered the Chicago Bulls and the NBA for the *Chicago Tribune* for more than two decades before becoming a writer for the Bulls' website in 2008. He received the Curt Gowdy Media Award from Basketball Hall of Fame in Springfield, Massachusetts, in 2012 and the Lifetime Achievement Award from the Professional Basketball Writers Association. His books include the *New York Times* best seller *The Jordan Rules*.

Wendell Smith (1914–72) was considered by many the best black sportswriter of his generation. He began his career in 1937 with the *Pittsburgh Courier*, then the most popular black paper in the country. He joined the *Chicago Herald-American* in 1948 and television station WGN as a sports anchor in 1964, while continuing to write a weekly column for the *Chicago Sun-Times*.

Ray Sons was a sportswriter and columnist for the *Chicago Daily News* and *Chicago Sun-Times* and served as sports editor of both papers. As the night city editor for the *Chicago Daily News*, he discovered and encouraged a young reporter named Mike Royko, who called him a masterful editor and Chicago's best sports columnist.

Rick Talley (1934–95) joined *Chicago's American* in 1968 before it evolved into *Chicago Today* and later became its sports editor. He assumed the role of sports columnist for the *Chicago Tribune* from 1969 to 1974. He wrote a number of books, including *The Cubs of '69*, which the *New York Times* called one of the best sports books of the year.

Rick Telander has been a sports columnist at the *Chicago Sun-Times* since 1995 and previously was a senior writer for *Sports Illustrated* and *ESPN: The Magazine*. He has written eight books, one of which, *Heaven Is a Playground*, has been named one of the top twenty-five sports books of all time. Telander played football at Northwestern and appeared in two postseason all-star games.

Bob Verdi was a staff writer and columnist for the *Chicago Tribune* from 1967 to 1997. He also served as a senior writer for *Golf Digest* and *Golf World*. In 2004, he received the PGA Lifetime Achievement Award in Journalism and in 2010 the Chicago Blackhawks appointed him team historian, a newly created position.

Arch Ward (1896–1955), the sports editor of the *Chicago Tribune* for twenty-five years, was called the Cecil B. DeMille of sports for his role in creating the baseball and football all-star games, his promotion of events ranging from boxing's Golden Gloves to horse races and concerts, and his creation of professional football's All-American Conference.

Gene Wojciechowski is a senior national sports columnist for ESPN. He was the national college football and basketball columnist for the *Chicago Tribune* in 1996 and 1997 and has worked at the *Dallas Morning News, Denver Post, Los*

Angeles Times, and *ESPN: The Magazine*. He is the author of nine books, including *Cubs Nation: 162 Games. 162 Stories. 1 Addiction*.

Frank A. (Fay) Young (1884–1957) spent fifty years as a sports editor, reporter, and columnist, most of it at the *Chicago Defender*, and was acknowledged as the dean of black sportswriters in America. He was a champion of black athletes and a long-time crusader for the integration of major-league baseball.

ACKNOWLEDGMENTS

This anthology would not have been possible without the cooperation of the newspapers in which the articles and columns it contains originally appeared. For permission to republish material from their papers, I am grateful to Joycelyn Winnecke, vice president and associate editor of the *Chicago Tribune*; John Barron, former publisher of the *Chicago Sun-Times*; Michael House, president of the *Chicago Defender*; and John Lampinen, senior vice president and editor of the *Daily Herald* of Arlington Heights. Thanks also to Jennifer Streff, the *Sun-Times'* licensing coordinator, Tina Kourasis, assistant general counsel of Wrapports/Sun-Times Media, and Courtney Price; Ayana Haaruun, the *Defender* archivist; and Mark Black, the *Daily Herald* copyright administrator.

I am also in the debt of *Tribune* librarians Elaine Varvatos and Lelia Bellinger for helping me find a number of columns from the *Tribune* and its former sister papers, *Chicago Today* and the *Chicago American*. Albert Dickens of the *Sun-Times* sports staff hunted down several columns from the *Sun-Times*, and the *Chicago Daily News* and *Sun-Times* librarian Virginia Davis allowed me to wander through those papers' archives. The Chicago Public Library's microfilm collection of every daily paper published in Chicago since the early 1900s was an invaluable resource. Tim Wiles, director of research at the National Baseball Hall of Fame in Cooperstown, New York, and Jack Bales, reference and humanities librarian at the University of Mary Washington Library in Fredericksburg, Virginia, were particularly helpful in locating a number of columns from earlier eras. Paul Dickson made the voluminous research he did for his fine book, *Bill Veeck: Baseball's Greatest Maverick,* available to me, and David Smith, formerly of the New York Public Library, was once again ready with valuable help and advice when called on.

It was a pleasure to speak with a number of the family members of the columnists in this book who are no longer living. They helped me find columns I might otherwise not have seen and were forthcoming with biographical information. Among them are Wyonella Smith, Wendell Smith's widow; Jane Daley, Steve Daley's widow; Joyce Banks, Lacy Banks's widow; Mary Ellen and Marty Gleason, Bill Gleason's widow and son, respectively; Woodson Jack Griffin, Jack Griffin's son; and Bob Kuenster, John Kuenster's son. Others who suggested some of the writers and columns in this book, and helped me find them, were Dr. David Fletcher of the Chicago Baseball Museum, Todd Musburger, Bettina Sons, Carol Marin, Chuck Davidson, Peggy Kusinski, Cheryl-Raye Stout, Mark Whicker, Bob Herguth, and Phil Rosenthal.

Thanks to Mike Downey for calling *The Greatest Sports Stories from the Chicago Tribune*, an anthology edited by Arch Ward in 1953, to my attention; to Taylor Bell, for tracking down the elusive Bernard Randolph; and to Jim Reiser, with whom I enjoyed speaking about his excellent book, *Black Writers/Black Baseball: An Anthology of Articles from Black Sportswriters Who Covered the Negro Leagues*. That book, and a series of articles about a number of major American sportswriters in *The Dictionary of Literary Biography*, contained much useful information about some of the writers in this book. Thanks also to Van Nightingale, a sports copy editor for both the *Chicago Tribune* and the *Los Angeles Times*, who read the manuscript at an early stage and made many useful suggestions.

At the University of Chicago press, I would like to thank executive editor John Tryneski for his early enthusiasm for the project and his help throughout, manuscript editor Yvonne Zipter for her careful reading of the manuscript and her many excellent suggestions, assistant editor Rodney Powell, and promotions director Levi Stahl.

I would like to extend a special thank you to my friends Paul and Adrianne Johnson for their hospitality while I was searching various libraries and archives in Chicago, and to John Schulian and Barbara Isenberg for lending a patient ear and offering a number of good ideas while I was putting this book together. Thanks also for their help to Terry Cannon, Bill Adee, Cathleen Karp, Colette Pauley, Don Hayner, and Rick Kogan.

Finally, I would like once again to thank the men and women I worked alongside during my years in Chicago who contributed to this anthology. I was pleased when virtually all of them seemed intrigued by what I was up to and a little startled when so many of them said they were flattered, or even honored, to be included.

The honor, of course, is all mine.

INDEX

303